GOOD FRAMES AND BAD

GOOD FRAMES AND BAD

A Grammar of Frame Writing, 2nd Edition

Susan Meyer Markle

Professor and Head of Programmed Instruction
University of Illinois, Chicago Circle

JOHN WILEY & SONS, INC., New York/London/Sydney/Toronto

Copyright © 1969 by John Wiley & Sons, Inc.

All Rights Reserved. No part of this book may be reproduced in any form, nor transmitted, nor translated into a machine language without the written permission of the publisher.

10 9 8 7 6 5 4 3 2 1

Library of Congress Catalog Card Number: 71-91153
SBN 471 57012 5 Cloth
SBN 471 57013 3 Paper
Printed in the United States of America

Preface

A lively field such as programed instruction is bound to change rapidly, and any book which purports to cover the basic concepts must change too. In the years since the publication of the first edition of *Good Frames and Bad,* new techniques have appeared, new systematic approaches have flowered, and, to our advantage, some old issues have died. The choices open to the programer have broadened as programers have adopted new media and developed greater sophistication in individualizing instruction. Programers are becoming flexible and eclectic. And yet, with this greater flexibility in what instructional product will be produced, there is at the same time a firm consensus on the basic process that is programing.

We know that programed instruction is not synonymous with "those funny little books," as J. H. Harless calls them. Some instructional products will turn out to be little books because books with questions in them happen to be the way to handle the problem. But books that can be called programs are the result of a problem-solving process beginning with analysis of the problem to be solved and ending with validation through empirical trials demonstrating that the solution works. The solution in many industrial settings may even by-pass training for a better designed environment. Instructional designers at times find that instruction is not the appropriate solution to a problem. The solution in education may turn out to be the creation of a set of procedures to be mediated by that most flexible of teaching machines, the instructor. Individual instruction by book or machine is not always the best solution to a problem. These applications are possibilities that are open to programers, along with the most frequent solution—the design of instructional materials for classroom or individual use. The primary emphasis of this book is on the latter, on the process and techniques that result in rationally designed instructional materials. If this is not all that programers do, it is nevertheless a significant portion of their task.

The creation of a good program is the result of a combination of talents and attitudes applied to the problem of designing an effective and efficient teaching tool. Not all of these talents and attitudes are easily trainable, certainly not within the short period a student works through this book.

In "Characteristics of Instructional Technologists," Gagné (1969) identified one of the key attitudes: "an instructional technologist should be able to choose approaches to instructional design and development that are capable of empirical test and public communication . . . whether or not they are personally or esthetically satisfying." Because of the difficulties of changing the attitude of many artistically oriented designers, he concluded that we need to *select* as programers "people who believe in empirical evidence as a source of truth and a preferred basis for action."

In the academic environment the programer also needs a firm commitment to student learning as his goal, since most of the reinforcers in his academic world are unrelated to this goal. His colleagues, if they attend to his instruction at all, will criticize the omission of technical terms, the simplification of basic concepts, and the failure to *cover* standard topics in standard order. His advancement will depend on the number of publications he can produce, not on the effectiveness of his instruction which can consume so much time. Even the students will contribute to his state of mind, as so beautifully described by Mager (1968): "They made me change the sequence of topics until it made sense to *them,* and showed no respect whatever for what was 'logical' to *me;* ripped out paragraphs I was very fond of and trampled them into oblivion; caused the demise of clever explanations that nobody seemed to understand; . . . and vetoed examples that didn't examp." Since the programing of any skill or knowledge is a long and difficult process, a programer will need a persistent commitment to changing student behavior and to gathering empirical evidence that he has done so.

Among the talents required to support these attitudes are the following:

1) Sophistication in the subject matter to be programed. In formulating the objectives of the program, in arranging the order in which concepts and skills are to be introduced, in generating examples, in relating one segment of the task to others, and in determining the adequacy and truth of statements made about the subject, an intimate knowledge of what is being taught is required. If the programer himself does not have it, he must work closely with someone who does.
2) Communication skills. There is no substitute for good writing and artistic use of any other medium. In this context, of course, we take artistry and communication skills to mean precision and clarity which gets through to the student rather than artistry designed for appreciation by connoisseurs.
3) Sophistication in the analysis of the behavior to be generated in the student and the techniques available to achieve it. The breadth of techniques now available permit each programer a wide range of choices.
4) Diagnostic skill in observing the learning process in the individual students who constitute the first "guinea pigs" in the developmental testing sessions.
5) Experimental sophistication in the final validation process. A knowledge of sound experimental design, test construction principles, and sampling procedures is helpful to anyone attempting to show the range of application of a set of instructional materials and procedures.

The primary audience for the book is those who will produce materials for educational consumption. Secondary audiences are industrial producers, evaluators of programed materials, and educational researchers who wish to do basic research on variables related to the effectiveness of programing techniques. A person who is sophisticated in the skills listed above is not only a good producer but also a critical evaluator and designer of research. The primary objectives of this program are that qualified students will be able to

a) identify errors in analysis and frame construction exemplified in a hastily prepared first-draft program—errors that should be repaired before the draft is tested on a student. This objective is tested by the "Editing Test" in the Instructor's Manual.
b) given an analyzed task, prepare a competent first draft sequence based on the principles stated in Chapter 5. This is tested by the first of the final outside exercises.
c) analyze a subject or skill and design an adequate first draft using more than one of the systematic approaches described in Chapter 3. (Most students find some of the approaches more congenial than others and not all approaches are equally easy to use with certain kinds of content.)
d) evaluate the adherence of existing published programs, in any medium, to basic programing principles and to the subsidiary principles of various "schools of thought." This skill is

tested by having students review various commercially available materials. (I have my own favorites, but this is not the place to admit it!)
e) discriminate rhetoric from the reality of actual practice in reading what has been written about "programed instruction" in general or particular styles and theories, and evaluate the weakness of various studies of the "effectiveness of programed instruction" or the "comparative effectiveness of programed versus conventional" instruction, a skill that depends on attainment of Item (d) above. As Skinner noted (1965), "Those who have had anything useful to say have said it far too often, and those who have had nothing to say have been no more reticent." Even in literature more recent than that which led to Skinner's comment, rhetoric out of touch with reality and just plain nonsense can be readily found.

A program such as this one cannot take responsibility for the student's sophistication in a subject matter nor his communication abilities. Advice is given throughout the book and in the Appendix on the "clinical" skills in developmental testing, but this advice is not thereby programed. I suspect that a book is the wrong medium for teaching that skill. And the full development of the experimental sophistication required for excellence in validating instruction is also beyond the scope of this small book.

The first edition of the book was written for and tested on graduate students in education. Since that time, I have been working primarily with psychology students, most of them undergraduates. Few changes in the present edition of the book were dictated by this change of population; most have arisen from new concepts and changes in emphasis that have occurred in the subject matter since the first edition. On entrance tests of psychological background, the present population has not proved more sophisticated than the earlier one, but I have become more concerned with the ability to "think like a psychologist" in precise stimulus-and-response terms. As mentioned early in Chapter 2, outside work is required for those who have had no practice in identifying the basic building blocks of operant learning theory: examples of discriminations and generalizations, and the rudiments of reinforcement theory. Being able to diagram chains or read cumulative records has not proved essential to programers, but the basic thinking patterns are. In addition to high verbal ability, of the sort that enables student to stay in school and make the grade into graduate school, an additional analytical orientation appears to be required. In his recent book, *Conceptual Learning,* Englemann (1969) notes: "Intuition is perhaps the greatest enemy of the kind of analysis offered (in his book) . . . The intuition that we feel about what we have learned has a negligible role in the development of efficient teaching programs. It is supplanted by the type of creative imagination used to solve problems of design." Well said. It is precisely what programing is. In conjunction with the attitude of empiricism noted by Gagné, it may be the most important ability which good programers must have before the knowledge taught in this book can be of use.

Chicago, Illinois SUSAN M. MARKLE
July, 1969

Acknowledgments

I gratefully acknowledge permissions granted by the following persons and companies to use materials written and copyrighted by them.

Addison-Wesley Publishing Company, for permission to reprint frames from *Labor Relations for the Supervisor,* By Joseph P. Yaney and Geary A. Rummler, 1968.

Basic Systems, for permission to use a chapter from *Vectors: A Programmed Text for Introductory Physics,* 1962; several frames from *Chemistry I: Atomic Structure and Bonding,* 1962; and frames from *Medical Parasitology,* 1963, 1964.

Doubleday and Company, for permission to reprint frames from the following Tutor Texts: *Trigonometry,* by Norman A. Crowder and Grace C. Martin, U.S. Industries, 1961; *Elements of Bridge,* by Charles H. Goren, U.S. Industries, 1961; *The Arithmetic of Computers,* by Norman A. Crowder and Grace C. Martin, U.S. Industries, 1960.

Harcourt, Brace and World, for permission to use a frame from *Poetry: A Closer Look,* by James M. Reid, John Ciardi, and Laurence Perrine, 1963.

Dr. Lloyd E. Homme, for permission to reprint parts of *The RULEG System for the Construction of Programmed Verbal Learning Sequences,* University of Pittsburgh, 1960.

Dr. Ralph W. Hunter, for permission to reprint frames from *The Spinal Cord,* by Ralph W. Hunter and Joan A. O'Connell, Trustees of Dartmouth College, 1963.

Macmillan Company, for permission to use frames from *Programmed English,* by M. W. Sullivan, Sullivan Associates, 1963.

Dr. Robert F. Mager, for permission to use frames from *Klystrons* by Robert H. Kantor and Robert F. Mager, Varian Associates, 1961; and for permission to use several frames from *The Language of Computers,* prepared for Learning Systems Institute S. A., Paris, France, 1964.

McGraw-Hill Book Company, for permission to use frames from *The Analysis of Behavior,* by James G. Holland and B. F. Skinner, 1961.

Scientific American, for permission to reprint paragraphs from B. F. Skinner, "Teaching Machines," *Scientific American* (November 1961).

Teaching Machines Inc., for permission to use frames from *Introduction to Modern Mathematics,* TMI, 1962; frames from *Multiplication and Division Games,* TMI, 1962.

John Wiley and Sons, for permission to use frames from *A Programmed Introduction to Vectors,* Robert A. Carman, 1963.

I am also grateful to Bert Holtby of the U.S. Forest Service and Robert Reynolds of Communicable Disease Center, U.S. Public Health, for calling to my attention excellent examples in the public domain. All other frames used in the program, when not identified as belonging to the preceding programs or some other source, or when not identified as being modeled after frames in said programs, were constructed by the author for the purposes of this program. Resemblance to frames in other programs is purely coincidental.

To the Student

Please Read Before Working Through the Program.

1. *Respond as you go.* As you work through this program, you are expected not only to read carefully, as you would with any text, but also to think out the answers to questions and problems. The large majority of frames *do not* require written answers, unless you so choose, because in many research studies, covert responding (that is, thinking) has been found adequate and far less time consuming than writing out a response. However, as its name implies, covert responding *is* responding. So keep thinking as you go. On occasion, you will be asked to write out your responses. Since frame designing involves writing, this seems legitimate enough. In cases of lengthy answers, it also facilitates your checking of your own answers.

2. *Use the mask.* Even the most honest eyes wander and you cannot think out for yourself something that you have just read.

3. *Format.* Most frames in this program are presented in this format:

> Example drawn from some other program.

Questions and commentary.

— — — — — — — — — — — — — — —

Answer (or suggested kind of answer) to question.

You need not try to answer the frames used as examples; in many cases you may not be able to, since they are drawn from a variety of subject matters. The text of my frames will point out what aspect of the example is important. Most students prefer to read the text to find out what to look for before they inspect the example. That makes sense, I think. Slide your mask down to the dashed line so that you can see everything above it.

4. *Timing.* The program has been prepared in sections, or in the case of extra long sections, in subsections, to enable you to cover a whole chunk at a time. Most of the sections or subsections should consume less than an hour of your time. Try to complete a unit before stopping, and take a running start by backing up a frame or two if you have to stop in the middle.

5. *Branching.* Since students differ, the program has been designed as far as possible to enable you to schedule your own reviews as well as to take different tracks at key points. You will find summaries at the end of sections and chapters, a Glossary in the back, and an Index to assist you in locating something you want to look at again. Don't overlook the Table of Contents as a tracking device! Directions are given in the text where branches occur, letting you get a hint if you need it, skip something you're not interested in, or review if you wish. At times your choice of answer will determine where you should go. Simply follow the directions.

6. *Errors.* Most programers advise students to reread the frame carefully, perhaps going back a frame or two, in order to be sure that they understand why the answer was as given before going on. That seems like sound advice. When your answer does not agree with mine, however, you may not have been in error. Not all the answers are a simple "yes" or "no" in a field as complex as programing. If you are seriously in doubt, discuss your answer with a colleague or an instructor, or write to the author. All programers welcome feedback.

Contents

Chapter 1	The Basic Programing Principles	1
	Section A. The Three Basic Principles	1
	Section B. A Close Look at a Segment of a Classical Linear Program	25
Chapter 2	The Basic Elements and Operations	56
	Section A. Priming	58
	Section B. Prompted Frames and Copying Frames	62
	Section C. Formal and Thematic Prompts	78
	Section D. Multiple Choice as a Prompt	94
	Section E. Visual Prompts	104
	Section F. The Sequence Prompt	111
	Section G. The Strength of Prompts	118
Chapter 3	Systematic Approaches to Design	131
	Section A. Matrices	131
	Section B. RULEG and EGRUL	138
	Section C. Mathetics: A Very Short Course	159
	Section D. An Essay on Concepts and Uncommon Sense	179
Chapter 4	Adaptive Programing and Individual Differences	186
	Section A. The Rationale of Intrinsic Programing	187
	Section B. A Close Look at a Segment of an Intrinsic Program	196
	Section C. Prompting in the Intrinsic Format	211
	Section D. The Problems of Adaptive Programing	220

Chapter 5 Editing	**238**
Section A. Relevance	239
Section B. How to Avoid the Copying Frame	250
Section C. The "Lecture" Frame and What to Do with It	258
Section D. Take the Holes out of the Swiss Cheese	260
Section E. The Role of the Formal Prompt	262
Section F. EGs, Non-EGs, and the Multidimensional Concept	266
Section G. Making the Most of an Elastic Prompt	275
Section H. Branching Frames	277
APPENDIX	295
BIBLIOGRAPHY	297
GLOSSARY	301
INDEX	307

GOOD FRAMES AND BAD

Chapter 1
The Basic Programing Principles

INTRODUCTION

Programers seek to solve educational problems by applying the techniques of behavior analysis. Most of us date the beginning of this application in 1954 with the publication of B. F. Skinner's article "The Science of Learning and the Art of Teaching." Unlike many other psychologists, Skinner saw a strong parallel between his activities in the laboratory and practices that would improve education. However apt the parallel may be, the fabled achievements in changing animal behavior in the laboratory did not lead to an immediate revolution in the schoolroom. If there was one great lie in the article, it was the statement in the concluding paragraph "There is a simple job to be done. . . . The necessary techniques are known." The years since 1954 have seen a gradual, often painful, growth in the technology of instructional design.

Historically, the first style of programing was the one called "linear," derived in part from Skinner's suggestions and in part from the characteristics of the first teaching machines. (Markle, 1962) Although the term *linear* describes only one characteristic of the most popular early style of programing, many other characteristics crept in and were soon regarded as essential. Indeed, linearity—meaning that each student proceeds in a straight line through a fixed instructional sequence—is one of the less salient attributes of what many people consider "Skinnerian programing" to be. When Schramm (1964) complained about the "hardening of the arteries" that he saw taking place in programing styles, it was not linearity *per se* that caused concern. Since each new convert to programing tended to imitate the programs he saw, a couple of bad apples in the barrel could spread their influence far and fast. Such imitation proved to be a sincere form of idiocy! And, as we shall see, much of the real activity in applying techniques of behavior analysis to education is, like the mass of an iceberg, below the surface and not visible in the final product. Copying the surface characteristics does not produce a program.

OVERVIEW: SECTIONS A AND B

Since history may help in understanding where we are now, this program will begin with an early article by Skinner. Although written seven years after the first one, it makes very similar points. From this, you will get a good look at the basic principles which are still relevant. Following these basic principles, we will look at an example of the traditional style. I hope some bits of that submerged iceberg (the work that went into producing this apparently simple sequence) will become apparent.

SECTION A. THE THREE BASIC PRINCIPLES

The case for linear programing is presented in the following article by Skinner. The sequence of frames that follow it are intended to start you thinking about the implications

2   THE BASIC PROGRAMING PRINCIPLES

of what he has to say. As you read the article, keep the following study questions in mind.
(a) The way that teaching materials are designed implies a theory of learning. What is required, according to Skinner, to produce learning?
(b) What role do individual differences among students have in determining the design of a linear teaching sequence?
(c) What is Skinner's attitude toward errors?

No question in the succeeding frames on this text will require that you have memorized it. However, it is not advisable to treat it as "light" reading. No student of mine has ever found Skinner "light"!

From "Teaching Machines", *Scientific American,* **November, 1961.**

Obviously the machine itself does not teach. It simply brings the student into contact with the person who composed the material it presents. It is a labor-saving device because it can bring one programer into contact with an indefinite number of students. This may suggest mass production, but the effect on each student is surprisingly like that of a private tutor. The comparison holds in several respects. There is a constant exchange between program and student. Unlike lectures, textbooks, and the usual audio-visual aids, the machine does not simply present something to be learned; it induces sustained activity. The student is always alert and busy. Like a good tutor, the machine insists that a given point be thoroughly understood, either frame by frame or set by set, before the student moves on. Lectures, textbooks, and their mechanized equivalents, on the other hand, proceed without making sure that the student understands, and they easily leave him behind. Like a tutor, the machine presents just that material for which the student is ready. It asks him to take only that step which he is at the moment best equipped and most likely to take. Like a tutor, the machine helps the student to come up with the right answer. It does this in part through the orderly construction of the program and in part with techniques of hinting, prompting, suggesting, and so on, derived from an analysis of verbal behavior. Finally, the machine, like the private tutor, reinforces the student for every correct response, using this immediate feedback not only to shape his behavior most efficiently but also to maintain it in strength in a manner that the layman would describe as "holding the student's interest."

A useful teaching machine will have several important features. Except in some kinds of stimulus learning, the student should compose his response, rather than select it from a set of alternatives, as he would in a multiple-choice scheme. One reason for this is that we want him to recall rather than merely recognize—to make a response as well as see that it is right. An equally important reason is that effective multiple-choice material must contain plausible wrong answers, which are out of place in the delicate process of shaping behavior because they strengthen unwanted responses.

The student must pass through a carefully arranged sequence of steps, often of considerable length. The machine must be designed so that the student has to take each step and take it in the prescribed order.

One of the great sources of inefficiency in modern education is due to our effort to teach a group of students at the same rate. We recognize that this is unfair to the student who is able to move faster, but we have no idea how much damage may be suffered by those who move slowly. There is no evidence that a slow student is necessarily unintelligent. . . . With properly designed machines and programs, a slow student free to move at his own normal rate of work may rise to undreamed-of levels of competence.

Difficult as programing is, it has its compensations. It is a salutory thing to try to guarantee a correct response at every step in the presentation of a subject. The programer will find that he has been accustomed to leaving much to the student, omitting essential steps, and neglecting relevant points. The responses made to his program may reveal surprising ambiguities. Unless he is extremely able, he may find that he still has something to learn about his subject. He will almost certainly find that he needs to learn a great deal more about the behavioral changes he is trying to induce in the student. His goal must be to keep refining his program until the point is reached at which the answers of the average child will almost always be right.

THE FIRST PRINCIPLE

1. In his article Skinner states "there is a constant exchange between program and student," and "the machine does not simply present something to be learned; it induces sustained activity."

    In these and other statements, Skinner makes clear his position on one of the main necessities governing learning. In order for learning to occur, the student must_____.

_ _ _ _ _ _ _ _ _ _ _ _ _ _ _

respond, or do something, or be active, etc.

4 THE BASIC PROGRAMING PRINCIPLES

2. From what Skinner says about "lectures, textbooks, and their mechanized equivalents," (refer to the text if you wish) would you say that *listening, reading,* and *watching* a film or TV presentation are responses of the sort that Skinner intends to have the student make?

    — — — — — — — — — — — — — — —

    The question asks what you would say. If you find yourself tending to say "yes," reread the first paragraph of Skinner's article. Note the emphasis on making sure that the student understands before he is allowed to go on.

---

3. A basic principle derived from the learning theory on which linear programing is based is:
    In order for learning to occur, a response must be made by the learner. It follows that if we give a student two bits of information, both of which we expect him to learn, he should respond to
    (a) either of them
    (b) both of them.

    — — — — — — — — — — — — — — —

    (b) both of them.

---

4. Suppose a student has been led to respond correctly to the question "What is the capital of France"? In psychological terms, we can say:
    In the presence of the stimulus "capital of France," the student responds "Paris."
    Is this the same situation as that represented by the following?
    In the presence of "Paris is the capital of what country?" the student will respond "France".

    — — — — — — — — — — — — — — —

    If your answer is "yes," go to item 4a.
    If your answer is "no," go to item 4c.

4a. Your answer was "yes." When the sentence "Paris is the capital of France" is broken into a *stimulus* part and a *response* part, it can be made into several different combinations of stimulus and response:

"What country is Paris the capital of?" is one question to which the correct response is "France."

"What is the capital of France?" is another question to which the correct response is "Paris."

According to the principle of active responding, the student who has learned the answer to the first question has *not necessarily* learned the answer to the second question. The principle has been supported—often to the chagrin of program authors who assume that reading is an adequate response—by data drawn from all levels of student age and ability.

Minor wording changes (what we call "synonymous" phrasing) may be made without changing the stimulus-response relationship. One item is different from another whenever the stimulus is changed and a different response is asked for.

Are the following questions the same or are they different?

> Q1. "What do we call the meaningful unit that goes in front of a root?"
> A1. "A prefix."
> Q2. "When a meaningful unit precedes a root, it is a_____."
> A2. "prefix."

— — — — — — — — — — — — — —

For any student for whom "precedes" = "goes in front of," the items are the same.

4b. In the presence of the stimulus "The particles that circle the nucleus are called . . . ," the student responds "electrons."

Is this the same situation as when in the presence of "Electrons circle around the . . . ," the student responds "nucleus"?

— —

4c. Answer to 4 and 4b: No.

Note. Although the question may seem obvious to you, the failure to discriminate that such situations are different has led to criticisms of linear programs as being too repetitive (i.e., asking the student to do the same thing over and over again), when in fact they might not be. Go on to item 5.

5. According to the *principle of active responding,* the student learns only what he has been led to do. Although "Madrid is the capital of Spain" is a single sentence, it is the answer to more than one question. Each of the possible questions might be a terminal frame (a test question) in a geography program.

To an unsophisticated reader who thinks of the sentence as one sentence instead of as the answer to several questions, a program based on the principle of active responding will appear to be repetitive. Yet each question (1. What is the capital of Spain? 2. What country is Madrid the capital of?) is different. How would you describe the difference between these two questions using the terms *stimulus* and *response?*

- - - - - - - - - - - - - - - -

You could say "Each question is a different stimulus asking for a different response" or "In the presence of different stimuli, the student gives a different response" or you could describe them by saying which is stimulus and which is response in each case (Spain-Madrid and Madrid-Spain).

---

6. Although much of what may appear to the unsophisticated reader to be repetition in a program turns out not to be, a programer may repeat himself—i.e., make use of review items. When can you legitimately call some item a review item? What characteristic must it have?

- - - - - - - - - - - - - - - -

It must ask for the same (or very similar) response in the presence of the same (or similar) stimulus as a previous item did.

Note. Changing the numbers in a mathematical problem and requiring the student to repeat the same problem-solving process could be said to be repetitive, especially if there were no increase in complexity. Just where the line is drawn between "same" and "different" will depend on many factors. What is "the same" for a college student may represent an enormous difference to a first grader!

---

7. Programers should keep in mind that familiar maternal phrase, "How many times do I have to tell you. . . ." Putting words in front of a student is no guarantee that he has noticed them, much less understood them. (Some sophisticated students look at the blank first and then read backwards to find the answer—a trick they have learned from taking reading comprehension tests. It sometimes saves a lot of reading!)

In this item, what information can be ignored without affecting the answer at all?

> Electrons, which have a negative charge, circle around the nucleus, which has a positive charge. The center of an atom is called a [nucleus/electron].

- - - - - - - - - - - - - - - -

The information about positive and negative charges may be ignored.

---

8. Assume that the following item is an introduction to the two key terms "prefix" and "suffix." In what way does it *not* satisfy the principle of active responding?

> A prefix is a meaningful unit that goes in front of a root. A suffix is a meaningful unit that goes after a root.
>
> In the word "hopeless," the unit "less" is placed after the root, so it is a_____.

- - - - - - - - - - - - - - - -

It includes two definitions and the student is only required to respond to the second one. (The item has other faults as well, to be discussed later.)

---

9. Suppose we take the above item and rewrite it in the form given below. Does it now appear to require students to attend to *both* definitions?

> Meaningful units that go in front of a root are called *prefixes*.
> Meaningful units that go after a root are called *suffixes*.
> Label the units in this word:
>
>   UN BEAR ABLE
>
> _ _ _fix   (root)   _ _ _fix

- - - - - - - - - - - - - - - -

Yes.

8 THE BASIC PROGRAMING PRINCIPLES

Research Note. The necessity to control what the student observes by requiring a response to anything we wish him to notice was learned "in the field", so to speak. Programers working on practical problems verified the principle to their own satisfaction—enough to have it included in How-To books like this one. Controlled laboratory research has since provided firmer evidence. *If you are not interested in such basic research, skip directly to the next frame.*

A cogent technique for determining which parts of a frame could be skipped by students without increasing the number of errors they made was developed by Holland (1965). His "blackout technique," as its name implies, consisted of painting over the unnecessary content in the frame so that students could not read what was originally there.

Holland demonstrated that his judgments of what was unnecessary were correct by having two groups of students go through the two versions of the frames. If students made no more errors on the painted-out frames than they did on the original version, it followed that noticing the "unnecessary content" was not required in order to answer. Frames 7 and 8 above have asked you to make essentially the same kinds of judgments about the examples given in them.

Once we can show by the blackout technique that the content blacked out isn't necessary, we can go on to show that it isn't learned. Even when it is not blacked out, posttest questions asking for it will show that most students paid no attention and consequently didn't learn it. Several studies along these lines are reported in Holland's chapter (1965). A more recent exhaustive review of the research can be found in Anderson (1967).

10. There is no reason to hide the prejudice of your author until later in the program, so here goes.

    An *active* response to all the content in a frame is obtained when the student is required to process all of it in order to respond. There is considerable evidence that active responding aids learning.

    There is, however, a distinction between requiring active responding to each bit of information and requiring the student to give each response separately. In many lists of the "characteristics of programed instruction" you will find the "principle of *small steps*" given as one of the necessary features. The word "small" has had unfortunate effects on the way some programers have designed instruction.

    On the opposite page is a frame from a program designed for medical technicians—adults who don't need to be fed in small bites. We'll call it one frame because confirmation of their responses is not presented until they have completed the whole frame. Glance at the frame briefly. Do you agree that this could NOT be called a "small step"? ⇨

    Now, inspect it carefully to answer this question. The student is to note five structures and three functions of a cell, and, with the help of the descriptions given, match each of these with the appropriate illustrations. Activity we certainly have! Can you locate anything in the frame that the student is NOT required to attend to in order to complete the exercise? If so, what?

    — — — — — — — — — — — — — — —

    Confirmation is at top of page 10.

THE THREE BASIC PRINCIPLES 9

The drawing below represents the STRUCTURE of the cell. In this case it is an AMEBA, a unicellular animal.

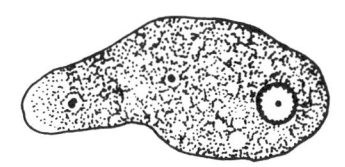

Using the following information, *you* draw arrows to and label the cell's STRUCTURES:

    NUCLEUS—the most prominent structure in the cell
    NUCLEAR MEMBRANE—the membrane surrounding the nucleus
    CELL WALL—the membrane surrounding the cell
    VACUOLE—cavity inside the cell
    CYTOPLASM (endoplasm, ectoplasm)—material inside the cell

The drawings below represent FUNCTIONS of the cell (ameba).

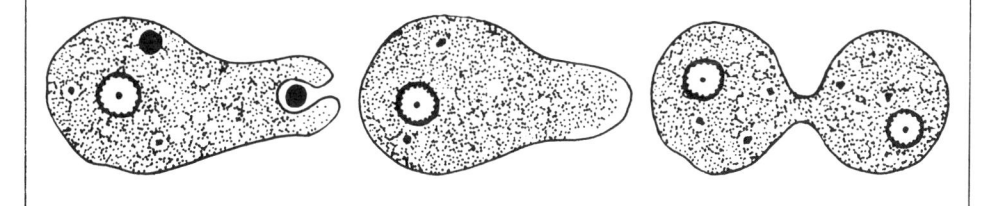

_____   _____   _____

Using the following information, *you* write in the FUNCTION represented by each drawing:

FEEDING—by surrounding food with pseudopodia
MOVEMENT—by thrusting of pseudopodia
REPRODUCTION—by binary fission

The first question asked for *your opinion.* Most people agree that this frame is a pretty big chunk.

If you could locate an unused bit of information, you probably selected the second sentence at the top. The parenthetical "endoplasm, ectoplasm" also appears unnecessary to most people seeing this frame without the frame that preceded it. Looking at this frame by itself, you would be correct in assuming that students could ignore the material in the parentheses.

11. An active response is not necessarily a small response to a small bit of information, as you just saw. The "responses" near the end of a program on writing computer programs could ask the student to write such a program and de-bug it on a computer, a "response" which might take him an hour or more. At the end of an art appreciation program, you might send the student out to spend an afternoon in the local art museum preparing a report on what he saw and felt. (This hasn't been done to my knowledge. But I still would call this a response—a very active foot-weary one!) Don't think of "active response" as a little twitch of the finger or writing a single word.

A further confusion about "active responding":

If you ask an arithmetic student to add a column of five numbers in his head and tell you the answer, you have an overt, observable response. Is this final sum the only response he made in doing the problem?

— — — — — — — — — — — — — —

If you said yes, try to do it yourself. I think you will observe yourself responding to the sum of the first and second, then this sum and the third, and so on. (You are the only one who can observe this response, since it is covert.)

12. Covert responding is active responding. It isn't, of course, observable to anyone else. If a programmer is trying out some new frames, can he let the student respond covertly and still know that the frames are producing good answers?

— — — — — — — — — — — — — —

No.

13. When the instruction is thoroughly tested, the programer doesn't need to hear (or see) responses from everyone going through it. At that point, we can raise the question about overt versus covert responding. When does writing down an answer or saying it aloud help and when is it just a time-consuming nuisance? Research is still going on, and the answers are not all in. (See Anderson, 1967.) Common sense is one guide, of course. Which of these subjects would seem to require overt responding?

(a) student is learning how to write in script, after he has learned how to print letters.
(b) student is learning some basic terms in geography (all about mesas, peninsulas, etc.)

– – – – – – – – – – – – – – – –

Common sense (mine, anyway) suggests that handwriting cannot be practiced very well covertly, although it might be possible to design a teaching sequence to do most of the teaching without having the student practice.

Research Note. *Skip to the end of this section, if you are not interested.* A fascinating example of this flying-in-the-face of "common sense" is found in a study by Evans (1961). Several youngsters who, on a pretest, could not form "good" numerals were taught to discriminate well-written numerals from poorly written ones by a sequence of multiple-choice responses (they picked the good one as the correct answer). Without any practice in writing them, the children wrote acceptable numerals on the posttest.

Moral: take common sense with a grain of salt.

End of subsection: Because this section is long, you may be running out of time. If so, this is a good place to stop. The next section will take up a second important principle.

THE SECOND PRINCIPLE

14. If a student must respond in order to learn, it may also be the case that the student will learn the response that he makes. According to this theory (with no further qualifications), what does he learn if he makes an error?

– – – – – – – – – – – – – – – –

The erroneous response (we said nothing yet about telling him that he is wrong).

12 THE BASIC PROGRAMING PRINCIPLES

15. There are many inconclusive experimental demonstrations of the role of errors in learning; the relationships involved are complex. There are subjects (and parts of almost all subjects) in which there are right answers and any other response is definitely incorrect. There are other situations in which several answers, even widely deviating ones, may all be correct. For the moment, we will ignore this latter type of situation.

    Consider the following as applying to relatively simple responses such as correct spelling of a word, naming of an object, or solution of an arithmetical problem.

    First, if a student responds "64" to the problem of "9 × 7", and he is not told that this response is incorrect, what response is he likely to give the next time he is asked the question? ____ .

    — — — — — — — — — — — — — — —

    64.

16. From this observation, then, we can derive the principle that, having made an error, the student should find out very soon that _____ in order to prevent his doing it again.

    — — — — — — — — — — — — — — —

    he is wrong (or equivalent).

17. Carry the principle a step further. If a student writes "Misisipi" on a history test and his paper comes back with a red line under that word, does he now know how to spell it? _____ .

    — — — — — — — — — — — — — — —

    No. He has many other possible spellings to try out on his teacher!

18. From this observation, we can derive a further principle. Not only should the student's error be brought to his attention, but also he should find out _____ , so that he will be right the next time.

    — — — — — — — — — — — — — — —

    what the correct answer is. (I did *not* say that he must be told—he may be required to look it up, but he should find it.)

THE THREE BASIC PRINCIPLES 13

19. Carry the principle one step further, and you are in the Skinnerian camp:
    Because "rhyme" and "rythm" (or is it "rhythm"?) were frequently contrasted in discussions of poetry, I learned somewhere that their spellings also contrasted. As a consequence of this, I have so frequently misspelled and so frequently corrected the latter word that two responses of absolutely equal strength exist in my repertoire. Confronted with the task of spelling the word, the rule that has been adopted is: Write the word, erase it, and spell it the other way. Half the time this rule works. There is nothing unusual about this situation. "I can never remember whether it's an x or a y" is a common complaint. Under such conditions, what is the probability of choosing the correct response?

    — — — — — — — — — — — — — — —

    If the responses are absolutely equal in strength, the probability of choosing the correct one is ½ or 50-50.

20. There seem to be times when an erroneous response, once made, is likely to recur although it is corrected. If every time an error is made the wrong response gets a little stronger, and then we correct it and the right response gets a little stronger, there is no way out. The probability of making the error remains high. If the effects of making an error are difficult to overcome, the programer should_____.

    — — — — — — — — — — — — — — —

    (something like) not let errors occur, (or) see that the student is right the first time.

21. The first principle derived from Skinner's theory—the principle of active responding—is carried to its logical extreme in linear programing. The student is to be led to make every response in the program that we can legitimately expect him to make when he is through learning. The second principle—correct responding on the first try—is also carried to its logical extreme. Although reading something is not considered an adequate type of response, Skinner has eliminated one type of question on the basis that a student might learn something by reading. What type of question is not allowed and why? (If your memory slips, see the second paragraph of Skinner's article, page 3.)

    — — — — — — — — — — — — — — —

    Multiple-choice, because the student might learn one of the plausible wrong answers.

14   THE BASIC PROGRAMING PRINCIPLES

22. In the Glossary the following definition of an error appears:

    Error.   A response not acceptable to the programer. Programers attempt to eliminate errors by revising the program. Erroneous responses may indicate: (a) a poorly designed item which fails to communicate and therefore needs to be rewritten; (b) a sequence in which prompts have been withdrawn too fast or inadequate practice given; (c) assumed previous knowledge which in fact the student does not have; (d) poor analysis of the subject matter, leading to a confusion not predicted by the programer.

    According to the criterion given here, does this definition imply that students should never be allowed to make responses that are in fact errors in the subject matter being taught?

    No. The criterion is "not acceptable to the programer." He might have a reason for getting some misconception out in the open–in order to show the student where the misconception would lead.

Note.   The need to openly "punish" previous learning where it represents error is not universally agreed upon. For the time being, an open mind is recommended on this issue.

23. One of the essential features of Skinner's approach to a science of behavior is control of behavior. An investigator can be said to understand *why* some behavior occurs when he can make it occur (and prevent it from occurring) by manipulating some variable. Programers following this line of thinking wish to *make* the student learn. To do this, they must control the student's responses.
    Consider the following:

    (a) If the programer believes that learning is facilitated by permitting the misinformed student to give an erroneous response, is the programer in control of the response when the student makes the error?_____.
    (b) If the programer predicts a correct answer to his "well-written" frame and the student makes an error, is the programer in control of the student's response? _____.

    (a) Yes (the error, which the programer is trying to get out of the student, is "acceptable to the programer").
    (b) No (he has not produced the response he predicted).

24. In the development of a program, the programer has to start somewhere. His first draft represents what he thinks is a reasonable order of presentation of the material. He includes what he thinks students may need and he excludes any material that he thinks students already know. Although, in the distant future, a perfect first draft may be produced, this has not yet happened.

The key to the effectiveness of the final product is the testing procedure. Many programers prefer face-to-face testing with the first few students who go through a program. Talking to one student at a time can be a great deal more valuable than compiling errors from a large group. If the student does not understand a particular item, he can often say exactly what word or phrase is giving him difficulty. That phrase gets dropped and the item rewritten. If the student cannot solve some problem, he can often say exactly where his difficulty is. The programer now knows that this source of difficulty will either have to be dealt with if it has not been or dealt with better if it has already been mentioned.

Eventually, of course, the program will be tested on a group of representative students. At this point the programer should be ready to show that his program is in working order. If he gets a large number of errors from the group, he may be in trouble. Why? What data will be hard to get from the group?

– – – – – – – – – – – – – – – –

It is hard to find out why the students made errors and exactly what they might need when they are not talking to the programer.

25. A programer writes a sequence that he thinks is adequate. He tries it out on a student. Parts of it do not work. So he rewrites these parts. Can he use the same student to test the second version? Why?

– – – – – – – – – – – – – – – –

No. The student has already learned too much about the subject. (Or, put less elegantly, the programer has already "ruined" the first student.)

26. The programer's credo might be stated thus: "If the student errs, the programer flunks." This statement has to be tempered with some common sense, of course. Even the best student makes a few careless mistakes. (Again, if you are talking with him, rather than reading his answer sheet, a careless error is easy to identify—the student readily recognizes what he should have done.) Truly errorless learning is probably unattainable and might be terribly tedious.

Any significant number of errors, however, is an indication that something is wrong and calls for revision of the sequence. Programers argue about the figure—2%, 5%, 10%—that is permissible. In testing the first draft, however, the programer may regard almost all errors as significant, depending on his discussions with his students. After revision, the second draft is tried on another student. If this second student makes a lot of errors and does not do well on a test, what should the programer do (if he believes his own credo)?

_ _ _ _ _ _ _ _ _ _ _ _ _ _ _

Revise again.

27. After the first student has located some of the gross errors, the programer rewrites the ineffective material and tries it again on a new "guinea pig." If it still doesn't work, he goes through the process again. What sort of rule of thumb does this suggest concerning how many students he will have to use in developing a programed sequence?

_ _ _ _ _ _ _ _ _ _ _ _ _ _ _

(in your own words) He will have to keep trying until the sequence works with an individual student. The number of students that he needs will depend on the programer's skill.

Note. Nothing has been said about the "representativeness" of these individual students used in developmental testing. I, for one, prefer a slightly "unrepresentative" type of student at this point in the process. The student with high motivation to learn the material and with the gall to "tell the teacher off" whenever the sequence goes wrong is, for me, the easiest to work with. Some students simply cannot believe that a programer blames himself for errors. If your student merely reports that he was careless each time he makes an error, the information is of little help. Other students have a hard time figuring out why they made mistakes or are too shy to say what they think. The student who tells you "I know what answer you expect here but . . ." is the one you want! Learn from him.

28. Watch what happens to a program as it goes through the testing procedure. Some students in any group will lack some bit of information that is important for progress through the program. If a linear programer is going to guarantee correct responses from almost all the

students, what should he do about this bit of information if 30% of the students that he intends to teach do not have it?

Include it in the program or teach it. (He could, of course, take the easy way out and change his mind about whom the program was supposed to teach.)

---

29. When starting to write a program, programers naturally make assumptions about what students know and do not know. Consider this one:

    If a programer assumes that students *do not* know something that they in fact do, he will put it into the program. If he assumes they *do* know something that they do not know, he will leave it out of the program.
    When he tests the program, which of his two erroneous assumptions will he find out about?

The second one. If they do not know something that he assumed, they will make mistakes. He will never find out by looking at the errors that he taught something that he did not need to teach.

---

30. The amount of practice that any one student needs in order to master some fact may differ considerably from the amount needed by another student. For any one individual, the amount of practice that he needs in one subject may be quite different from the amount that he needs in another. If the linear programer is going to guarantee acquisition of some fact by all of his students, how much practice does he need to put in the program?

The amount required by the person who needs the most.

---

31. Errors by students will tell a programer when he has [too much/too little] practice.

Too little (groans may tell him when he has too much!).

32. We can deduce that, on the average, the more a program is tested and adjusted to produce errorless learning, the [longer/shorter] it gets!

─ ─ ─ ─ ─ ─ ─ ─ ─ ─ ─ ─ ─ ─ ─

Longer. The answer is pretty obvious!

33. Among the early principles given as advice to programers was the already mentioned principle of "small steps": the subject or skill to be acquired should be broken into "small" units easily digested by students. Historically, we may blame the resulting size-of-steps on two factors: first, the amount of space provided in some of the early teaching machines (you simply couldn't get more than thirty words in those small windows!) and second, on faulty design of frames. The idea that learning can proceed with minimal errors is basic. So if you can't design good teaching exercises that enable the student to handle large amounts of material (as shown in Frame 10's example), then the only other solution seems to be that of making the steps so small that students can figure them out even if they are badly written.

In terms of what's "in" and what's "out," we can definitely say today that small steps are out. Does this mean that programers have to abandon errorless learning as an ideal?

─ ─ ─ ─ ─ ─ ─ ─ ─ ─ ─ ─ ─ ─ ─

I think not. Instead we might give up the teaching techniques that necessitated small steps. Bad frames are out too!

Relevant Quote. The reader will recognize that 'errorless' learning is a conceptual convenience similar to the physicist's 'perfect' vacuum or the chemist's 'perfect' gas. (Evans, 1965.)

34. The theoretical necessity of guaranteeing mostly correct responding creates a dilemma for programers. In the ordinary language and in statistical talk, the "average" person is in the middle of the distribution of some attribute.

If the "average" student in any grade level makes few errors on a program, then we would expect the "above-average" student to make no errors and the "below-average" student to make many errors.

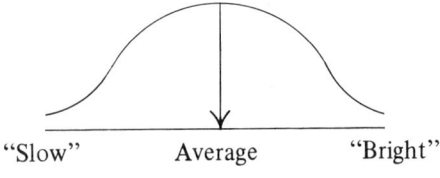

"Slow"   Average   "Bright"

But *(watch this logic, now!)*, the program is therefore NOT adequate for the below-average student. Our *average* student, who in the above diagram would be in the *middle* of the curve for his grade, becomes the *bottom* of the population for which the program is any good.

Suppose we produce and thoroughly test a program in ninth-grade algebra until it performs well with all ninth graders who score at the eighth-grade level or better in reading

THE THREE BASIC PRINCIPLES 19

and have C's or better in arithmetic. (We're a bit below average on reading, but are presumably at the average in arithmetic.)

(a) Will there be some students in a typical ninth-grade class who will make too many errors on this program?
(b) Who, in Skinner's sense, is the "average" child for whom this program is adjusted to produce a high percentage of correct responses?
(c) Is the student described in (b) above also the "average" student who can successfully take the program? (Consider all students who could succeed.)

— — — — — — — — — — — — — — —

(a) Yes—the below-average students will have trouble.
(b) The eighth-grade reader with C's in math.
(c) No. He is at the bottom of the distribution of students who can use the program successfully.

---

35. At some level of IQ, reading ability, previous training, etc., we would expect a program to "bottom out"; students would start making too many errors and show less than adequate performance on a test of what they had learned. In this case, the programer is justified in stating that the program is not written for these students (and that he will not revise it to make it easy enough for them). If a program has a "floor," would you expect it also to have a "ceiling"? _____ . How would you find out about this?

— — — — — — — — — — — — — — —

Yes. Certainly a program for seventh graders would insult a college student even if he didn't know the subject matter.
   There are many possible answers, such as "try another program that goes much faster and see if they learn as well from it," or "ask the students whether they're bored," and so forth.

---

36. In his article, Skinner notes that teaching a group of students at exactly the same rate is a great source of inefficiency in education. In proceeding through a linear program (linear = straight line), each student does every item. How then, do students go at different rates?

— — — — — — — — — — — — — — —

(in your own words) Some do the items faster than others.

Note. Carried to its logical extreme (one frame for each possible response), the principle of active responding leads to a lengthy program. The problems discussed above indicate that the second principle, minimal errors, also has a tendency to produce long programs.

Problem for Consideration. (No answer is required at the moment.) Is the notion of bringing each student up to mastery at his own rate—that is, with maximum efficiency—simply an impossibility? Revision of existing frames is no solution to the problems of differences in previous knowledge or in rate of acquisition (amount of practice needed) for the material being taught. The need for a solution (but not necessarily *the* solution itself) will appear again and again in this program.

37. The only way to revise an item that leads to error is to break the idea into smaller steps. True or False?

_ _ _ _ _ _ _ _ _ _ _ _ _ _ _

False. Perhaps expressing it better or coming up with a more apt example would clear up the difficulty. In breaking some ideas down, we are likely to lose the whole picture.

Relevant Quote. (The) student cannot fail. If he doesn't get where you want him to go, you have failed. (Gilbert, 1960.)

If you have to stop soon, stop here.

THE THIRD PRINCIPLE

38. Immediately after writing (or thinking or speaking) his response, the student proceeding through a linear program is provided with "knowledge of results." He compares the answer that he gave with the correct answer provided by the programer.

    If he is correct, his response is "confirmed." If he is incorrect, he has at least read the correct response, which raises the probability (but does not guarantee) that he will give the correct response the next time he is asked a similar question.

    Several experiments have been done with this variable—knowledge of results. The question often asked, "Is it necessary?" might better be phrased, "*When* is it necessary?" Consider the following:

    (a) I ask you to guess which whole number I am thinking of that lies between 4 and 6. You respond. Do you need to have your response confirmed?_____. Why?

_ _ _ _ _ _ _ _ _ _ _ _ _ _ _

No, providing we are using the same number system. The answer is completely obvious and you cannot really be said to be guessing.

THE THREE BASIC PRINCIPLES 21

Consider this situation:

(b) I ask you to guess which number I am thinking of that lies between 1 and 10. You respond. Do you need to have your response confirmed?_____. Why?

- - - - - - - - - - - - - - - -

Yes. You have no way of knowing what number I am thinking of, so you cannot evaluate your own response.

---

39. When the student is completely unsure of the correctness of his response, the teacher must provide "knowledge of results." When the student is completely sure (correctly so) of the correctness of his response, the teacher does not need to provide "knowledge of results." Does this latter case mean that learning can occur without knowledge of results?_____. What is the difference between the first and the second case here?

- - - - - - - - - - - - - - - -

No. In the latter case it is the student who provides himself with knowledge of results. The difference is in who provides it, not in whether it occurs or not. (See Klaus, 1965, and Gilbert, 1962, for further argument on this subject.)

---

40. For most of you, the following frame presents a new fact.

> Since aardvarks find uncles indigestible, they eat_____.
> (demonstration frame) Klaus

Figure out the answer to this "riddle." Do you need your response confirmed?_____. Why?

- - - - - - - - - - - - - - - -

Most people say "no," once they have figured out the answer. There is only one answer that "fits," and it obviously fits. Most riddles have this property—the answer may be difficult to get but you know when you've got it. (Those who pronounce "aunts" and "ants" differently are in trouble, of course.)

22   THE BASIC PROGRAMING PRINCIPLES

---

41. If you already know about aardvarks' appetites, you'll have to take the point made by the frame on faith. For those who do not know about aardvarks, it should be obvious that a student confronted with a new fact that he has just generated could [sometimes/never] provide himself with knowledge of results.

    — — — — — — — — — — — — — — —

    sometimes (frames of this type are rare, but such obviousness can also be brought about by clever sequencing).

---

42. A program is supposed to proceed in logical fashion as it leads a student through a subject. There are rote drill aspects of many subjects in which we really can't say that an answer is supposed to seem "sensible," but if a subject has a structure—mathematics, for instance—we would hope that the answers required of students "make sense" to them. When you come up with an answer that makes sense to you, can you be fairly sure that you are correct?_____.

    — — — — — — — — — — — — — — —

    Most would say "yes."

---

43. If the program in a machine (or out of a machine) asks the student to "take only that step which he is at the moment best equipped to take," is it likely that the student will know that the response he is making is the correct one?_____.

    — — — — — — — — — — — — — — —

    Yes.

---

44. However,
    (a) Is it possible for a student to be certain he is correct when he is in fact incorrect?_____.
    (b) Is it possible for a student to be correct but to be uncertain that he is?_____.
    (c) If thirty or more students are taking the same program, is it likely that the next step is *the* step for which all thirty are absolutely prepared?_____.

    — — — — — — — — — — — — — — —

    (a) Yes, it happens. (Answers to arithmetic problems are an obvious example—minor errors can occur without the student's feeling unsure.)

(b) Yes. For some "anxious" students, this happens frequently.
(c) No. It is unlikely that they are all alike. The step could be too big for some, who will therefore be unsure of their responses.

---

45. On the basis of the questions in the preceding frame, we may deduce that (a) a particular student may or may not need confirmation of his correct response or correction of his incorrect response on any particular frame in a program; and (b) that the program will be used by large groups of students who may vary in their reactions to any particular frame. Therefore, the programer should provide knowledge of results on [every frame/those frames that he thinks are hard/those frames that his students missed in the trial of the program]. (Which?)

— — — — — — — — — — — — — — —

every frame (unless his whole program reads like the "aardvark" frame!).

---

46. In an experiment by the author (Meyer, 1960) 16 eighth graders completed a program with no immediate confirmation of their responses. The group as a whole made significantly more errors and gained significantly less knowledge than a comparable group given knowledge of results in the usual way. However, two students in the "no-answer" group turned in an almost errorless performance and gained a great deal from pretest to posttest. How would you explain the data from these two students? (They did not cheat and their pretest scores showed they had much to learn.)

— — — — — — — — — — — — — — —

The best guess is that the program moved at a rate of progress that was right for them—they could take the next step correctly, and they knew that they were right.

---

47. If the "fit" between the size of the steps forward that the program asks for and the size of steps that an individual student can take happens to be good, this particular student may "know he is right" and do very well without ever having to check the correct answer. (Indeed many students can be observed doing just this—paying no attention to the answers.)
   If the size of step in the program is too small for the student—that is, if he could have gone faster than the program allows, is he likely to do well without checking his answers?

— — — — — — — — — — — — — — —

Yes.

48. In any good program, the condition in which the student is guessing wildly (for example, "what number am I thinking of?") will not happen. (This does not mean that he won't be asked to guess, but his guess is left as a guess and not called wrong.) This was one condition under which it was necessary to provide knowledge of results.

For any particular student, what other *conditions* might arise in which he would need to be given knowledge of results even in a fairly good program?

- - - - - - - - - - - - - - -

(a) Whenever he is unsure of his response and needs it confirmed or corrected, and (b) whenever he is wrong but thought he was right.

Note. Pragmatically, most programers adopt the conventional system of providing an answer or a model of kinds of good answers immediately after each frame, as you are experiencing in this program. Other solutions have been tried, such as having answers available if needed at the bottom of the page or back of the text. Certain kinds of teaching machines can "confirm" a correct answer by moving on to the next problem, without revealing the correct answer if the student errs—the machine simply waits.

An example of a program which provides no confirmation is *Child Management: A Program for Parents* by Judith M. and Donald E. P. Smith. (1966) Here "frames" consist of presentation of material describing a general principle they are advising parents to adopt, followed by two or more "cases"—one of which illustrates the principle and the others of which do not. The reader is expected to be able to make the choices and to have the correctness of his choice as obvious as was the answer to the Aardvark frame (presented in Frame 41). The answer to whether this procedure works is found, as always, in research with students, not in theoretical arguments. Each program is an individual case in itself.

Summary: Principles of Skinnerian Programing

The programer's task is to create instructional materials which embody these principles:

1. Active Responding. The student learns what the program leads him to do.

An active response is not necessarily a small one nor is it necessarily (in the final version of the program) an overt one.

2. Minimal Errors. By good design of the instruction, and by repeated tryout and revision of the instruction, errors made by students in responding to frames and in exhibiting the final desired behavior are held to a minimum.

An error, as we defined it, is a response that the programer did not expect or does not wish students to make.

3. **Knowledge of Results.** In some fashion, a student should be given such feedback on the adequacy of his response. This may be provided by skillful design, which leads a student to be right and be sure he's right, or by providing an answer as a guide to checking himself if he is unsure or in error.

The status of confirmation as "the reinforcer" in the sense intended by Skinner and his colleagues is open to question. The glossary presents a brief discussion of this point, if you are interested, under the definition of *reinforcement.*

SECTION B. A CLOSE LOOK AT A SEGMENT OF A CLASSICAL LINEAR PROGRAM

INTRODUCTION

The first rule of "program inspecting" is: YOU CAN'T TELL BY LOOKING AT IT WHETHER IT WORKS, OR WHETHER IT'S TOO EASY OR TOO HARD. As a matter of fact, you can't even tell WHETHER IT'S A FULLY RESEARCHED PROGRAM.

Any program is a particular product resulting from a long and grueling process. This process begins with a careful analysis of the subject matter or skill to be taught. The programer has to identify all the necessary principles, technical terms, manipulations, and the range of examples to which these principles, terms, or operations can be applied. He has to, in effect, analyze the behavior of subject matter experts, if he is not one himself, in order to specify clearly and in measurable terms what it means to "know" and "understand" the subject. When he can describe what these behaviors are and how they can be measured or tested, he then studies his intended student population in order to determine what needs to go in the program. Knowing what students can already do and what he wants to lead them to be able to do, he is ready to draft a design for instruction.

But first drafts are only first drafts. The final product is the result of taking drafts to students, carefully observing these students as they work through the instruction *and* try to perform like experts on the final test. (A low error rate is NOT enough!) Programers set standards of how well they want the program to work and they keep at the research-and-development until the program comes up to these standards. (Markle and Tiemann, 1967.)

Section A presented some of the things that happen to a program when it goes to its trial-by-student. When a program has been thoroughly tested, you can see the effects of these changes. But, unless you can get hold of *both* the first draft and the actual responses of students to the final product and to its test (data, in other words), there are some things you cannot decide about the program by looking at it.

1. Using common sense, what you learned in Section A, and the brief description above, decide which of the following can be found out by looking at a published program and which would require supporting documents such as a description of data obtained from a sample of students.

(a) The programer makes use of multiple-choice frames occasionally. [program/data?]
(b) The program provides enough practice for "average" students in its intended population. [program/data?]
(c) The program provides review frames, repeating former frame content, at fairly regular intervals. [program/data?]
(d) The program omits certain key terms in the subject matter. [program/data?]
(e) The program has been thoroughly tested on appropriate students. [program/data?]

— — — — — — — — — — — — — —

(a) Kinds of responses, as well as other variables such as size of frames, adherence to "active" responding versus much irrelevant material, can be determined by looking at the program.
(b) "Enough practice" is an empirical dimension—you'd have to look at data to determine this.
(c) Review frames (see Frames 5 and 6 in Section A) can be located by inspection of the program. How regularly they occur, of course, is just a matter of counting.
(d) Subject matter *coverage,* in contrast with subject matter *learned by students,* can be determined by looking at the program. What is learned can only be gleaned from looking at the test and the data.
(e) At the beginning of the introduction, I said that you can't tell whether it's a program (according to my definition of a program) by looking at it. This is why—only data can demonstrate that a program has been thoroughly tested. Without such data, I would call it a first draft, not a program.

2. A segment of a program follows this page (pp. 27-36). Before getting down to a critical look at it, glance at it for the answers to the following "quickie" inspection questions:

(a) Does the programer use any multiple-choice questions?
(b) Would you say that these are "small steps," at least in terms of the amount of material in them?
(c) (This will take a little more time.) Does the programer vary the way he asks for a response or does he restrict himself to one format, such as an incomplete sentence with a blank to be filled?

When you have answered these inspection questions, return to this page for confirmation.

— — — — — — — — — — — — — —

(a) This program is theoretically "pure," according to the Skinnerian position in 1960. It contains no multiple-choice questions. (b) It also proceeds in the classically small-step fashion, with very little variation in frame size. (c) It does, however, use a variety of techniques in asking for responses—questions, incomplete sentences, and requests such as "define" or "explain."

A CLOSE LOOK AT A SEGMENT OF A CLASSICAL LINEAR PROGRAM

At this point, you should assess your own knowledge of the subject matter. The program was designed to teach high-school physics students, and since it was thoroughly researched to do that job, it should be effective in teaching you as well.

If you do not know (or are not sure you know) all about DISPLACEMENT, MAGNITUDE, VECTORS, and SCALARS, it would be a good idea to take the programed sequence right now.

Frames 5-38 have been replaced by a brief description of their content. If you find yourself making errors in the immediately following frames, it is my description of their content, not the original program, that is at fault!

If this subject is familiar to you, go directly to Frame 4 on page 36. There we will go through the program frame by frame observing the techniques used in frame and sequence construction.

Segment of a Classical Linear Program

The program presented below, *Vectors,* a Basic Systems program, is published in a programed text with "through-the-book" format. The student turns the page in order to find the correct answer and the next item. For ease of inspection, it is here presented in "down-the-page" format. Some of the illustrations have been omitted. *The program begins with these four frames*:

1. A person walks three miles north. He takes a rest and walks another three miles north. How far has he walked altogether?

   _ _ _ _ _ _ _ _ _ _ _ _ _ _ _

   Six miles.

2. A boy walks one mile north and then walks one mile south. How far has he walked?

   _ _ _ _ _ _ _ _ _ _ _ _ _ _ _

   Two miles.

3. A boy walks one mile north, then two miles south. Draw a diagram of his path; show his starting point and his finishing point.

   _ _ _ _ _ _ _ _ _ _ _ _ _ _ _

   (Diagram provided in answer space.)

28 THE BASIC PROGRAMING PRINCIPLES

4. If a boy walked one mile north, then two miles south, how far was he from his starting point when he stopped walking?

— — — — — — — — — — — — — — —

One mile.

At this point, we have removed 35 frames. These frames teach the student that DISTANCE means "how far an object has moved", that MAGNITUDE means "size", and that DISPLACEMENT means "how far and in what direction an object is from its starting point." The magnitude of a displacement is how far the object is from the origin, while a full description of displacement must also include the direction. A typical problem is this one:

A person walks from A to B to C.
What is the distance he walked?
What is his displacement?

— — — — — — — — — — — — — — —

(The distance is 8 miles—5 + 3.)
(The displacement is 4 miles East of his starting point.)

39. Things that have direction and magnitude are called vectors. Is displacement a vector?_____. Explain your answer.

— — — — — — — — — — — — — — —

Yes. It has magnitude and direction.

---

40. A boy walks ten miles south and then six miles north. What distance has he walked?

— — — — — — — — — — — — — — —

Sixteen miles.

---

41. What is a vector?

— — — — — — — — — — — — — — —

A vector is a quantity that has magnitude and direction.

42. A displacement has direction and magnitude. A distance has_____ but not_____. Is distance a vector?_____. Explain your answer.

— — — — — — — — — — — — — — —

magnitude, direction.

No. A vector has magnitude and direction, and a distance has only magnitude.

---

43. This arrow has a length. We call this length the magnitude of the arrow. The magnitude of arrow $\overline{AB}$ is_____inches. (Use a ruler for measuring.)

— — — — — — — — — — — — — — —

one-half.

---

44. What is the magnitude of arrow $\overline{PQ}$?

— — — — — — — — — — — — — — —

One inch.

---

45. The magnitude of an arrow is equal to its_____.

— — — — — — — — — — — — — — —

length.

---

46. In what direction does arrow $\overline{AB}$ point?

— — — — — — — — — — — — — — —

North.

30 THE BASIC PROGRAMING PRINCIPLES

47. What are the magnitude and direction of arrow $\overline{ST}$?

Three-quarter inch, east.

---

48. The displacement of an object as it moves from one point to another is defined as the distance and direction from the first point to the second. Why is displacement a vector?

Displacement is a vector because it has magnitude and direction.

---

49. All vectors and all arrows have _____ and _____.

----

direction and magnitude.

---

50. Arrow $\overline{AB}$ represents a vector. What are the magnitude (in inches) and direction of vector $\overline{AB}$?

One inch, north.

A CLOSE LOOK AT A SEGMENT OF A CLASSICAL LINEAR PROGRAM   31

51. Arrow $\overline{PQ}$ represents a displacement vector. What are the magnitude (in inches) and direction of $\overline{PQ}$?

    — — — — — — — — — — — — — —

    One and one-eighth inches, south.

---

52. We can use arrows to represent vectors because both arrows and vectors have _____.
                    (complete the sentence)

    — — — — — — — — — — — — — —

    magnitude and direction.

---

53. Define displacement.

    — — — — — — — — — — — — — —

    The displacement of an object as it moves from one point to another is defined as the distance and direction from the first point to the second.

---

54. Explain why displacements can be represented by arrows.

    — — — — — — — — — — — — — —

    Displacements are vectors and therefore can be represented by arrows.

32 THE BASIC PROGRAMING PRINCIPLES

55. Suppose each inch represents twenty miles, and $\overline{AB}$ represents a boy's displacement from his starting point. What is the boy's displacement?

— — — — — — — — — — — — — —

Fifteen miles north.

56. $\overline{PQ}$ represents a person's displacement. If one inch represents four miles, what is his displacement?

— — — — — — — — — — — — — —

Five miles south.

57. A distance has magnitude but not direction. Therefore distance is called a scalar. Quantities which have magnitude but not direction are called _____.

— — — — — — — — — — — — — —

scalars.

58. All numbers are scalars because they don't have _____ and do have _____.

— — — — — — — — — — — — — —

direction, magnitude.

59. A quantity which has magnitude but not direction is called a
 _____.

— — — — — — — — — — — — — — —

scalar.

---

60. Give two examples of scalars.

— — — — — — — — — — — — — — —

Sum of money, distance, length, numbers, etc.

---

61. What is the difference between a vector and a scalar?

— — — — — — — — — — — — — — —

A vector has magnitude and direction. A scalar has magnitude only.

---

62. Explain why a sum of money such as $302.79 can be called a scalar.

— — — — — — — — — — — — — — —

It has magnitude but not direction.

---

63. Define displacement.

— — — — — — — — — — — — — — —

The displacement of an object as it moves from one point to another is defined as the distance and direction from the first point to the second.

34 THE BASIC PROGRAMING PRINCIPLES

---

64. Explain why we say that displacement is a vector.

— — — — — — — — — — — — — —

It has magnitude and direction.

---

65. A farmer walks around his rectangular corn field from *A* to *B* to *C* to *D,* stopping at *D.* What is the distance he has traveled?

— — — — — — — — — — — — — —

Thirteen miles.

---

66. What is the magnitude of his displacement?

_____.

What is his displacement?

_____.

— — — — — — — — — — — — — —

Three miles.

Three miles north.

---

67. Distance has only magnitude, it has no direction. Therefore, distance is a _____.

— — — — — — — — — — — — — —

scalar.

---

68. What is a scalar?

— — — — — — — — — — — — — — —

A scalar is a quantity with magnitude but not direction.

---

69. Define displacement.

— — — — — — — — — — — — — —

The displacement of an object as it moves from one point to another is defined as the distance and direction from the first point to the second.

---

70. Since displacement has both magnitude and direction, displacement is not a _____. Displacement is a _____.

— — — — — — — — — — — — — — —

scalar.

vector.

---

71. A difference between displacement and distance is that _____ has only magnitude, while _____ has both magnitude and direction.

— — — — — — — — — — — — —

distance, displacement.

36 THE BASIC PROGRAMING PRINCIPLES

72. Displacement is a _____. Distance is a _____.

--- --- --- --- --- --- --- --- --- --- --- --- --- ---

vector.

scalar.

---

73. Explain what we mean by scalar and vector.

--- --- --- --- --- --- --- --- --- --- --- --- --- ---

A scalar has magnitude but not direction. A vector has magnitude and direction.

From here on, you'll have to indulge in some page-turning to locate the answers to questions about the construction of the Vectors program.

4. The first four frames, pages 27-28, belong in the first section of the program; then we skip to the second section starting at Frame 39.

In the first section (#1-38), the technical terms "distance," "magnitude," and "displacement" were introduced, their definitions memorized (data show), and various problems involving them presented for solution. Inspect the first four frames. Are any of these technical terms used in these four frames?

--- --- --- --- --- --- --- --- --- --- --- ---

No.

5. The programer is dealing with already known material in the first four frames, but he is leading up to the distinction he wants to teach between "distance" and "displacement." The first three frames ask questions about distance. In the fourth one, the question is about displacement:

> 4. If a boy walked one mile north, then two miles south, how far was he from his starting point when he stopped walking?

Displacement is a *two-dimensional* concept. It includes both
  (a) how far from the starting point
       and
  (b) in what direction from the origin.

Frame 4 is one step, and this program is proceeding one step at a time. If the programer is consistent, he still has one more question to ask about displacement before he introduces the term. What content would you predict for Frame 5 if he proceeds in the fashion shown so far?

— — — — — — — — — — — — — — — —

The student will be asked to say in what direction from the starting point an object is at the end of a trip. (In fact, this is not the content of the next frame, but it does appear, predictably, before the student sees the technical term "displacement.")

---

6. Given a two-dimensional concept such as displacement, the programer asks the student to respond to each dimension: one response for "how far from the starting point" and a second response for "in what direction from the starting point."

What principle of programing does this two-questions-for-two-dimensions exemplify?

  If your memory has slipped, see the Summary for Section A on page 24.

— — — — — — — — — — — — — — — —

The principle of active responding. These frames also represent adherence to the idea of "one-step-at-a-time" or "small steps", although true believers in small steps might be upset about the length of some of the responses and the number of responses asked for per frame in some of the later frames in the second section!

38 THE BASIC PROGRAMING PRINCIPLES

Now for the second section of the program, beginning with Frame 39 on page 28.

7. From what you see in the first four items of the second section, this program involves (a) single-word responses; (b) sentence-length responses; (c) both of these; (d) neither of these.

— — — — — — — — — — — — — — —

Both of these (or c). Note especially the answers for Frame 42, which included all three kinds of stimuli–blanks to fill in, direct questions, and requests for sentences. The responses, thus, were both short and long.

---

8. In the first 38 frames of the program, the student has been led to define the term "displacement," to calculate distances covered and displacements represented by trips of different lengths and directions around triangles and rectangles, and to define and use the term "magnitude."
    Here is frame 39:

> 39. Things that have direction and magnitude are called vectors. Is displacement a vector?_____. Explain your answer.

This frame represents (a) a rehearsal of old learning; (b) an introduction of a new concept; (c) both of these; (d) neither of these.

— — — — — — — — — — — — — — —

(c) both of these–displacement has been taught and the frame introduces the concept of 'vector'.

---

9. > 40. A boy walks ten miles south and then six miles north. What distance has he walked?

Frame 40 represents (a) a rehearsal of old learning; (b) an introduction of a new concept; (c) both of these; (d) neither of these.

— — — — — — — — — — — — — — —

(a) a rehearsal of old learning–calculating distances was practiced in the first section.

A CLOSE LOOK AT A SEGMENT OF A CLASSICAL LINEAR PROGRAM

10. At this point, it is time to read through the second section of the program in detail, looking at its construction. (If you've already read through it to learn the subject matter, you probably weren't looking at the way the frames were put together and sequenced. So you'll need to go through it again from this new point of view.)

This is what you should be looking for and taking notes on:

(1) Skinner noted that there are two techniques that help the student to come up with the right answer before he has permanently learned it:
   "orderly construction of the program" and
   "techniques of hinting, prompting, suggesting."
We may take the objectives of the Frames 39-73 to be:
   the student will be able to define the terms 'vector' and 'scalar' and
   the student will be able to identify examples of each concept.
These behaviors are what the last frames ask for.

On a large piece of notepaper (to save you from turning back to this page all the time), you will take notes on three facets of the program. Here is the first:

(1) You are looking for all the frames relevant to the first objective: the student will define 'vector' and 'scalar.' These fall into two categories: (a) those asking for the definition and including some kind of hint or prompt, and (b) frames asking for the definition but giving no help. Frame 73, asking for the definition of both terms, will belong in your list for each term in the no-help section.

Set up a two-by-two table like this:

	help	no help
vector		, 73
scalar		, 73

(2) Teaching on the concept 'scalar' begins at Frame 57. Some of the frames, which you will have listed above, require the student to give the definition. There are also several other different kinds of frames, asking for other kinds of responses. Look for the different kinds of questions on the concept 'scalar.' How many kinds are there? Give each kind you find some sort of name and note which frames belong in each category.

(There are no "correct" names. You will be using these notes shortly, and if the names make sense to you, you're in good shape.)

(3) How many direct repetitions do you find? These must be the same question with the same answer. All but the first frame that you list in the "no-help" section of your notes on items asking for the definitions [in (1) above] will be repetitions. There are others in this segment of the program.

As you take notes, write down the frame numbers. Then you'll be able to find particular frames easily.

When you've finished taking notes, check the "interim" confirmation. You may wish to fill out your notes further, if you overlooked something important.

--- --- --- --- --- --- --- --- ---

Here is an interim confirmation of what you should have in your notes. We'll go into greater detail in later frames in this program.

(1) There are SEVEN frames in which the student is asked to define 'vector' WITH help. Consider yourself sharp if you located five, eagle-eyed if you've listed all seven.

There are THREE frames in which the student is asked to define 'vector' with NO help, including the example we gave you, Frame 73.

There are TWO frames in which the student is asked to define 'scalar' WITH help.

There are THREE frames in which the student is asked to define 'scalar' with NO help, including Frame 73.

(2) There are ELEVEN frames in which 'scalar' is part or all of the subject matter. One category "give definition" you have listed in (1) above. You should be able to get at least three other categories. (What you call them doesn't matter.)

(3) This was the roughest question to answer. Consider your list satisfactory if, along with the repetitions of the definition of 'scalar' and 'vector' that you have in your "no-help" part of (1), you also noted the three direct repetitions of the definition of displacement which occurs first in Frame 48.

If you also included solving the same kind of problem with only the numbers changed, you may have at least three other sets of repetitions.

If you have to stop soon, this would be a good spot. SAVE YOUR NOTES!!

---

11. At the beginning of this section (on page 25), we noted that you cannot judge from looking at a program whether it contains "enough" practice. This is an empirical question. There is enough practice IF students can perform well on the terminal test and, in a long program, remember for use later in the program what they learned early in the program.

    In the Teacher's Manual for the *Vectors* program, evidence is given that there is indeed enough practice for the students used in the validation study. They did well.

    Look at it from another point of view. In your notes for Frame 10, you have documented how much practice there really is in this section of the program, at least on certain types of questions. With this evidence gained from your inspection of the program, do you THINK there is too much practice?

    If you think so, are you justified in stating that *it is a fact that* there is too much practice?

If you say "no" to that last question, what would you have to do to prove that there is too much practice?

———————————————

The first question asked for your opinion. You are in the majority if you said you think there is too much. Many people make judgments of this sort without going through the documenting that you did.

It is NOT a fact. As with the question of "enough", "too much" is an empirical question, not a matter of opinion. Only data drawn from appropriate students can answer it.

The only proof that would hold water would be revising the program by eliminating repetitions and then trying out your new version. If it worked just as well, you could conclude that the "fat" version has too much practice. You would have to be especially careful, of course, to include among your test students the "slowest" ones that this "fat" version works with.

12. The order in which information is introduced is not an integral part of any general theory of linear programing. (In Chapter Three, we'll look at some approaches to this subject.) You will find linear programs going from the concrete (examples or lower level concepts) to the abstract (higher level generalizations and concepts) and from the abstract to the concrete (beginning with general principles and leading into application of these). There are some that proceed in spiral order (Bruner, 1960), which requires concepts to be introduced at a simple, almost "intuitive" level, followed by gradual elaboration and precise presentation. Each concept to be treated is, therefore, handled several times (hence, the spiral) at each increasingly sophisticated level.

From what you have seen of the *Vectors* program, the programer is proceeding (a) from concrete to abstract or (b) from abstract to concrete. (a or b?)

———————————————

(a) The program begins with very concrete low-level examples before introducing the low-level concepts which, in turn, are used to introduce the higher level concepts.

42   THE BASIC PROGRAMING PRINCIPLES

13. A prompt is a hint to the student that aids him to give the correct answer. Are there any prompts given in the text of frame 41?

> 41. What is a vector?

No. It is a direct question with no hint as to the number of dimensions that must be specified, no example to suggest what is asked for, or any other kind of hint.

---

14. The *Vectors* program is a tested program. Therefore, we can assume that few students will make errors on any of the items in it, and we have to allow that students will answer item 41 correctly. Also, because of the format of the program, students would have to turn back two pages if they wished to copy item 39. Yet, the student cannot be said to have "really learned" the definition already, as the programer shows by giving many more items on the subject later.

If (a) there are no prompts in the item, (b) the student does not look back at item 39, (c) the programer does not assume that the student has mastered it yet, and (d) the student answers the item correctly, what is going on—how can he give an answer he has not fully learned yet? What makes it easy for him?

Note. If you are not sure and want a hint, drop down to the next line. If you are sure, skip the hint.

Hint. When you look up a new phone number, you may say it to yourself and run to the phone to dial it. (Assume you cannot take the phone book with you.) Most of us can retain a number sufficiently accurately to get the place we want to call. Yet an hour later, you would have difficulty recognizing the number you called placed among other numbers (a multiple-choice question) and would be unable to recall it. You had not learned the number "for keeps," but you got your party. Could the same thing be going on in item 41? Why can the student answer the question?

The student saw the answer (or gave the answer) a moment earlier.

15. Item 49 reads:

> All vectors and all arrows have _____ and _____ .

Item 52 reads:

> We can use arrows to represent vectors because both arrows and vectors have_____.

The first part of the sentence in item 52 changes the context slightly but it is not a prompt. Item 52 is more difficult than item 49. A prompt has been withdrawn. Why is it easier for the student to come up with the complete response "direction and magnitude" in the first item than in the second?

— — — — — — — — — — — — — —

(in your own words) he is told that he has to produce two words in the first item. In the second one he is not told how many words to produce.

---

16. Suppose we wrote this item:

> What two properties must a vector have?

Such an item is [easier/harder] than

> What is a vector?

— — — — — — — — — — — — — —

easier (the number of blanks is not the only way to ask for two!).

44 THE BASIC PROGRAMING PRINCIPLES

---

17. In the Glossary (under *Terminal behavior*) a terminal frame is defined thus:

> A terminal item contains NO prompts
>   AND
> is placed far enough from the training sequences to measure more than immediate memory.

Frame 41 of *Vectors,* as we just saw, does not qualify as a terminal item.

Choose between items 67, 68, and 69. (You will have to locate them, on page 34, to inspect the items preceding them as well.) Which of these items most nearly qualifies as a terminal item? Why does each of the other not qualify?

    (a) Item_____ does not qualify because_____.
    (b) Item_____ does not qualify because_____.
    (c) Item_____ most nearly qualifies.

— — — — — — — — — — — — — — —

(a) Item 67 contains a strong hint (the first sentence) that distance is a scalar, so it doesn't qualify.
(b) Item 68 directly follows an item on the same subject, so it doesn't qualify.
(c) Item 69 most nearly qualifies—it is somewhat separated from the last discussion of the concept and contains no prompts.

---

18. When a student understands a concept, he can do many things with it. Among the possible responses he can make are the following:

(a) given the term, he can give its definition;
(b) given its definition, he can give the term;
(c) given an example of it, he can correctly <u>name</u> what class the example belongs to;
(d) he can give examples of the term;
(e) given a non-example of it, he can correctly identify it as not an example.

Further kinds of items are elaborations of these. For instance:

(f) given two concepts, he can compare and contrast them; this is really a combination of two items of type (a), since contrasting means saying what each is and noting the difference.
(g) given a set of examples which exemplify two or more concepts, he can correctly classify all of them; this is a more complicated version of (c) and (e).

In a good program, we'd expect items of each one of these types that was relevant to the objectives of the program. In a classical linear small-step program, we'd also expect repeti-

A CLOSE LOOK AT A SEGMENT OF A CLASSICAL LINEAR PROGRAM 45

tions of these item types, with early ones being heavily prompted, later ones not prompted at all, and, perhaps, delayed reviews.

At this point, your notes on "scalar" are relevant. Whenever they are not complete enough, you'll have to go back and look at the frame again. You were asked in Frame 10, question 2, to note all the different kinds of items teaching "scalar." Your terminology may not agree with the list above, but hopefully it will save you some page flipping.

The term 'scalar' is introduced in Frame 57. This is a highly prompted item. (In the next chapter, we'll introduce the idea that it is a copying frame which is so prompted that it isn't what Skinner meant by prompting.) Since, given the definition, the student responds with the term, this is an item of type (b) in the above list of item types.

The second item in the sequence, #58, is prompted and it is of type (a)—the student fills in at least part of the definition of 'scalar'.

Now, using your notes when possible and referring to the original frames (they begin on page 32), fill in the rest of this table, using the seven different item types.

Write. You couldn't hold all this in your head until the confirmation—and you will be working with the whole table.

	Type of item	Prompted (yes or no)
Item 57	b	yes
Item 58	a	yes
Item 59	___	___
Item 60	___	___
Item 61	___	___
Item 62	a	yes
Item 67	___	___
Item 70 (first response)	___	___
Item 72	___	___
Item 73	___	___

19. In confirming your response to the last frame, you should review the definitions of item types and take another look at the frames in *Vectors* if you made any mistake in the *first* column. If you disagree with the rating on prompting in the second column, don't worry. That's the subject of the next chapter and you're playing it by ear at the moment.

Here is the outline of that part of *Vectors*.

Item 57 Definition to term	(b)	Prompted
Item 58 Term to definition	(a)	Yes
Item 59 Definition to term	(b)	No
Item 60 Give example	(d)	No
Item 61 Contrast terms	(f)	Yes
Item 62 Term to definition	(a)	Yes
Item 67 Label an example	(c)	Yes
Item 68 Term to definition	(a)	No
Item 70 Identify non-example	(e)	Yes
Item 72 Classify examples	(g)	No
Item 73 Contrast terms	(f)	No

Inspect this outline to answer the following:

A. In teaching this one concept, are all types of items used (a - g)?
B. Taking (f) to mean $(a_1 + a_2)$—in other words, an item of type (a) for two concepts, and
taking (g) to mean $(c_1 + c_2)$—in other words, label examples of two concepts,
is there any place in the sequence outlined above where the student is asked to do the *same* thing twice in a row? [Does an (a) follow an (a) or a (b) a (b), etc.?]

— — — — — — — — — — — — — —

Yes, there is at least one of each type.

There is only one direct repetition—61 and 62 are both (a) types; both ask the student to define 'scalar.' In 61, he has to define 'vector' too.

[Note to the dubious: In Frame 62, the example, $302.79, is a help, or prompt, should the student have any difficulty in remembering the definition. In that frame the student does not have to judge whether or not the money is a scalar; he is told. So it is not a frame of type (c).]

A CLOSE LOOK AT A SEGMENT OF A CLASSICAL LINEAR PROGRAM

20. *Vectors* moves in far smaller steps than is now considered fashionable, especially for programs designed for similar populations. (It was designed for upper high-school students taking physics and can be used by college students as well.) It is, however, an excellent example of effective early linear programing. You would be hard put to find irrelevant material in the frames that would reduce its adherence to the principle of active responding. There is real variety in the types of responses asked for, which somewhat reduces the "boredom" that some students feel in going through such small steps. This variety also fosters what most of us mean by the word "understanding"—the student can do far more than spout a rote-memorized definition of a term. From these small segments of the program, you can get some feel for the orderliness with which the concepts are sequenced, building from common knowledge in the first few frames to low-level concepts to higher-level concepts. You can see the occurrence of at least one set of really terminal items—the review frames on the definition of 'displacement'.

As you may have guessed, the orderliness that produced your outline of the small segment on 'scalar' did not happen by accident. Programers may have different ideas about how to design instruction, but there is one point of agreement among all. The work that *precedes* the production of frames is the key to good instruction. *Vectors* represents an example (though not the only acceptable kind of example) of what Skinner proposed in the article you read at the beginning of this program.

On the following page is an example of a different style of programing. It is also in a different format, in which the student is expected to cover the edge of the page where answers are given next to each blank. He moves a mask down to reveal each answer as he fills in each blank. We are interested in the programing *style* rather than the format.

Question: In what ways does this "style" differ from the programing in *Vectors?* Name at least three differences you observe.

Do you think it represents an acceptable example of the three principles of programing described by Skinner? Which one or ones would be violated, do you feel?

1. Programers have given a name to certain techniques employed for insuring correct responses. Some call them "cues" while others call them *prompts*. A cue or_____ is a technique for insuring a correct response.	prompt
2. When a student knows nothing about a subject, he needs more than a hint or_____to help him respond correctly. When he knows all about the subject, he	prompt
doesn't need_____s to help him respond correctly.	prompts
3. A question or an incomplete sentence is a kind of stimulus to which a student responds. If he already knows the answer, we should not give him a_____.	prompt
4. Because we want the student to be correct, we provide him with_____s to help him respond to material he has not yet thoroughly learned.	prompts
5. A question or an incomplete sentence is a kind of stimulus to which a student responds. If he already knows the answer, should we give him a prompt? (Yes/No)	No
6. If a student needs to be given ten items on a particular subject in order to master it, the third item in this sequence should have more_____s than the seventh.	prompts

— — — — — — — — — — — — — —

The above "program" is a revision of some frames I wrote. It represents a style which I have called "Swiss Cheese." (More about that later.) It differs from *Vectors* in (1) repetition of the same response, (2) rigidity in the way the response is asked for, (3) large amount of irrelevant unresponded-to material in each frame, and (4) no examples of the concept. You may have thought of others, too.

It does provide knowledge of results and would probably produce minimal errors, but it is a gross violation of the principle of active responding.

21. Programs in academic subject matter usually cover material quite similar to that of the *Vectors* program. "Understanding" the discipline means mastering many concepts and the relations between them, which are the "principles" or "laws" of the subject. (Gagné, 1965.)
    One part of mastery, of course, is being able to talk about the subject. This is best exemplified by items that require the student to define terms or to state principles. Another part of mastery, too often overlooked, is being able to apply the terms and principles to the real world being talked about, in other words to recognize examples of concepts and be able to use principles to solve problems. The best test of "real understanding" of a concept is correct classification of examples the student never met in the teaching sequence. (Markle and Tiemann, 1969.)

A CLOSE LOOK AT A SEGMENT OF A CLASSICAL LINEAR PROGRAM 49

In the *Vectors* program, the concept of 'scalar' was exemplified by several different kinds of examples. If you check back (or remember), the only example of a vector at this point in the program was displacement. Later, the concept is extended to include other examples.

We can, of course, apply this approach to programs about programing, as well. If, in a sequence of items, I teach you to define *terminal frame* (mentioned in Frame 17 above and applied to one frame in the *Vectors* program), what do I still have to do to apply the principle of active responding to your "understanding" of *terminal frame?* What further kinds of responses should be asked for?

— — — — — — — — — — — — — — —

If you "really understand" it, you should be able to recognize all sorts of examples of it. Maybe you should be able to produce such frames too!

If you have to stop soon, this is an appropriate spot. The next stopping point is the end of the chapter.

22. Frame 55 asks the student to calculate a displacement from a picture of a 3/4 inch arrow pointing north. It begins with the phrase "Suppose each inch represents twenty miles . . ." The sequence developing the whole skill required to answer this item begins with Frame 43, and continues through 44, 45, 46, 47, 50, and 51.

    In order to answer frame 55 correctly, the student should be able to (a) give the direction of the arrow, (b) measure its magnitude, (c) know that these two represent displacement, and (d) multiply the length of the arrow by 20 in order to get the answer in miles.

    From what you see in the preceding frames (beginning with 43), does the programer instruct the student in all of these or does he assume that students can do one of them? If so, which one?

— — — — — — — — — — — — — —

The programer does not instruct the student in what to do with "suppose an inch represents 20 miles."

50   THE BASIC PROGRAMING PRINCIPLES

23. Which bit of behavior seems more complex to you: using a ruler to measure an arrow or translating 3/4 of an inch into 15 miles?

_ _ _ _ _ _ _ _ _ _ _ _ _ _ _

Your opinion. I vote for the latter.

24. The *Vectors* program was *tested* on a good many students. From what you know about the development of a linear program, why did the programer instruct the students to use a ruler in order to measure the arrow (Frame 43) but not in the apparently more difficult translation of inches into miles?

_ _ _ _ _ _ _ _ _ _ _ _ _ _ _

The best guess would be that the programer *found* (not *assumed*) that some students were approximating the measurement of the arrows and needed to be reminded to be precise, whereas no errors were made on the "translation" problem. If your answer was incorrect, do items 25 and 26. If correct, skip to 27.

25. When you inspect the *first draft* of a program, you may talk about what the programer *assumes* that students can do. If, in a trigonometry program, the programer assumes that students know about right triangles, will he tell them that a right angle has 90°?_____.

_ _ _ _ _ _ _ _ _ _ _ _ _ _ _

No. Why waste space?

26. If a programer is wrong in his assumption about how much students know (or remember) from geometry, he will discover his mistake from his initial test of the program. Students will make errors, and he will repair his program accordingly. Suppose you look at the final version of a program. You find that the programer has not taught something that you would have taught, had you written the program. If the program has been well tested, what do you know about your assumption of what students need to be told?

_ _ _ _ _ _ _ _ _ _ _ _ _ _ _

For the students whom he used in the test, your assumption is wrong. (It may not be wrong when a different group of students is tested.)

A CLOSE LOOK AT A SEGMENT OF A CLASSICAL LINEAR PROGRAM 51

27. We could line up the properties of the two concepts, vector and scalar, thus:
    vector: magnitude, yes; direction, yes.
    scalar: magnitude, yes; direction, no.
Inspect items 58 and 62. In both items the student is asked to say why an example (numbers in one case, money in the other) of a scalar is an example. Item 62 is considerably harder than item 58. In terms of the analysis of the concepts above, name two ways that make it harder.

- - - - - - - - - - - - - - -

The student has to know that there are two properties, and know the "yes-no" part that goes with the two properties in item 62. In item 58, he has two blanks and is given the "yes-no" part.

---

28. One item is a repetition of another if, in the presence of the same or a similar stimulus, the same or a similar response is asked for. When we ask for more of a response from the student (as in the comparison of items 58 and 62), the response has changed. If we add a prompt to the item (more information, an example, a definition, or even an indication of the number of words to be given) we have changed the stimulus.
    No one would have any doubt that item 63 ("Define displacement") is a direct repetition of item 53 ("Define displacement").
    Is item 73 close enough to item 61 in both stimulus and response characteristics to be called a repetition?_____ .

- - - - - - - - - - - - - - -

I would say "yes." The wording has been changed slightly, but neither item contains a prompt and the response is identical.

---

29. Is item 56 a repetition of item 55?_____ . Why?

- - - - - - - - - - - - - - -

I would say "yes." The numbers have been changed but they are otherwise the same problem.

52   THE BASIC PROGRAMING PRINCIPLES

30. The student is asked three times in this section (items 53, 63, and 69) to define displacement by a direct question. How many other times in these 34 items does he have to *define* or *explain* displacement (not classify or solve it) in order to answer a question?_____.
Which questions require this?_____.

Hint. Watch the answer spaces for "magnitude and direction." If that is the response and displacement (not vector) is the stimulus, you have the right question.

— — — — — — — — — — — — — — — —

Three times. Items 39, 48, and 64 require him to say what displacement is in order to tell why it is a vector. Data obtained in research with this program show that students actually add a fourth item, 54, and answer that question by giving the definition of displacement as the reason.

---

31. There are further review items later in the program on this definition. It should come as no surprise to you that the question "Define displacement" is on the final examination for this program. Why did the programer provide so much practice on a definition that he wants the students to learn?

— — — — — — — — — — — — — — — —

Because some students needed that amount of practice in order to retain the concept (*not* because that was the amount of practice the programer thought was about right).

---

32. The *Vectors* program asks this pair of questions:

> Item 59. A quantity which has magnitude but not direction is called a_____.
> Item 68. What is a scalar?

Let us say that the proposition that the programer is teaching is represented by the formula $a = b$. (Let a be the term and b be its definition.) In mathematics, if $a = b$, then usually $b = a$.

According to the theory of learning represented by the *Vectors* program, if the student has practiced the response b in the presence of the stimulus a, he
 (a) now knows that $b = a$;
 (b) should be led to say that $b = a$. (Choose one.)

— — — — — — — — — — — — — — — —

(b) (should be led to say it).

A CLOSE LOOK AT A SEGMENT OF A CLASSICAL LINEAR PROGRAM   53

33. If a student can correctly define a term, he can discriminate between instances (examples) of it and noninstances of it. True or false?_____.

─ ─ ─ ─ ─ ─ ─ ─ ─ ─ ─ ─ ─ ─ ─ ─

False. (The definition may be merely a bunch of words, which the student can repeat without any idea of their meaning.)

34. Errors made by each individual trial student in the process of testing a program produce a change in the program. Further adjustments may be made following group tests (or field tests) of the program. The final product is a series of frames leading to nearly perfect responding from the "average" child in some *specific* and carefully defined population. In the light of this developmental procedure, would *you* say that a linear program does not take account of individual differences?

─ ─ ─ ─ ─ ─ ─ ─ ─ ─ ─ ─ ─ ─ ─ ─

The question asked what *you* would say. Many people do say that. In my opinion, a tested linear program takes account of individual differences in one very clear way: everything that *any* of the tested students needed has been put into it. In another sense it does not: each student gets everything whether he needs it or not.

35. A student learns only what a program leads him to do. Data from the testing of programs have supported this theoretical statement many times. Take, for example, data from my program in Latin-derived prefixes.
    Students who had correctly responded to two frames in which the definition "around" was the correct answer when the prefix was "circum" showed a relatively high number of errors when asked to give the prefix that meant "around."
  The objection that only one of these responses is difficult—the other is a common English word, and the pair should have been taught the other way around—does not hold up.
    Students who could correctly respond "inter" when given the definition "between" made the same number of errors as before when asked to give the definition of "inter," a response that is a common English word.
  In the *Vectors* program, the student emits the response "scalar" in the presence of its definition and gives its definition in the presence of the question "What is a scalar?". The same principle is in operation.
  Many people feel that classical linear programs are too repetitive, and often this feeling arises from the habit that linear programers have of asking every question in every possible way. If, as you develop a program, you feel that students who can answer one question do not need to be asked another, what might you do to prove this?_____.

─ ─ ─ ─ ─ ─ ─ ─ ─ ─ ─ ─ ─ ─ ─ ─

Try it out. You might be right. The testing of a program may be an occasion for upsetting certain "theoretical" assumptions. But do not be surprised if the data come out in favor of the theory.

Summary: What Can Be Seen By Inspection of a Program

As with any set of instructional materials, many facets of a program may be judged by inspection. In judging its "goodness," one obvious dimension is the content. By this I mean the content included, *not* the content learned, which only data can show. You can look at the adequacy of definitions, the range of examples included, the types of problems presented to students, and, as a subject matter expert, make judgments about how relevant this is to the student's needs and the objectives of the course in which the program might fit.

No matter what the medium in which the program is presented (and just about all of them have been used to some extent) you can judge the effectiveness with which the programer used the medium, in the sense of "good writing" or "good visualization techniques."

In the specific area of programing techniques, the program's realization of the "principle of active responding" can be calculated by hard work (as you should be well aware after this last section!). The number of *different* relevant behaviors involved in the teaching of each concept is observable. So also is the amount of repetition, if you keep in mind:

(a) Within the theory of programing, a prompted item differs as a stimulus from the same question in which no prompts are given.
(b) Given the principle of active responding, labeling examples is a totally different stimulus-response situation from giving a definition, and responding to one dimension of a multi-dimensional concept (like vector) is different from responding to another.

The programer's assumptions about entering behavior, if they are not fully stated in a manual, can be deduced from inspection of the program. The critic's opinions about the validity of the programer's assumptions are, along with opinions about the amount of practice, merely opinions!

Outside Exercise.

At this point, you should have achieved the following objectives: You can

(a) identify terminal frames;
(b) identify repetitions in a sequence;
(c) locate frames which, while they cover the same concept, require different types of responses and therefore illustrate active responding;
(d) discriminate between "legitimate" judgments which can be made about programed sequences on inspecting them and those judgments which can only be verified by empirical evidence.

If you have access to a library of programs, select a commercially available linear program in a subject matter with which you are familiar. It is to your advantage to find one that has an accompanying instructor's manual containing data. (Not all things called "programs" have data, and some well-researched ones do not provide data in the instructor's manual—one has to ask for it.) Inspect a section of the program.

(a) What does it present to students? What is your reaction to the content?
(b) What is your reaction to the use of the medium?
(c) Does it appear to satisfy the principle of active responding?
(d) How much repetition does it contain?
(e) What assumptions does it make about student knowledge? If you are inspecting a later section of a program, you'll have to check earlier sections to verify your hypotheses.
(f) If you have had experience teaching the kinds of students the program was produced for, what are your predictions about its effectiveness? Are your predictions matched by data?

I find that great fun and much fur-flying can be had by getting two subject-matter experts together to analyze a program. It should be just as much fun to compare the reactions of two teachers who handle the appropriate kinds of students!

Chapter 2

The Basic Elements and Operations

INTRODUCTION

This book is called a grammar because it tries to do what a grammar of a language would do. It contains a classification scheme of the basic elements (or structures) and operations (or procedures) and a survey of the possible ways of combining these elements and operations into "good" forms. As with many grammars, you could also expect considerable practice aimed at eliminating from your repertoire certain inelegant or unpermitted ways of combining the elements and operations.

Programing is a rapidly changing technology. Classifying different frames as being this or that type could become an academic exercise if you were led to believe that all possibilities had been covered. So let me point out right now that new possibilities will be discovered— perhaps by you. Likewise, all rules are made to be broken, as the history of attempts to make rules about frames illustrates. So there will be more emphasis on what is "bad" design and why than on the way you "ought" to write frames. In the last analysis, only the students you are producing instruction for can tell you what is "good" design—by learning.

The concern of this chapter is with the operations of priming and prompting, with special emphasis on the latter because of its complexity. A third operation, testing, has already been considered in our discussion of terminal frames in Chapter One. The basic elements to which these operations are applied are the various types of behaviors to be learned. While some scholars feel the need for more than four categories (see Gagné, 1965, with eight), many programers use the four-way categorization: discriminations, generalizations, chains, and concepts.

The following unprogramed review is provided for the benefit of those whose laboratory psychology is rusty. Those who do not meet the prerequisite of familiarity with basic terminology and procedures in operant conditioning may wish to branch to a suitable text, such as Ferster and Perrott (1968), Mechner (1967), or Englemann (1969). Students who do not need to review these terms may skip ahead to page 58, Section A. Priming.

The smallest number of categories found workable is the operant conditioning model, which has the four: discriminations, generalizations, chains, and, for more recent work in verbal subject matters, concepts. With only four categories into which you can put all "mastery behavior," you should be able to deduce that these categories are quite broad! The broader a category (or concept) is the more difficult it is to master because one example may appear to be so completely different from another.

Here are the four categories, with examples.

Discrimination: In the presence of an appropriate stimulus, a learner makes an appropriate response, a response he does not make to other stimuli. In other words, he can tell two or more stimuli apart.

Example: When he sees the letters P-I-N, the reader says "pin", not "pan" or "pit" or "din". And he doesn't say "pin" when he sees P-E-N or B-I-N.

Example: When a triangle with equal sides is presented, a geometry student says "equilateral triangle" not "isoceles".

Example: On a freeway, a sign saying "squeeze left" leads to appropriate behavior from drivers in the right-hand lane. (Other discriminations—the presence of cars next to them—affect *when* they change lanes!)

Discrimination, as we will see in Chapter Three, is to some programers the major teaching problem. The student can be said to know what response to make, to know what to do; the primary teaching problem is to enable him to discriminate when *he should make such a response.*

Generalization: In a situation which differs in some way from ones the learner has met before, the learner gives a response learned for earlier similar situations.

Example: Having learned to use the past tense sound, -ed, with "wanted" and "mended," a child says, for the first time and with no coaching, that his toy is "busted." *(N.B. Generalizing such a rule on the basis of limited experience can often lead to error—the child could report that a stick is "bended.")*

Example: Having learned to try out his paper-and-pencil frames on students, a programer tries out his slides and scripts for audiovisual programs.

Example: Having experienced success and challenge in algebra and geometry, the student arrives at his trigonometry class eager to learn. (An attitude is generalized.)

Concept: A concept is a class or set containing members varying in many ways but sharing certain properties which, by definition, make them members of the set. A student "has" a concept when he can correctly identify a *new* example (he generalizes within the set) and correctly exclude a *new* non-example (he discriminates between members and non-members). Conceptual learning includes both generalization within the class and discrimination outside the class. The term is useful not only because it means *both* simpler processes but also because most concepts are far more complex than the "stimuli" in typical discrimination problems. We may speak of discrimination between "b," "d," "p," and "q" (difficult as that is for first graders), but we find it more useful to think of large sets like "dog" as a concept, since there is such wide variation among members such as great danes and chihuahuas.

Example: Having learned to identify examples of "sonata form" in classical music from Bach to Brahms, the student can tell when Shostakovitch is or isn't employing the same form.

Note: any one instance of "sonata" contains many dimensions, such as tonality and style, which are not the defining property of "sonata"—there is variation within the set "all sonatas".

Example: Having learned to identify examples of "discrimination learning" in standard laboratory situations, the student can correctly classify human learning in real-life situations as being examples or non-examples of the same type of learning.

Chains: Beginning at the beginning of a lengthy procedure, the learner can follow a relatively fixed sequence of steps in which completion of one step serves as the stimulus for beginning the next one.

Example: Given a film in a can and a projector in a case, the student can follow the steps to produce a focused image on a screen and sound at a reasonable volume.

Example: Without consulting a cookbook, the chef can start with an unmeasured set of ingredients and arrive at a baked alaska. *(There may be some leeway in the order in which he does things, but not much. You can't whip ingredients you haven't combined.)*

Example: The statistics student can calculate a product-moment correlation from raw unordered sets of data.

These four categories (discriminations, generalizations, concepts, and chains) are quite useful in categorizing frames and sequences according to which of the behavior types the programmer is aiming for. In Chapter Three we will consider them in more detail.

SECTION A. PRIMING

"Simply waiting for behavior to occur so that it can be reinforced is inefficient—indeed, for many parts of a terminal repertoire, quite useless. Shaping behavior by progressive approximation can be tedious. There are better ways of solving the 'problem of the first instance'." (Skinner, 1968.) One solution, frequently used by programmers is priming. (The term may be new, but this kind of behavior by instructors is not!) If you think carefully about how you would handle the problem of the first instance—getting the student to give a response early in instruction that bore some relationship to the terminal behavior you want to produce, you may find yourself "intuitively" understanding what *priming* means. Let's look at some examples and non-examples of the concept.

The following excerpt is taken from a slide-audiotape program designed for preschool children in Harlem and presented on the Edison Responsive Environment machine, better known as the "Talking Typewriter." (See Gotkin and McSweeney, 1967.)

The child is presented with a discrimination task: when he sees the letters "P-O," he is to say "pah" (as in "pot") and when he sees the letter "P," he is to say "puh" (the initial consonant sound). The audiotape frequently asks for several responses while one slide is on, as shown here.

(Tape)	*(Slide)*
(1) "His name's on his shirt. Say 'Hi, Puh.' "	
Child says "Hi, Puh."	
(2) "What's his name?"	
Child says "Puh."	

The *first* statement (both sentences) on the tape is a PRIME.

The following frame resembles many in beginning reading programs. It too asks for discrimination—which set of letters match the name of the object pictured. The student can say "rat"—he has to learn to say "rat" to r-a-t. This frame is NOT primed.

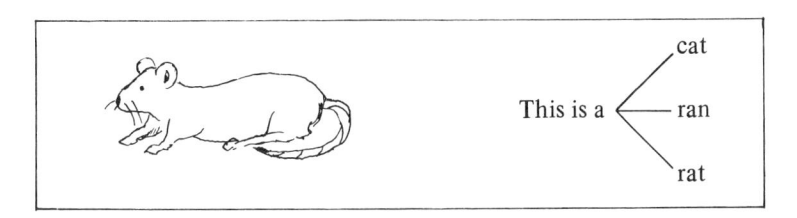

![rat picture] This is a ⟨ cat / ran / rat

The following frames are from *The Language of Computers,* a short demonstration program prepared by Robert F. Mager. The program is presented in a small ring binder; below, each new page is treated as a frame by being separately boxed.

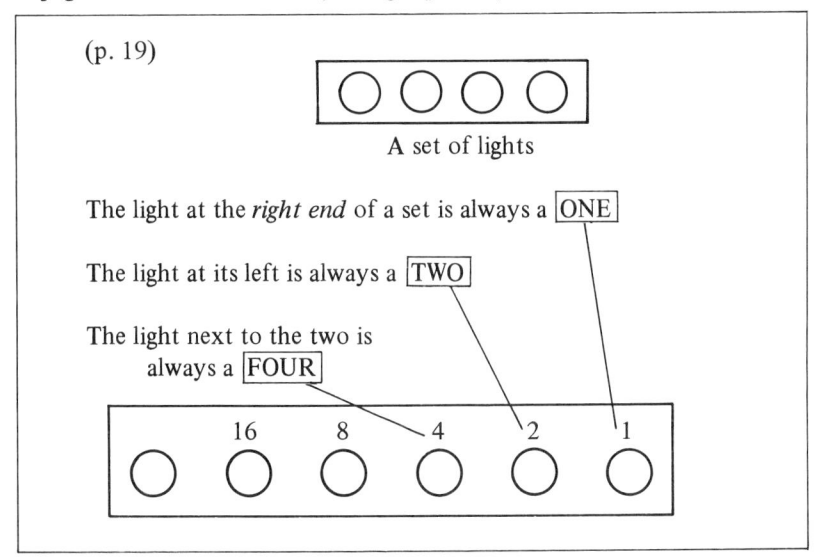

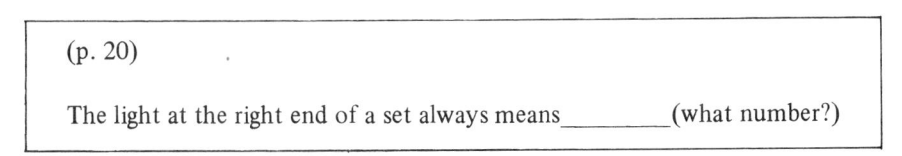

(p. 19)

A set of lights

The light at the *right end* of a set is always a ONE

The light at its left is always a TWO

The light next to the two is always a FOUR

16 8 4 2 1

(p. 20)

The light at the right end of a set always means _____ (what number?)

The information on page 19 of Mager's program *primes* the response asked for on page 20.

60 THE BASIC ELEMENTS AND OPERATIONS

1. Which of the following frames is a prime?

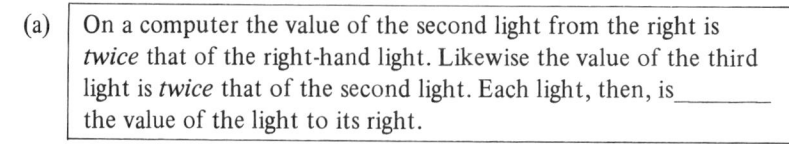

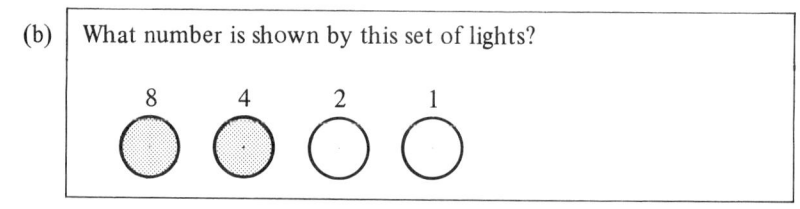

   (a) | On a computer the value of the second light from the right is *twice* that of the right-hand light. Likewise the value of the third light is *twice* that of the second light. Each light, then, is _____ the value of the light to its right.

   (b) | What number is shown by this set of lights?

   8 4 2 1
   ● ● ○ ○

- - - - - - - - - - - - - - -

(a) It is similar to the request "Say, 'Hi, Puh' " and to the statement on page 19 of Mager's program which the student repeats on page 20. (b) is page 29 of Mager's program teaching the chain "reading a set of computer lights." Since real computer lights are not conveniently labeled with the numerical value they represent, this frame is prompted—by the numbers above each light.

2. The word "prime" is a marvelous metaphor for those old-timers and woodsmen who know that, to get a hand pump to draw water, you have to pour water in it to get it started—a process called "priming the pump." "Primes," as described by Skinner (1968, Chapter 10) serve a similar purpose for mastery behavior. They are the simplest solution to "the problem of the first instance," how to get the student to give, the first time, the response you want to bring to mastery level.

   One kind of prime is seen in many programs, seen, I think, far too often. This is the copying frame, where the student is told something and asked to copy one or more words of what he is told. Here, we may say, the stimulus is a written text and the response is reproducing some part of the text.

   Another kind of prime, absolutely necessary in teaching pronunciation of a language or phonics in reading, is what Skinner (1957) calls an "echoic response," where the stimulus is a sound pattern and the response is reproducing (or echoing) what is heard.

   A third kind of prime, also useful on occasion, you should be able to figure out. If the terminal response you want is for the student to be able to get a tape recorder out of its case, plug it in, load it with a tape, and record his own voice, you have two fairly obvious ways to solve the problem of getting him to go through this chain of behavior the first time. Name one way to prime this behavior.

— — — — — — — — — — — — — — — —

One way is to show him by doing it yourself while he watches. Then he imitates the model you have provided. (If you have to teach a lot of students, you might end up with your "prime" on film, of course!)

The other way is to give him a complete and adequate set of directions which he reads and follows step-by-step through the chain.

3. When an audiotape tells a child to "Say 'Hi, Puh' ", and the child echoes it, has the programer solved the problem of getting the child to say "puh" when he sees the letter P?

— — — — — — — — — — — — — — —

No. As a matter of fact, the child could ignore the letter printed on the slide. In other words, the stimulus you want him to respond to in the end (P) is not what gets him to say "puh" when it is primed by "Say puh."

4. If a student can follow a carefully worded set of directions for loading a tape recorder and recording his voice, has he now mastered the making of tapes? Why?

— — — — — — — — — — — — — — —

If you take "mastery" to mean doing it with no help, which is what I would take it to mean, then you agree that he has not mastered it since he still uses directions to get him to take each step in the chain in the proper order.

Summary

Priming by showing or telling is one way, but not the only way, of solving the problem of getting the student to give an adequate response the first time he is asked to give the response. It does not guarantee that he will be able to give the response at the right time for the right reasons (under appropriate stimulus control, a psychologist would say) without a prime. In many cases, priming can be the wrong first step for a programer to take. It will slow down the progress towards the unaided mastery response.

Relevant Quote: Priming repertoires are misused when the teacher accepts the simple execution of behavior as a goal regardless of whether the student is likely to behave in the same way after the primes have been withdrawn. The belief that men 'learn by doing' encourages the mistake. The student repeats what the teacher says, and the teacher leaves it at that. (Skinner, 1968.)

SECTION B. PROMPTED FRAMES AND COPYING FRAMES

Both the design of a frame and its position in a sequence determine whether it is a prompted frame. This section will concentrate on design alone. At the end of the section you should be able to determine by looking at the design whether a frame is designed to prime some response, to prompt it, or to test its final mastery. Since most programs are written, we will be most concerned with the copying frame as the major example of priming.

In the Glossary, you will find that the word *prompt* has several meanings, depending on who is using it. If you are planning to read the experimental literature that has grown up in this area, you will need to make the distinctions. For the purposes of this program, however, the word is used in the Skinnerian sense. (See Skinner: *Verbal Behavior* and *The Technology of Teaching.*)

A prompt is a supplementary stimulus, a hint or bit of assistance that helps the student come up with a correct response, but it is not a prime—it does not tell him the response. In other words,

(a) something has been added to the terminal stimulus to make the frame easier, and
(b) what has been added is not sufficient to produce the response by itself.

PROMPTED FRAMES AND COPYING FRAMES 63

1. Copying frames are a peculiar kind of priming that consists of instructions for the student to copy one or more words. These instructions may be given implicitly, (by syntax, in other words) rather than (as you might see at the beginning of a spelling sequence) by asking the student to copy a word.

   Classify the following frames as (a) terminal in design, (b) prompted, or (c) copying frame. (The frames are from *Medical Parasitology,* a Basic Systems program.)

   _____ 1. | An endoparasite is a parasite established_____ the host. (Remember the Greek root words EXTOS and ENDON.)

   _____ 2. | Every parasite must have a host. The organism upon which or within which a parasite lives is its_____ .

   _____ 3. | A relationship between two organisms from which one derives benefit while the other suffers injury to some degree is termed_____ .

   - - - - - - - - - - - - - - -

   1. (b) prompted—the reminder about the Greek roots, which the student had learned earlier, is the prompt.
   2. (c) copying frame—the first sentence primes the word "host," which is to be copied into the blank.
   3. (a) terminal frame—in the presence of the definition, the student is to give the correct term.

2. The two frames below are from *Programmed English,* Macmillan Co., programed by M. W. Sullivan. How would you classify them? Copying, prompted, or terminal?

   _____ 1. | We say that the form BOY is singular but that the form BOYS is [singular/plural] .

   _____ 2. | We say that DOGS is the_____ form of DOG.

   - - - - - - - - - - - - - -

   The first is heavily prompted, but is not a copying frame since the student has to choose the answer with all sorts of hints.

   The second is a terminal frame, asking him to correctly classify an example of a plural form with no prompts.

64 THE BASIC ELEMENTS AND OPERATIONS

3. This frame is one of many terminal items that we might construct to test whether the student can multiply powers of numbers.

$$(x^4)(x^7) =$$

Suppose, earlier in the program, we have included a solved example in a frame, thus:

$$(a^3)(a^4) = a^7$$
$$(x^2)(x^6) = \underline{}$$

Have we helped the student solve the problem?____
Have we told him the answer?____

— — — — — — — — — — — — — — —

Yes, it is some help, though it might not lead to correct answers if we used that prompt on the first frame.

No. He has to do the calculations on the second one himself.

4. Suppose, instead of hinting at the procedure by showing an example all solved, we tell the student what to do by providing a rule (in language he can understand, of course.)

To multiply powers of a variable, add the exponents.

$$(x^2)(x^6) =$$

Have we helped him?____
Have we told him the answer?____
Is this a copying frame?____

— — — — — — — — — — — — — — —

Yes. (Unless we've used language over his head.)
No. He has to apply the rule to get the correct answer.
No. To be a copying frame, the answer must be provided in the text.

PROMPTED FRAMES AND COPYING FRAMES 65

5. Which of these frames is a copying frame?

> _____ 1. In Latin, the plural of a word ending in *us* is formed by dropping *us* and substituting *i*. Thus, the plural of *nucleus* is N_____.
>
> _____ 2. The plural of NUCLEUS is NUCLEI. If one atom has one nucleus, then two atoms have two_____.

— — — — — — — — — — — — — — —

The second (from *Chemistry,* a Basic Systems program) is a copying frame. The first one is certainly primed since it states a general rule and asks the student to apply it to an example.

---

6. To illustrate a solution to the "problem of the first instance" by prompting rather than priming, we'll analyze an imaginary frame from an imaginary program on mythical animals. Assume the following:
   (a) The objective of the program is that students will be able to describe the animals, as evidence that, when a reference to one of these animals occurs in their reading, they "know" the referent of the name. If Pegasus is one of the animals, then, a terminal frame would be "Describe Pegasus."
   (b) The students read English, know the properties of common classes of animals, and have never heard of Pegasus. Perhaps they are third or fourth graders studying mythology.
   (c) This is the first frame on the subject.

> Pegasus was a most unusual animal. Like a horse, he had four legs, and like a bird, he had two_____.

This is obviously not a copying frame. Although I have never tried it out, I would predict that it is a pretty easy frame to answer. It is loaded with prompts. We can add or subtract prompts bit by bit to look at their function. Each prompt limits the answer in certain ways. One obvious limitation for speakers of English (which we assumed the students were) lies in the kind of word that belongs in that slot in a sentence. No one would put a verb there. What is the most likely *kind* of word?

Given the number of words that are of that kind, is this prompt a strong prompt for the particular word wanted?

— — — — — — — — — — — — — — —

It is most likely to be a noun in that position. Since nouns are one of the largest classes of English words, the probability of the particular noun "wings," is rather low.

A PROMPT-BY-PROMPT ANALYSIS

7.   Pegasus was a most unusual animal. Like a horse, he had four legs, and, like a bird, he had two _____ .

Prompt No. 1 is syntax. With no other prompts, the answer is at least restricted to the class of plural nouns by the single prompt shown in frame A:

A. Pegasus had two _____ .

All the other prompts are contextual or semantic in character. Pegasus might have had two of many things, but a further limitation is suggested on the class of plural nouns that might be acceptable. Consider these:

B. Pegasus had four saddles and two _____ .

or

C. Pegasus had four successes and two _____ .

when compared to this:

D. Pegasus had four legs and two _____ .

For the horsey set, the first of these, frame B, contains a very strong prompt. Most of them would think of "bridles." For most of us, the usual response to "successes and . . ." in frame C would be "failures." It is clear that neither "bridles" nor "failures" belongs in the third version, frame D.

Whether you call this prompt "appositional parallelism" with the grammarians, "level of abstraction" with the logicians, or "intraverbal" with Skinner, the word "legs" obviously restricts the size of the class of possible correct responses.

For students who do not know about Pegasus, does this prompt (the parallelism in frame D) force them to come up with *the* correct answer? _____ .

What sort of answer do you think a student might give to frame D, with *just* this prompt and no previous instruction about Pegasus? _____ .

— — — — — — — — — — — — — —

No (Pegasus could be a four-legged chair with two cushions!).

Your choice. Depending on the age of the student, "four legs" might suggest all sorts of things. I would bet on "ears," "eyes," and other characteristics of animals.

8. | Pegasus was a most unusual animal. He had four legs and two_____. |

"Animal," of course, is a prompt. We now know that we are not talking about furniture and that whatever Pegasus has two of, at least some other animals also possess.
  Have we eliminated "ears" and "eyes" with the word "animal"?_____.
  Does the frame above suggest that "ears" and "eyes" are not adequate responses? _____. Why?

— — — — — — — — — — — — — — —

No.

Yes. "Unusual" prompts an unusual response. Something is wanted that will be an unusual property when combined with four legs.

9. | Pegasus was a most unusual animal. He had four legs and two _____s. |

What new restriction is put on the class of correct answers in this frame?

— — — — — — — — — — — — — — —

A four-letter word (or five in the plural) is needed.

10. | Like a bird, Pegasus had two_____. |

If the student knows nothing about Pegasus, is this prompt by itself sufficient to guarantee a correct response?_____. (*Hint:* Are there any other sensible answers?)

| Pegasus was a most unusual animal. He had four legs and two_____. |

Would it make sense (disregard facts) to respond "heads" or "tails" to this item?

— — — — — — — — — — — — — — —

No. Birds have two legs and other pairs as well, any of which would be sensible answers.

Yes. Either answer certainly would be unusual enough.

11. A prompt is a supplementary stimulus which
   (a) is added to (and therefore can be subtracted again from) the terminal stimulus to make the item easier and
   (b) is not sufficient in itself to produce the response.

In summary, here are the prompts in this one item (none of these are technical terms to be mastered; use your own terminology):

1. Syntax—restriction to plural nouns:	Pegasus had two _____.
2. Parallel levels of abstraction:	Pegasus had four legs and two _____.
3. Class restriction on subject of discourse:	Pegasus was an animal. He had two _____.
4. Exclude any "usual" responses to pairs of things belonging to a four-legged animal:	Pegasus was a most unusual animal. He had two _____.
5. Another restriction on class of subject:	Pegasus, like a bird, had two _____.

Do you agree that no one of these prompts by itself will reliably produce "wings" from students who know nothing about Pegasus?

— — — — — — — — — — — — — —

If you disagree with the question, you might try out the frames on any student who demonstrates ignorance of Pegasus.

PROMPTED FRAMES AND COPYING FRAMES   **69**

---

12. Here is the total frame:

> Pegasus was a most unusual animal. Like a horse, he had four legs, and, like a bird, he had two _____ .

What phrase have we not discussed? Does this phrase seem to you to have any function in making the correct answer more probable?

— — — — — — — — — — — — — — —

We did not discuss "like a horse," which, from my point of view, is there because of the demands of good writing—it completes the parallel structure of the sentence. "Horse" was, of course, determined by the nature of Pegasus; "dog" would do just as well for completing the structure. Neither name is likely to make a student think of wings.

---

13. Although any one prompt operating alone may not be sufficient to produce a response without some previous "softening up" or "exposure" of the student to the desired response, a combination of them can be as powerful as a copying item.

> Pegasus was a horse with wings. Like a horse, he had four legs, and, like a bird, he had two _____ .

> Pegasus was a most unusual animal. Like a horse, he had four legs, and, like a bird, he had two _____ .

No data have been collected on either of these frames, but I assume they are equally easy. Which one is more interesting?

Can you think of a more interesting (probably) and more complete way to help a student visualize Pegasus?

— — — — — — — — — — — — — — —

Your choice. You know what I think, but at this point you have seen the frame so many times that you may have lost interest in it!

Again, your choice. I think a picture could save a lot of words here.

70 THE BASIC ELEMENTS AND OPERATIONS

14. This frame might have occurred in the *Vectors* program (it does not):

> A. | A vector has direction and magnitude. We call distance a scalar. Therefore, scalars must have _____ but not _____ .

A prompt is a stimulus which is added and which, therefore, can be subtracted. This does not mean that we can subtract them in "any old order" and be left with a sensible item! It should be obvious that the middle sentence above could not be removed without producing a very odd pair of sentences.

Suppose you remove the first sentence:

> B. | We call distance a scalar. Therefore, scalars must have _____ but not _____ .

Is frame B more difficult than frame A? _____ . Why?

— — — — — — — — — — — — — —

Yes. The first sentence in frame A reminds the student of the relevant terms, whereas frame B depends solely on the student's previous training with "distance."

---

15. | A vector has direction and magnitude. We call distance a scalar. Therefore, scalars must have _____ but not _____ .

The presence in the frame of the words that are the correct responses does *not necessarily* produce a copying frame. Try to look at the frame above strictly as a grammatical sequence forgetting the knowledge you have of the connection between vectors and distance and scalars.

Could a student with *no* previous instruction in the subject matter be sure what was wanted in the blanks on the basis of the grammar alone? _____ .

— — — — — — — — — — — — — —

Yes. Go to 16a.

No. Go to 16b.

16a. Your answer to (15) was "yes." Consider the following frame:

> A deciduous tree has no leaves in winter. We say that the arctic hare has protective coloration. Therefore, arctic hares are _____ in winter.

The above frame is similar in grammatical construction to the previous frame on scalars. Yet you know that the answer is not "leafless." You know this because you know that "protective coloration" and "deciduous" are not related terms. The first sentence is no prompt at all for the answer. Indeed, the item borders on the illogical, because there is only a tenuous connection (conditions in winter) between the opening sentence and the rest of the item.

Compare the vector item and the arctic hare item carefully and proceed to 16b.

16b. Your answer to (15) was "no." You are correct. If the student does not know that distance *is not* a vector, the first sentence is no help. The frame is a *non sequitur* if the student cannot supply the relationship involved.

> A vector has direction and magnitude. We call distance a scalar. Therefore, scalars must have _____ but not _____ .

Therefore, which of the following statements about this frame is correct? The first sentence is

  (a) a stimulus for a copying response
  (b) a supplementary stimulus serving as a prompt.

— — — — — — — — — — — — — — —

(b)

72 THE BASIC ELEMENTS AND OPERATIONS

17.
> A vector has direction and magnitude. We call distance a scalar. Therefore, scalars must have _____ but not _____.

The total item produces a very strong tendency for the student to give the correct response. The frame is probably too easy.

To see another reason why the frame cannot be called a copying item, we remove the middle sentence and edit the frame.

> A vector has direction and magnitude. However, a scalar has _____ but not _____.

The grammar of the frame certainly suggests that the properties listed in the first sentence are the answers to the second sentence. Does the grammar of the item give a clue as to *which one* of these properties belongs in *which* blank? _____.

— — — — — — — — — — — — — —

No.

18. A.
> We call distance a scalar. Therefore, scalars must have _____ but not _____.

Reminding the student (or telling him, if you have not told him before) that distance is an example of scalars enables him, if he knows, to come up with a property that distance has and another one that it does not have. This is a prompt that can be removed.

B.
> Scalars have _____ but not _____.

(We also removed the word relating the two sentences. Programers are supposed to write English!)

How does the item B above differ from the terminal item actually used in *Vectors:* "What is a scalar"?

— — — — — — — — — — — — — —

(In your own words.) It still informs the student that there are two relevant things to be said about scalars—one property that they possess and one that they do not—whereas the actual terminal item contains no hints at all.

19. Inspect these two items:

> To DISGLOP the xeron, you must first revurl the CORASCIS. The
> _____ is always revurled before the xeron is_____ed.

> The grammel is a bloober because it has both chinders and t_____s.

(a) Do you understand either item?_____.

- - - - - - - - - - - - - - - -

No, and neither does the author of them.

(b) Can you answer the first frame?_____.

- - - - - - - - - - - - - - - -

Yes. If you can read this program, you can do the first frame.

(c) Can you answer the second item?_____.

- - - - - - - - - - - - - - - -

No, and neither can I.

(d) What do you know about the answer to the second item? Name at least three prompts that "help" you choose the right word.
1.   2.   3.

- - - - - - - - - - - - - - - -

There are more than three if you keep working at it: (1) it is a noun; (2) it begins with *t*; (3) it has seven letters in the plural; (4) it is comparable to "chinders" in class or category; (5) it is something a "grammel" might have.)

(e) It is true that we can locate prompts in the first frame. Capital letters, underlining, and the ending *-ed* assist the student in copying the right word into each blank. The strongest stimuli, however, are the models provided and the grammatical transformation of the first sentence into another with essentially the same meaning. Where the main controlling stimuli consist of a model and grammar, the frame *is not* a prompted frame. We give it a name with a slight sneer: it is a _____ frame.

- - - - - - - - - - - - - - - -

copying

20. Copying frames, like other inadequate designs we will be looking at, stand in the way of the programer's real task, which is to get the student to mastery efficiently. Operant conditioners often point out that punishment is such a prevalent way of attempting to control another's behavior because it is reinforced—it suppresses the unwanted response, at least temporarily. Perhaps the wide use of copy frames in programs is a function of the same phenomenon—that is, because they are so easy to write and because students rarely miss them, programers descend to this alternative as a way to get behavior started.

Suppose the nonsense frame about *disglopping the xeron* were part of a training sequence for laboratory assistants. [They could be audiovisual assistants, who, the programer hopes, will pitch in after instruction and help teachers show films in the classroom; or they could be medical assistants who, after instruction, will be responsible for setting up, using, and dismantling complex laboratory equipment.] Presumably all these assistants would answer the frame correctly. But the programer has done a very poor analysis of what he wants to teach—a chain of responses in which each step will set the stage for the next step.

In completing the frame, the students will have learned something about the spelling of *disglop* and *xeron*. Is this a step in the direction of handling the machinery?

— — — — — — — — — — — — — — —

No. Whatever referent you can think of for that little phrase *disglopping the xeron*—in other words, whether the programer wants the student to operate a machine, decline a Latin verb, create an English composition, run a statistical analysis, or determine a historical trend—merely repeating a phrase of this sort represents no progress at all.

---

21. When is a frame a copying frame? A frame may present a choice of words, one of which will be correct in the blank, thereby giving the student a chance to copy its spelling. However, if he has a choice based on "understanding" the item or on some previous exposure to the content, that is not what is meant by a copying frame.

In its simplest form a copying frame requires two sentences—the first to introduce a term or fact, and the second to get the student to repeat it (or part of it) back to the writer.

> Paris is the capital of France. Paris is the capital of _____ .

Here there would be no disagreement. Suppose we change the grammar of the second sentence a bit:

> Paris is the capital of France. The capital of France is _____ .

Or use a question:

> Paris is the capital of France. What city is the capital of France?
> _____.

This is still copying. A three-year-old speaker of English could figure out which word was correct even though he had no idea about the meaning of "capital," "France," or even "city," and was only going on the basis of what he knew could be done with the verb "is." You, as sophisticated speakers of English, can figure out far more complex transformations, as was illustrated in the preceding nonsense frame.

Although frames of this oversimplified nature are a temptation to all programers (they always work if you write within the grammatical level of the students), they are, I think, an insult to students. Although each step in a program should be within the student's capacity if we wish to prevent errors, copying or repeat-after-me frames represent a step that is too [small/large] for students under almost all conditions.

- - - - - - - - - - - - - - -

small

---

22. > Paris is the capital of France. Situated on the Seine, it is the location of many famous buildings and monuments, as well as the seat of the French government. What city is the capital of France?

Does this elongated frame still contain an introduction to a fact and a repeat-after-me instruction? _____.

It [is/is not] a copying frame.

- - - - - - - - - - - - - - -

Yes.

is (it has the required parts, even though it has more than these).

---

23. Does successful completion of a copying frame demonstrate that the student understands what he has been led to say? _____.

- - - - - - - - - - - - - - -

No.

76   THE BASIC ELEMENTS AND OPERATIONS

24. Does successful completion of a copying frame indicate that a student has observed the spelling of the word that he copied?_____. Might this be a legitimate goal for a frame? _____.

— — — — — — — — — — — — — —

Yes. (If he copied correctly, he has the letters in the right order. This is, of course, no guarantee of permanent learning.)

Yes, it might. There is no reason in science programs, for instance, to allow students to practice misspellings. (See Chapter Five for ways to control spelling while requiring more than copying.)

25. In the fourth paragraph of his article (p. 3), Skinner describes one of the most important functions of the response in a linear program. It provides important feedback to the programer on the effectiveness of the explanations and examples used in the teaching sequence. An error provides a great deal of insight into what the student is actually thinking. A programer hopes that correct responses are a function of the effectiveness of his teaching.

If students respond correctly to the blanks in a copying item, what has the programer learned about his students?

— — — — — — — — — — — — — —

(In your own words.) They are capable of translating or transforming sentences from one structure to another; i.e., they read English and they can copy it.

Summary

A prompt is a supplementary stimulus, which can be added to the terminal stimulus in order to make an item easier for a student to answer correctly. Any single prompt acting alone is, according to Skinner's definition, incapable of producing the correct response by itself; i.e., it is a hint, not a "giveaway." With the exception of syntax, which is a very weak prompt, a terminal item should contain no prompts.

A frame in which the grammar is a clear instruction to copy one or more words is a copying frame. It has a function in forcing the student to pay attention to and reproduce the spelling of a word, but it has a distinct disadvantage: it can be answered without any understanding.

By combining several prompts, an item may force a student to come up with a correct answer on his first try, although any one of the prompts by itself would not do so.

Self-Test: Copying Frames, Prompted Frames, and Terminal Frames

If you can label the following correctly, you have achieved the discrimination. Are they copying, prompted, or terminal frames?

1. CANIS FAMILIARIS is the technical name for man's best friend. CANIS FAMILIARIS means_____.

2. Performing animals are sometimes trained by giving them reinforcers for good performance. When a hungry porpoise is trained by giving it a fish for a good performance, the fish is a_____.

3. The unit *deca* means "ten," while *octo* means "eight." Which animal has more legs, an OCTOPUS or a DECAPOD?

4. What do we mean by the intersection of two sets?

5. Give the German word for "mother":_____.

6. 7 X 9 = _____.

7. When we add *-ing* to a word like *rope,* we get *roping.* Add *-ing* to *brake:*_____.

8. The center of an atom has a positive charge and is called the nucleus. Circling around the nucleus are particles called electrons, which have negative charges. Electrons circle around the_____.

9. (microscope program)
   What do you see on slide No. 5?

10. As you look at the map, you will see that the Caribbean Sea has a very large island, Cuba, a smaller island with two countries—Haiti and the Dominican Republic—two still smaller islands—Puerto Rico, which is a territory of the U.S., and Jamaica—and many very small islands. The large island in the Caribbean Sea is_____.

Answers

Copying: 2, 8, 10.
Prompted: 1, 3, 5, 7.
Terminal: 4, 6, 9.

Scholarly Footnote: The concepts *prime* and *prompt* fade into each other. There is a middle ground where discrimination between them is difficult. If you found yourself wondering about #7, you faced this problem. Because the rule (drop the e) is not stated but merely exemplified, we can say that the frame is closer to being prompted than primed.

SECTION C: FORMAL AND THEMATIC PROMPTS

1. Prompts are classified into two broad types: formal and thematic (Skinner, 1957). As with the meaning of the word "prompt" itself, there is some disagreement about which category certain prompts belong in. The following discussion represents one approach. Again, in reading other authors, you have to figure out what they mean when they use the terms.

    The terminology "formal" and "thematic" may not seem appropriate to you unless you are familiar with terms used in the fine arts and literature. Discussion of the form and theme of particular works is common.

    (a) In music, opera is a [form/theme] that a composer can use.

    ----

    form

    (b) A poet has decided to construct a poem in four-line stanzas with the rhyme scheme a-b-a-b. Does this tell him what to write about? The decision about the poem's structure determines the [form/theme] of his poem.

    ----

form (this form can be employed on themes ranging from the futility of life to such dubious "messages" as that of the Jabberwocky).

(c) In a sonata, the melody would be a [formal/thematic] characteristic. (Think. Could the composer use the same melody in an opera?)

— — — — — — — — — — — — — — —

thematic (it can be used in many forms).

(d) If you know that a book is a collection of essays, you know something about the [form/theme] of the writings in it.

— — — — — — — — — — — — — — —

form (they could be about anything, but you know they are not poems).

(e) The title "Artists Look at War" tells you about the [formal/thematic] aspects of an art show.

— — — — — — — — — — — — — — —

thematic (from the title you do not even know whether the form is sculpture, oils, or photography).

80   THE BASIC ELEMENTS AND OPERATIONS

2. | This is a *v*_____. |

   Does the prompt *v* tell the student anything about the structure of the response he is to make?_____.
   Does the prompt *v* tell the student anything about the meaning of the response he is to make?_____.
   The letter *v*, then, is a_____prompt.

   – – – – – – – – – – – – – –

   Yes (the word begins with a *v*).

   No (it could mean anything).

   formal

---

3. | Like a bird, Pegasus had two_____. |

   Does the prompt "like a bird" tell the student what the word that he should give will look like?_____.
   Does the prompt "like a bird" tell the student what category of things the word he should give will name?_____.
   The phrase "like a bird" is, therefore, a_____prompt.

   – – – – – – – – – – – – – –

   No (a technical synonym from anatomy might be substituted for "wing" without violating the prompt at all—the two words would differ in form).

   Yes.

   thematic

---

4. | Like the American flag, the French flag is_____, _____, and_____. |

   The American flag is many things: saluted by citizens, raised at dawn, lowered at sunset, flown on flagpoles, etc. But none of these responses fit. What is the prompt that makes

"red, white, and blue" the most likely response?
Which category would you put this prompt into?

― ― ― ― ― ― ― ― ― ― ― ― ― ― ―

The three blanks separated by commas and an "and."

I would call it formal. It implies a parallel series but does not indicate whether the subject matter of the series is color, size, material, etc.

5. | The French flag is _____, _____, and _____ .

With the formal prompt, this is still not a terminal item ("What color is the French flag?"). It is fairly difficult, however, and would hardly get a correct response from a student who had not seen or read about the French flag.

Inserting the prompt "Like the American flag" brings to the student's mind a lot of things that he knows about the American flag. Among these past associations is "red, white, and blue." Getting the student to use such past associations involves using a _____ prompt (which type).

― ― ― ― ― ― ― ― ― ― ― ― ― ― ―

thematic (the American flag is the theme about which you can say many things).

82 THE BASIC ELEMENTS AND OPERATIONS

6. Terminal item: | What are the colors of the French flag?

    Add formal prompt: | The French flag is_____, _____, and _____.

    Add thematic prompt: | Like the American flag, the French flag is_____.

Since national flags vary from two to many colors, the plural "colors" is not much help in the first frame, and we can call it a terminal item.

The addition of a formal prompt specifying a series is not much help either, but it considerably limits the number of responses that fit. The student's problem is coming up with a response that fits the formal prompt. If he searches for all the things usually occurring in series that he knows about flags, he might come up with color. (He might also come up with another reasonable series.)

The thematic prompt sets a train of thought going about all the things that could be said about the American flag.

Combine the prompts: | Like the American flag, the French flag is _____, _____, and_____.

How does a student behave when confronted with this item? Does he generate all the three-word series that he knows and then see which ones apply to the American flag? Or is it more likely that he thinks about the American flag and selects a response to it that is usually given in a serial order?

— — — — — — — — — — — — — —

In organizing thoughts, most of us decide the broad subject matter before we get down to specifics. The thematic prompt probably operates first, although it would be possible to go at it the other way.

7. Consider the following side issue:

   Traditional grammar spoke of nouns as "names of persons, places, and things," which definition, in a broad sense, specifies their meaning. Modern grammar calls nouns a "form class" to which you can do the following things: add -s for plurals; add 's for possessives; etc. Modern grammar is often called structural grammar. If you are a traditionalist, you might say that a prompt indicating the syntax (such as plural nouns, verb in the present or

FORMAL AND THEMATIC PROMPTS 83

past tense, adjective, etc.) is thematic. If you are a modernist, however, you would have to put such a prompt into the other class.

The programer is a modernist. Syntax, which tells you the structure rather than the meaning of the word, is a _____ prompt.

--- --- --- --- --- --- --- --- --- --- --- --- --- ---

formal (until you finish this program!).

---

8. > When copper is present, the flame contains the color of grass. When copper burns, you will see _____ in the flame.

Does "color of grass" tell the student anything about the sound or structure of the word? _____.

Except for people from the bluegrass country, this frame is certain to get the response "green." The association between "color of grass" and "green" makes this a _____ prompt (which type)?

--- --- --- --- --- --- --- --- --- --- --- --- --- ---

No.

thematic

---

9. > Meaningful units that go after the root are called _____ fixes.
> (*Words,* Markle)

By the time a student reaches this item in the program, there are two reasonable answers to such a question—either "prefixes" or "suffixes." (Although this is a constructed-response format, the question has some aspects of a multiple-choice response.)

The word "after" is not a prompt. It is part of the terminal stimulus "meaningful units that go after the root" to which the student is being trained to respond "suffix." However, there is a prompt in the item. Which kind of prompt is it? _____.

--- --- --- --- --- --- --- --- --- --- --- --- --- ---

formal (three letters).

84 THE BASIC ELEMENTS AND OPERATIONS

10.
> Meaningful units that go after the root are called ___ fixes.

Does the formal prompt in this item help the student select between the two possible responses, "prefix" and "suffix"? _____ .
What do you suppose it is doing there, then?

— — — — — — — — — — — — — — —

No (they both have three letters before -fixes).

That was a guess, so your guess stands. I used the three blanks in order to control spelling, since the responses "sufixes" and "preffixes" turned up too often from eighth-grade spellers.

---

11. Is a prompt formal or is it thematic? In a language as rich in synonyms as English, there is an opportunity for a great deal of variability. Within certain limits (broad or narrow, depending on your interests and philosophical sophistication), it is possible to say essentially "the same thing" in completely different words. The same event can be described in technical or nontechnical terms, slang, or stiff prose.

It is true that most of us behave in very similar ways when confronted with a stimulus such as "the opposite of 'good' is '_____.' " Most will say either "bad" or "evil" (depending on a formal interpretation of the ambiguous grammar of the word "good"). But wouldn't "foul," "wicked," "lousy," and "terrible" also indicate understanding?

If I ask you for a four-letter word rhyming with "ham," you may have all sorts of thoughts on the subject, but you will not deviate from the prompt. The final sound is determined as is the number of letters that you have to work with. If I ask for a noun (and you know what nouns are), you will respond in a way that grammarians, if no one else, find predictable.

(a) If you know what the response is going to look like or sound like but not what it is going to mean, the prompt is_____.
(b) If you know what the response is going to mean but not what it is going to look like or sound like, the prompt is_____.

— — — — — — — — — — — — — — —

(a) formal.
(b) thematic.

12. Formal prompts could really be thought of as reductions from a copying frame. In a copying frame, the *whole form* of the word to be copied is provided for the student. In a formally prompted frame, *part of a word's form* is given—for instance its first letter, the number of letters in it, its sound (from something it rhymes with), or its stress pattern. Both copying and formal prompting, of course, may be used with larger responses than a single word.

In teaching a foreign language, formal prompts might have utility when the student is practicing pronunciation from a text he is reading (you might hum the stress pattern of a word to him, for instance) or is practicing spelling from dictation. In such cases, the objectives the frames are aiming at are what we might call *"formal behavior."* Like correct form in a tennis swing or a high jump, the student's pronunciation will have the correct form as a result of instruction.

The analogy between correct form in pronunciation and a correct tennis swing suggests something about correctness of form. It is quite likely that the novice who keeps his elbow in the right place will miss the ball despite his form! His swing is controlled by the feel of it but is still not under the control of the position of the ball in space. Can you think of a parallel that could happen to a Spanish student who had got the Spanish double-l (as in caballo, brillo) down pat in the language laboratory? What element might be lacking in his mastery of these words despite his correct form?

— — — — — — — — — — — — — —

It is quite possible that the student with "native" pronunciation after his drills hasn't the least notion what the words mean or when to use them. When presented with a written word (a text) he might pronounce a word correctly, but when presented with a picture of a "caballo" have no idea what to call it. Likewise, of course, without the formal training, he might butcher the sound of the word although he knew when to say it!

86 THE BASIC ELEMENTS AND OPERATIONS

13. Suppose a programer is teaching ninth graders about the powers of the various levels of government—federal, state, and local. After some discussion of taxation, he gets around to defense. He is afraid that the students don't really read the newspapers and don't watch the appropriate educational television, so he figures he has to help them out a bit. He prepares the following miserable frame:

> For defending the whole country, the Armed Forces are maintained by the f_____government. Police, however, who operate in a smaller territory, are maintained by the l_____governments.

If the students have had a little practice in talking about federal, state, and local governments, a frame like this should be confronting them with a discrimination—which has which power. Consider first: Are students likely to make errors on this frame as given?

A student has three potential responses in each blank: federal, state, or local. Look carefully at the way the blanks are set up. Does he need to read the whole frame in order to determine which of these three responses belongs in each of the blanks in the item?

— — — — — — — — — — — — — — —

If they can name the three types of government, it would be almost impossible to miss this frame.

No. Since only one of the choices begins with an f, that is *all* the student needs to look at to fill in the first blank. The l in the second blank serves the same function.

---

14. *Rule:* Formal prompts (foster/reduce) the necessity to pay attention to the important discriminations in a frame.

— — — — — — — — — — — — — — —

reduce the necessity.

---

15. It isn't possible to state a dogmatic rule that formal prompts should never be used. Obviously they have their uses—in the precise field that their name suggests. When the objective of the frame has something to do with the *form* of the response (its spelling, its pronunciation, or its sound) as would be true in a spelling program, a foreign language program, or a program teaching students to sound out words in beginning reading, then formal prompts relate precisely to what the programer is teaching.

Hinting at the form of a response when the frame's objective is related to the meaning of the response results in "miserable" frames of the type illustrated in Frame 13. Rarely can a formal prompt be used to control the form of a response (the spelling, for instance) at the same time that the theme or meaning is left undetermined. Such a lucky accident was illustrated in the "___fixes" frame, in which the meaningful choice between *pre*fix and *suf*fix could not be made on the basis of the three-letter prompt.

The example you are about to consider is provided to make a serious point about formal prompts. You are to observe carefully what *you are doing covertly* as you try to respond to this "frame".

> To select a useful prompt, the programer has to know something about the students' r_____res—both what they know and what errors are likely.

– – – – – – – – – – – – – – –

Go to next frame.

---

16. The frame about "selecting prompts on the basis of knowing something about students' r_____res" was one of the most miserable frames I ever wrote. I can't, of course, tell you how you responded—only you know that. I can, however, report what most people go through in that situation. Perhaps you did too.

    Thematically, a great many thoroughly adequate answers could be given to the frame. If you ignore the formal prompts (the first and the last three letters), you can respond with "previous knowledge," "most frequent errors," "tendencies to make errors," "likely responses," just simply "responses," and many other ways of saying what should be said. In an open frame, with no formal prompts, any of these responses might have occurred. They may have occurred to you as you struggled with it.

    Unfortunately, I was concentrating too hard on a technical term. I wanted students to say "repertoires," a term frequently used by operant conditioners to describe whole families of response tendencies. In initial testing of the frame, students just wouldn't give that word! Adding a formal prompt, the initial R, increased the number of people who responded with "responses." It seemed that the only way to get the technical term was to insert the last three letters so that "responses" would be prevented. Notice that anyone who uses the non-French form of the word *(repertories)* is now completely blocked.

    What a formal prompt does to students is beautifully illustrated by this miserable frame! It causes them to reject thematically adequate responses and concentrate on the form of the word. For many, the process is one of checking all the words that fit the form, throwing meaning to the winds. By the time some students have found a word with the correct form, they are no longer attending to the point the programer is trying to make. If, of course, they have been subjected to lots of practice with the particular word "repertoires," the blank with its "r_____res" will be enough to prompt the correct response *without any attention* to the point the programer is trying to make.

Dogmatic Conclusion: Formal prompts are dangerous when the objective is not form.

Relevant Quote: *The reviewer believes that the most compelling stimulus in a frame is the question which must be answered or the blank which must be completed. The student's attention is directed primarily to making the correct response. A strong prompt, such as underlining, permits the student to answer correctly without attending to other aspects of the material, not even, for example, to the definition of an underlined or capitalized technical term.* (Anderson, 1967.)

---

17. Here is a test question on the classification of prompts and their effects on *solving* a frame. After you have read the question, you may do one of three things:

(a) If you feel you are ready for it, go ahead.

(b) If you feel shaky about following the thinking patterns of students under the influence of prompts, further practice is provided on page 89.

(c) If you want to review the classification types, go back to page 79.

Take the objective of the "program" to be: Given the name of any animal in the zoo, the zoo animal-feeder trainee will be able to state its preferred diet.

Here's the first frame in the program:

> Since aardvarks find uncles indigestible, they eat_____.

Tear the frame apart the way we tore "Pegasus" apart. What kinds of prompts are used (in basic English) and which class does each belong to (in technical terms). In what order, roughly, do they operate? (What did you have to figure out first?)

Write your answer._____

Confirmation is provided on page 91.

FORMAL AND THEMATIC PROMPTS   89

Optional Sequence

From Frame 17 (b). The following is a programed analysis of the effects of formal and thematic prompts.

1. > Finish the poem:
    > Nine times seven and just one more
    > Is eight times eight, or _____.
    >
    >   (*Multiplication and Division Games*, TMI)

   This is a rather complicated item. Among the prompts at work here is one that makes the last digit in the answer absolutely certain, even if the student cannot multiply 9 × 7. "More" prompts "four." What class of prompt is this poetic hint? _____.

   ― ― ― ― ― ― ― ― ― ― ― ― ― ― ―

   Formal (the sound of a word and its meaning are two very different things).

---

2. The poetic prompt "more" controls only one aspect of the response that the student gives. It must rhyme with "more." Does this formal prompt tell him that it has to be a number? _____.

   ― ― ― ― ― ― ― ― ― ― ― ― ― ― ―

   No. Many many words rhyme with "more."

---

3. What class of prompt would control his choosing a number instead of "sore" or "door" in that item? _____.

   ― ― ― ― ― ― ― ― ― ― ― ― ― ― ―

   Thematic

---

4. Once the student has decided on a number word for the response, can he fail to get the last digit of the answer correct? _____. (Don't guess. Check the digits.)

   ― ― ― ― ― ― ― ― ― ― ― ― ― ― ―

   No. Only one of the ten digits rhymes with "more."

> Finish the poem:
>   Nine times seven and just one more
>   Is eight times eight, or _____.
>
>   *(Multiplication and Division Games,* TMI)

5. Follow the student through the item. As he reads, what is the first subvocal response that you would expect him to make? (What should he solve first?)

— — — — — — — — — — — — — —

He should get the answer to 9 × 7 first.

---

6. Suppose he is rather poor in arithmetic. He thinks "65." With that answer, what is the next response he will make subvocally in order to solve this problem? _____.

— — — — — — — — — — — — — —

66 (just one more).

---

7. If the student has 66 in mind at the end of the first line, what happens to this response when he gets to the end of line two and finds it does not rhyme?

— — — — — — — — — — — — — —

We hope that he rejects it. Otherwise the formal prompt is not helping him.

---

8. Suppose that he is very poor in arithmetic. In response to 9 × 7, he thinks "73." Now what does the formal prompt do for him?

— — — — — — — — — — — — — —

It confirms his last digit, but it will not help eliminate the response in the wrong decade.

9. With the possible exception of syntax (which sometimes does not operate at all, as you will find when you look at answers that your students give you), most formal prompts come into play at the [beginning/end] of a student's search for the correct answer.

— — — — — — — — — — — — — — —

end (he has to have something in mind before he can test whether it fits).

Note. The preceding description of logical search patterns is hypothetical. It is not intended to suggest that such patterns are conscious on the part of most students or, in some cases, even followed. Neither does it imply that even a logical pattern involves putting each stage into words.

Go back to page 88 and solve the aardvark problem.

— — — — — — — — — — — — — —

Answer to the aardvark frame, page 88 (your order may vary somewhat and the amount of detail may also vary):

First: A noun (formal).
Second: An "edible noun" (thematic–limitation of category).
Third: A class of nouns parallel to "uncles" (thematic).
Fourth: Probably the opposite of "uncles"–prompted by "since" and the relation between "indigestible" and "eat" (thematic).
Fifth: This must be a riddle, because animals do not eat "aunts" (thematic).
Sixth: The homonym "ants" will do (formal).

The third and fourth may be combined into "opposite of 'uncles.'" Where you put the fifth one depends on the way you solve it.

18. *A final qualification.* Technically, we should not speak of any part of the terminal stimulus as belonging among the prompts in a particular frame. In reality, however, it is often difficult to separate an item into such clear parts.

Obviously, if you want a student to say something about something, you will have to ask him a question or provide him with an incomplete sentence. Either of these gives him some strong thematic guidance as to what response is wanted.
  (a) "What do aardvarks eat?" is a terminal question and it certainly provides thematic cues—an edible substance is required. The answer to a "what" question is a noun, which is the weakest kind of formal prompt.
  (b) "Aardvarks eat _____" is also a terminal stimulus. Like the question above, but even more obviously, it contains a formal prompt. Although a "how" adverb is possible, a noun is the likely answer that the teacher would be looking for.

There is a subtle difference between the two terminal items (a) and (b). The thematic material is identical. Which one has a stronger formal prompt? _____. Why do you say so?

— — — — — — — — — — — — — — —

(b). The single blank informs the student that he only needs one noun. The answer to the first might be an extensive list.

---

19. *A final discrimination.* A formal prompt, such as the initial letter of a word, or the beginning and end of a word, is such an obvious concept that it can easily be overgeneralized. There are instances in which a letter or two might be *the critical response* and provision of the rest of the letters does not prompt this critical response.

For example, a programer might be teaching the rules for assimilation in the spelling of prefixes, describing how the negative *in-* changes to agree with the first letter of the root. The student might be required to fill in the following:

> *In-*, meaning "not" and *legal* can be combined to produce a word meaning "not lawful":
>
> i____egal

Here, of course, the FORM *is* the response and the other letters around the key letters do not prompt the correct response. If, on the other hand, the programer had been trying to teach when to use the English *un-* and when to use the Latin *in-*, a frame like the one above would qualify as MISERABLE—it defeats the purpose.

> A word meaning "not legal" is i_____l.

In this frame the student doesn't have to make the intended discrimination between *un-* and *in*. *In-*, to say the least, is prompted!

Which of the following frames is formally prompted?

A. From a reading program, teaching long and short vowels:

This is a r___t.

B. From a program teaching classification of animals.

This is a r___.

- - - - - - - - - - - - - - - - -

B. (The "r" reduces the choices to 'rat,' 'racoon,' 'rabbit,' and such.)

---

20. Enough thematic material has to be provided even in a terminal item to let the student know what is wanted. This is an old principle in testing, not a new finding by brilliant programers!

If you want the student to tell you what the colors of the French flag are, is this question fair?_____.

The French flag is_____.

- - - - - - - - - - - - - - - -

Emphatically "No."

---

21. The incomplete sentence is an accepted design for a terminal item in programs. Although a question may be at least slightly preferable in some cases, most programers use both kinds of terminal items.

An X is called a_____.
A Y is called a_____ _____.

For that terminal item, two questions would be better than the two incomplete sentences. Why?

- - - - - - - - - - - - - - -

The one and two-word formal prompts should not be there. (But using a single blank in the latter part might confuse the student.)

Summary

There are two broad classes of prompts, which have different functions in controlling the student's response.

(a) Formal prompts provide the student with information about the structure of the acceptable response but not its meaning. Examples are: the number of letters in a word or the number of words in a response; various rhetorical forms such as serial responses; the sound pattern of the word as indicated by rhyming; syntax, including such structural features as plurality and past tense forms; and any indication of one or more letters in a word. A formal prompt aids the student to select from among responses that other cues lead him to generate.

(b) Thematic prompts provide the student with information about the meaning of the response but not its structure. Examples are: indication of the general category of a response such as equivalence to some other word or phrase; indication of relationships such as opposites; indication that some past association is relevant to the new situation (e.g., the color of the American flag is relevant to the color of the French flag). A thematic prompt aids the student to generate responses within the universe of discourse relevant to the item.

A terminal item has to include at least some thematic and formal indicators so that the student will answer the question that the programer has in mind. Those aspects of the preterminal item that aid the student in coming up with the answer but that will be removed in the terminal item are prompts.

SECTION D: MULTIPLE CHOICE AS A PROMPT

1. In the sense that the student is not allowed to construct an answer in his own words, a multiple-choice item utilizes a formal prompt. The form of the answer is dictated.

   > The borogoves were [shuzzy/mimsy/grully].

   Even if we require the student to copy his choice of answer, a multiple-choice item such as this is not a copying frame. Why?

   _ _ _ _ _ _ _ _ _ _ _ _ _ _ _

   We have not told him, by grammar or directions, which word to copy. Some previous exposure is still required if the student is to select the correct answer other than by chance. Lewis Carroll fans would have no difficulty with the item.

2.
> 71. A difference between displacement and distance is that _____ has only magnitude, while _____ has both magnitude and direction.
>
> (*Vectors,* Basic Systems)

If you go back to page 35, you will see that the item immediately preceding this one required the responses "scalar" and "vector." In this item, those responses are incorrect, but they can and do occur.

First, the student has learned to say "scalar" when he sees "only magnitude" and "vector" when he sees "magnitude and direction."

Second, the student has learned to say "vector" when he sees "displacement" and "scalar" when he sees "distance."

Operating against this tendency is a very subtle grammatical prompt of a sort that students often disregard—namely, we say "a vector" but "displacement"; the latter requires no article. The same is true of the other pair of terms.

Is the above item essentially a multiple-choice item despite its format? _____.

— — — — — — — — — — — — — — —

Yes. Only two pairs of terms (scalar–vector or distance–displacement) are likely to be emitted because of strong thematic prompts.

3. If the item were put in multiple-choice format:

> [Distance/displacement] has only magnitude, while [distance/displacement] has magnitude and direction.

would the effects of the immediately preceding frame have a chance to interfere? _____.

— — — — — — — — — — — — — — —

No. He cannot possibly say "vector" when you give him two forms to choose from.

96 THE BASIC ELEMENTS AND OPERATIONS

4.
   A. | Meaningful units that go after the root are called ____ fixes.

   B. | Meaningful units that go after the root are called [prefixes/ suffixes].

As was pointed out earlier, the first frame is essentially a multiple-choice frame. The student has two possible responses based on previous learning: either "prefix" or "suffix." The formal prompt in the item does not help him select the correct answer, since both have three letters.

If the objective of the frame is the correct word correctly spelled, which frame requires more of a contribution from the student? A or B?

_ _ _ _ _ _ _ _ _ _ _ _ _ _ _

(A) the first one. He has come up with the correct (or at least a set of) three letters (such as "prefix"). In the second one, he merely copies the spelling, if he is writing on an answer sheet, or circles the word.

---

5. | We say that the form BOY is singular but that the form BOYS is [singular/plural].
   | *(Programmed English*, Sullivan)

A copy frame is a sure bet to produce a correct response from an English-speaking student. The above frame is not a copying frame. It is, however, the first occurrence of the word "plural" in the program.

Is this frame a sure bet for correct responses? _____. Why?

_ _ _ _ _ _ _ _ _ _ _ _ _ _ _

Yes. The response "singular" makes no sense after the "but," and there is only one other choice.

---

6. A strong thematic prompt combined with a formal prompt of the two-choice type produces a forced choice.

   | The glamsen is always grobal, but the bloober is always [grobal/clamfy].

What difficulty does a frame of this type share with the copying frame? (*Hint:* Can you answer that frame?)

———————————————

A student can answer it without the slightest idea of what it means.

---

7. There is more than one way to design forced-choice frames. In the one given above, the forcing is done by syntax. We could characterize such a frame in the abstract as:

> An X is always A, but a Y is always (A, B).

As a matter of fact, that should give you another look at how simple the frame is to answer without anything approaching comprehension. The variables X, Y, A, and B have no content (no meaning), yet obviously B is the correct answer.

If you designed a discrimination frame (the student is to tell the difference) in the following way:

> Z is a (D, E)

could the student get the answer without knowing something about D or E?

Could he probably get the answer if he knew something about either D or E but not both?

———————————————

No syntax tells him which to choose. He has to know something.

I have heard many students solve multiple-choice test items by saying "Well, I know it isn't a or b, so it must be c." This is a bit different from knowing that c is the right answer.

8. In a sense, we can force a choice by making use of this kind of processing on the student's part. Here is an example where previous learning forces a student to choose an answer he has never seen before. In other words "the problem of the first instance" is solved.

> MULTITUDINOUS is a [monosyllabic/polysyllabic] word for LOTS.

What do you know students know if they answer this correctly without having ever seen "poly-" before?

- - - - - - - - - - - - - - -

If the students have never seen "poly-," then they must know what "mono-" means. It's pretty obvious even to eighth graders that MULTITUDINOUS is not a one-syllable word. (The frame is from *WORDS.*) In a sense, they are forced to choose the strange answer because the other familiar word is rejected.

---

9. The absolute dictum against the use of multiple-choice responses is increasingly ignored by all but the purists. Although some will not allow the multiple-choice format to qualify as a terminal item (standardized tests notwithstanding!), it has a significant place when the programer is confronted with certain problems. Here is one such situation.

   Neophyte programers often write frames like this:

   > Beethoven wrote _____ symphonies than Brahms.

   and get answers as 'nicer,' 'deeper,' 'louder,' 'shorter,' etc., instead of the desired 'more.' To correct this situation they cue the answer by writing 'm . . . e.' While such a frame can be depended upon to produce a 'correct' answer, the response will not show whether or not the student actually knows which composer wrote more symphonies. In this case, a more significant frame would be:

   > Beethoven wrote [more/fewer] symphonies than Brahms.

   Here you not only restrict the possible answers but leave the important choice to the student. (Basescu, 1962.)

Following Basescu's advice, cure this frame:

> Mount Wilson is .... than Mount Washington.

Write.

_ _ _ _ _ _ _ _ _ _ _ _ _ _

Your choices of what responses to ask for—[wider/thinner], [snowier/sunnier], [taller/shorter], etc.

Note. [Steeper/not so steep] adds a grammatical prompt; the second alternative is not good English in the sentence. Check your choices for that error.

---

10. The insertion of words in multiple-choice format is one cure for the problem of the sentence

> Beethoven wrote ... symphonies than Brahms.

It isn't the only alternative you have, however, to repair the frame in a way that would prevent the overly free range of answers. Can you suggest another kind of repair that would cause the student to make essentially the same point under essentially the same degree of prompting?

Drop down one line for a hint, if you want one.

_ _ _ _ _ _ _ _ _ _ _ _ _ _

Hint: Programs are often supposed to resemble question-and-answer techniques, but the majority of frames appear to be sentences with words left out. Tradition, not necessity, causes this format to dominate the field.

If you ask the student "Who wrote more symphonies, Beethoven or Brahms?", you get the same effect. The sentence with a hole in it is not sacred!

11. The precise meaning of the phrase "essentially multiple-choice" was not specified above. It is a rather slippery term, which is most easily defined by pointing to extreme cases. Of the following pair of questions, which question would probably elicit the wider variety of answers from students who were halfway toward mastery of the subject matter? (A) or (B)? _____ .

> A. | Multiply the following: $(.02)^{-3}(1.67)^2$ |
>
> B. | The European nation with the largest colonial empire in 1905 was _____ . |

- - - - - - - - - - - - - - - -

I would say that the potential of the first question (A) is vast—a multiplicity of creative errors could be made—whereas the second one has only a few possible alternatives, if the student knows which nations are (or were) European, and even fewer alternatives if he is "halfway" toward knowing which of those were the colonizing nations.

---

12. A question could be called "essentially multiple-choice" if only a limited range of answers is plausible.
    (a) *If* we know that the student knows the five colonial powers (excuse the history, but multiple-choice questions usually stop with five alternatives), and
    (b) if we want to test his knowledge of the largest empire, would a multiple-choice, five-alternative format be any easier for him than the constructed-response format in (B) above? _____ .

- - - - - - - - - - - - - - - -

I think not. The constructors of standardized tests think not. Intrinsic programers, whose style of programing is discussed later, think not. You may disagree.

---

13. If there were *twelve* colonizing nations in 1905, and we provide the student with a *five*-alternative multiple-choice format, have we made the question easier? _____ . Why?

- - - - - - - - - - - - - - - -

Yes. We have eliminated seven wrong answers, leaving him only four possibilities for error.

14. You may feel that we are playing logical rather than realistic games with item-design problems. You are right. The argument for the multiple-choice format is based on "plausible alternatives." Even if you think that you know all you need to know about the plausible responses that the student might make, what data do you lose when you translate an "essentially multiple-choice" question into multiple-choice format?

— — — — — — — — — — — — — — —

You lose the data from the student who is lost, creative, careless, or asleep. With a constructed-response format, you always get a certain proportion of really interesting responses!

---

15. The teaching value of a multiple-choice frame is only as good as its alternatives, a bit of wisdom long known to those who design multiple-choice testing items. A forced-choice frame, as illustrated in Frame 6 above, represents very little progress toward unaided mastery of the subject matter.
    The same effect as that produced by the combination of a thematic prompt and the formal choice

    "X is A, but Y is (A, B)"

    can also be produced by making the first choice "sensible" and the second choice "idiotic."

Programmers have an advantage over multiple-choice test writers, since the former usually don't have to come up with a standard number of alternatives. For the test writer problems are created when the format of the test dictates five alternatives and only three are sensible. Idiot alternatives frequently result! Programmers don't need to get trapped. If there are only two good alternatives, make do with two.

With two alternatives, however, as all of us know, the student has a 50% chance of being correct with a wild guess. One suggestion to increase the sensitivity of a basically two-choice situation is sometimes called the NABB frame (from Neither-A-B-Both) or, in other circles, the BABOON frame (from B-A-BOth-Or-Neither). (Tosti, 1964.)

As an illustration, consider a situation in which a programmer is attempting to teach two concepts which overlap at some point or in which one concept is a subset of the other. In the case of overlapping concepts, any particular example could be

    a member of both sets
    a member of the first set only
    a member of the second set only
    a member of neither (a non-example)

In language study in English, such overlapping sets occur in the two concepts "words" and "roots." Some roots are words and others aren't, and conversely some words are roots and others aren't.

A BABOON or NABB frame testing student understanding of this overlap might look like this:

> In the word FOOTLESS, the unit FOOT is
> A)   a root
> B)   a word
> Both
> Neither

As multiple-choice test writers have found and as NABB frame writers should remember, the alternatives "Both" and "Neither" have to be the answer now and then. Students quickly learn that "None of these" is what a test-writer uses when he has to write that last alternative and there isn't a sensible one! (In the case above, the answer would be "both." We could also generate examples for "neither".)

The NABB frame, its authors claimed, is also a good one to encourage students to process both alternatives when a frame is intended to teach the spelling of a technical term. In an ordinary two-alternative frame, the student wouldn't have to look at the second alternative if he could judge the first one immediately. (If the first one were the wrong spelling, you lost the chance to get him to observe the correct spelling.) When the alternatives "both" and "neither" are offered, he has to look at both.

Try your hand at producing a BABOON frame. Assume you are teaching the classification scheme for animals. The objective of your frame is to check whether students know that some vertebrates are mammals but all mammals are vertebrates. Pick any example you like.

Write.___

- - - - - - - - - - - - -

Your frame should resemble the one on "FOOT" in structure, with alternatives in any order you choose. The example could be any type of animal that is a vertebrate, whether or not it is a mammal. (E.g., chicken, dog, aardvark.) The only example that wouldn't test what you're trying to get at would be one that wasn't a vertebrate. To test that particular objective, the answer can't be "neither."

16. A multiple-choice format with more than one correct answer lends itself to certain kinds of objectives. When the student is expected to learn multiple relationships (for instance, several contributing causes of some event or several alternative effects of some event) the good old one-step-at-a-time format can get in the way. The subject matter gets fractionated and, like Humpty Dumpty, is hard to put back together again.

In a medical program, for instance, you might see something like this:

> If your patient is running a fever of 102° and reports many aching muscles, your diagnosis might be:
> _____virus a
> _____virus b
> _____Hongkong flu
> _____high blood pressure
> _____etc.

More than one answer might be correct. Sometimes, in some programs, all happen to be correct; more rarely, none is correct. The student has to process each one. But he processes them together, which keeps related ideas connected with each other.

If you insisted on having NO multiple-choice items at all in your program, what would you have to ask the student to do to show that he had mastered the multiple possibilities in the case above?

Which frame is harder—the multiple-choice above or your suggested revision of it?

— — — — — — — — — — — — — —

The simplest revision would be to ask him to list all the possibilities.

Most of us would assume that it is harder to construct a list than to recognize what belongs in it and what doesn't. This assumption is difficult to prove, however, as years of conflicting research results show.

Summary

Multiple-choice, which once was "out" on theoretical grounds, at least among Skinnerians, is now "in." Rigid adherence to *none* of it, like rigid adherence to *only* multiple-choice, is gradually disappearing. Whenever there are a limited number of plausible choices of the correct answer, and especially when the design of the frame produces too many wild guesses along wrong dimensions, multiple-choice seems a good move, though not the only one. It lends itself beautifully to teaching discriminations, and, with some sophistication in design, to teaching overlapping concepts, multiples causes, and multiple effects.

SECTION E. VISUAL PROMPTS

Programing began in a highly literate environment (we can say that about Harvard, I think) with a group of very bookish people (you can tell that by the number of books and papers they've written as well as read). Although pictures and diagrams as stimuli to which the student was to respond were used in the earliest programs, other visual assists were not.

One exception to this, unfortunately, was the tendency to underline the already over-prompted response in a copy frame. A better way to *guarantee* that the student will IGNORE everything else in the frame has not yet been invented! (See Anderson and Faust, 1967, for experimental evidence on this point.)

Programed texts and their counterparts for machine presentation looked like ordinary books, crowded with print and relatively unaffected by layouts designed to aid the student. Among the earliest pioneers to insist that layout be part of designing lessons was Gilbert (1962b). Here is an example drawn from his essay. The behavior being taught is a chain—the sequence of responses which must be followed to do long division. The frame, as you can see, is heavily primed.

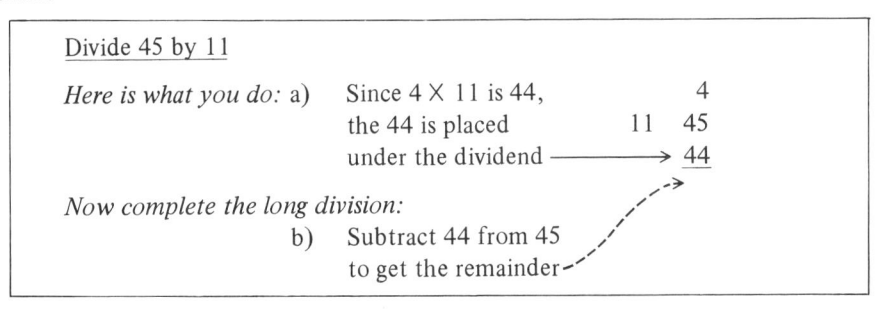

```
Divide 45 by 11

Here is what you do:  a)   Since 4 × 11 is 44,              4
                           the 44 is placed         11   45
                           under the dividend ───────→  44

Now complete the long division:
                      b)   Subtract 44 from 45
                           to get the remainder
```

Another example of Gilbert's influence can be seen in the frame from the *Ameba* program on page 9.

1. An excellent example of a layout that aids the student in processing all the information in a priming frame is this one from Mager's *Language of Computers.* The pictures of the set of lights are the stimuli to which the student is learning to respond—they are not prompts, therefore. What different kinds of visual assists do you see in this frame?

VISUAL PROMPTS   105

```
          ┌─────────────┐
          │ O  O  O  O  │
          └─────────────┘
            A set of lights
```

The light at the <u>right end</u> of a set is always a ONE

The light at its left is always a TWO

The light next to the two is
    always a FOUR

```
       16    8    4    2    1
    O   O    O    O    O    O
```

- - - - - - - - - - - - - - - -

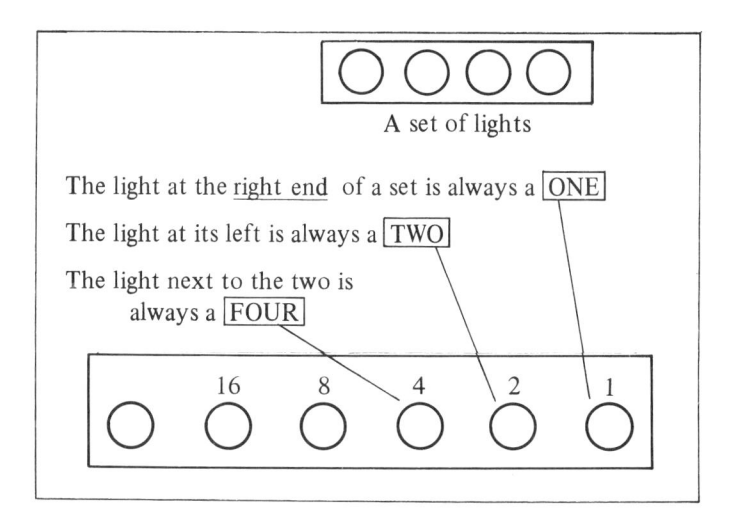

The words right end are *underlined* to focus the student's attention on the starting point of the numerical progression, each number is in *capital letters, boxed,* and with a *line* drawing the eye to where the number is found in the computer's set of lights. If you also noticed that the three numbers in boxes are in the same order from right to left as they appear on the set of lights, you have a good eye for visual design.

---

2. Here is another example from a much smaller-step program for eighth graders. What slight assist is given in this frame?

> The words SUBTERRANEAN
>   and   TERRESTRIAL have the same root.
> The root is   _____, meaning "ground."

- - - - - - - - - - - - - - - -

Positioning the two roots in a line made it less likely that students would include either the *a* or the *e* from the suffixes as part of the root. (From *WORDS.*)

3. In an earlier program, (Markle, 1961) typographical features such as underlining, capitalizing, italicizing, and so forth were given the name *emphasis prompts*. What we call them doesn't really matter. These types of typographical tricks for attracting the reader's attention are a subset of the larger set of tricks we might call *visual prompts*.

An Important Discrimination: Arrangement of material on a page and attractiveness of visual materials such as slides are important to producers of such materials on *aesthetic* or *artistic* grounds. The visual tricks we are discussing here have a different purpose. The important dimension is the *ease with which the student can process the instruction*. The ultimate referee of the goodness of the instructional layout is the student, not the artist. Our measurements of this variable are not very precise. However, I can suggest two:

(a) How long does the student spend processing the instruction and could this be reduced by a better layout?
(b) How often does the instruction have to be repeated because it didn't come through the first time?

You may think of or discover other signs as you watch students struggling with your own frames.

For programmers who deal with poor readers or with wide ranges of reading ability, the whole range of visual tricks is worth keeping in mind. Poor readers and even many fairly good readers can have trouble with

>logical connectives like *and, or,* and *but,*
>the very important little word *not,*

and especially double contingencies like

>*If x AND if y, then z.*

Here's a useful little spelling rule that is relatively difficult to teach because of this double-contingency problem:

>*If* a two-syllable word ends in a single consonant preceded by a single vowel *AND if* the accent is on the second syllable, *then* the final consonant is doubled when adding a suffix beginning with a vowel.

Written out like that, the rule is likely to lose the student (who could make good use of this regularity in the general chaos of English spelling!). Since the rule holds only if both if-clauses are satisfied, breaking it into small steps isn't the best answer. How do you make it easier for a student to take in all the parts without losing the whole?

You could try a whole bag of tricks or use only one or two in the first draft. You can rearrange the parts, of course, to fit your visual design. There are many potential variants, and probably many of them would work. Here's one:

> When adding a suffix beginning with a vowel
>
> > to a TWO-syllable word,
> >
> > you double the final consonant
>
> IF the word ends in a single consonant
>
> > preceded by a single vowel
> >
> > AND
>
> IF the accent is on the *second* syllable.

Here's another, perhaps better version, using an example to help make the point:

> Given a TWO-syllable word ⟶ RE PEL
>
> to which you are adding a suffix ⟶ ING
> beginning with a vowel ⟶ ↑
>
> you will double the final consonant ⟶ LL
>
> ONLY IF the accent is on the
> *second* syllable ⟶ re PEL
>
> AND
>
> IF the word ends in a single consonant ⟶ L
>
> preceded by a single vowel ⟶ E

Neither of the illustrative frames has been tested. Trying to teach the rule without visual tricks *has*—it is very hard to get across to eighth graders!

Try applying visual tricks to the double contingency, to the "not," and to any other key words you wish in this definition of "prompt."

A supplementary stimulus is a prompt if it makes the frame easier and if it is not sufficient to produce the response by itself.

Write out your design on a separate sheet of paper. This is one response you can't "think." (You may abbreviate at will.)

— — — — — — — — — — — — — — —

There are many ways of doing it. Good designs would probably separate the two if-clauses, emphasize at least the "and" and the "not," and perhaps emphasize other key words. For instance,

    (a) A supplementary stimulus is a prompt if it makes the item easier
                      and
        it is NOT sufficient, etc.

or (b) If a supplementary stimulus makes a frame easier
                    AND
        if it is *not* sufficient, etc., then it is a prompt.

108   THE BASIC ELEMENTS AND OPERATIONS

A Bit of Data. The following report from a Reading Improvement Project (RIP) indicates that this variable item design is worth keeping in mind.

> A poor reader may grasp at anything he sees to eke out his understanding of what is required of him. In testing of the RIP lessons, accidents of visual layout were often found to be responsible for errors.... Division of sentences into lines had finally to be governed by sense rather than space. In an early sequence on the word "accumulate," this frame appeared. [See (A) below.] Out of a group of ten students, five read the first line as a sentence and dutifully copied the whole list.... Such instances led the programmers to arrange all sentences into easily grasped units of meaning, each incomplete as a guide to responding, thus encouraging the student to read the whole before answering. [Frame (B) is the rearrangement of frame (A).] (Knight, 1964.)

A. | Write out all the words in the list below that mean *the same as* ACCUMULATE.
gather
pile up
rot
collect

B. | Write out all the words
in the list below
that mean *the same as* ACCUMULATE.
(etc.)

4. In one of these frames, the illustration functions as a prompt. In another, it functions as a prime—we cannot call the frame a copying frame in the usual sense. In the third, it functions solely as an illustration. Which frame is which?

1. | Two early methods of telling time at night or on cloudy days were the _____ and the _____.

(*Introduction to Modern Mathematics*, TMI)

The function of the illustration is _____.

VISUAL PROMPTS 109

2. The bushel is used for [liquid/dry] measurement.

(Introduction to Modern Mathematics, TMI)

The function of the illustration is _____.

3. A collection of things or objects is called a _____.

(Introduction to Modern Mathematics, TMI)

The function of the illustration is _____.

- - - - - - - - - - - - - - -

1. a prime
2. a prompt (apples are dry—at least they are not liquid).
3. solely as an illustration.

---

5. The second frame in the preceding set of examples employed an illustration as a thematic prompt for the response "dry." Suppose we verbalize the thematic prompt:

> Apples are measured by the bushel. The bushel is used for [liquid/dry] measurement.

Which frame seems more fun to you?

- - - - - - - - - - - - - - -

Your opinion.

110   THE BASIC ELEMENTS AND OPERATIONS

6. Two other uses of visuals are found in some programs. The examples in Frame 4 from a TMI program illustrate a cartooning style which appealed to children. Cartoons, sometimes relevant, sometimes irrelevant (as in the third example), were sprinkled through TMI's programs at random in the hopes that they would reinforce children for working through the rest of the unillustrated frames. In other words, they were motivational devices designed to lighten the load of serious learning.

Popham (1965) used visual humor to good effect (in other words, students report they like it) in an audiotape-filmstrip program on behavioral objectives. Like verbal wit, visual wit may be irrelevant to the cognitive objectives of a program but highly relevant to attitudes toward the subject matter and toward the instructional materials.

Several cautions might be offered to those who have skill with verbal and visual wit and could put this skill to work in designing programs. Suggest one or two.

You may have thought of all sorts of cautions. One that occurs to me is the assumption we all tend to make that what is funny to us is funny to others. Another is the potential distraction from the serious parts of the teaching that wit could cause. A third is the possibility of a student taking seriously a remark made in jest. (For example, if I remarked somewhere in this program, "Let's look at this *great* frame," meaning the opposite, some readers might misinterpret the intent and write such frames!)

---

7. This program does not attempt to teach future programers to be witty! Nor does it attempt to teach the other use of visualization which is worth knowing about and using if you already have the skill. This skill is the effective use of visual imagery, whether by picture or words, to help students remember something. An example of such a useful image occurred in the "Talking Typewriter" program from which we have drawn examples before. The letter S was called the "snake letter," a name which not only begins with the appropriate sound, but also suggests the multiple-curvature of the letter's shape.

The programers did not have such an image for each letter. If you try to think up such a visual association which really fits for each of the letters *and* which would be understood by four- and five-year-old children in a Harlem kindergarten, you will understand why.

Programers did not invent imagery, any more than they invented wit or multiple-choice formats or many other elements discussed in this chapter. Each of these elements, when and if they are used, have a purpose in the frame or sequence. This purpose is not to satisfy the programer or influence the purchaser of instructional materials. Rather it is because such elements can be shown to have the desired effect on _____ (whom)?

— — — — — — — — — — — — — —

STUDENTS (Although that response appears to be an irrelevant one, given the content of the frame, it NEVER is. It is good to remind ourselves, especially when discussing this artsy area, that the student is the ultimate proof of the pudding. Artistry that goes over his head is irrelevant.)

Relevant Quote: One man's humor is another man's wisecrack. (Gotkin and Goldstein, 1964.)

SECTION F. THE SEQUENCE PROMPT

1. The following frame, from Mager's *The Language of Computers,* is actually page 23, the fifth frame in the sequence on reading the sets of lights in a computer. The word *set,* then, has a fairly specific meaning to the student at this point.

    Do you think that the average college graduate could answer this frame as it is without *any* previous instruction?

    Without previous instruction, would the student's time to complete the item be longer, shorter, or about the same as when taken in sequence?

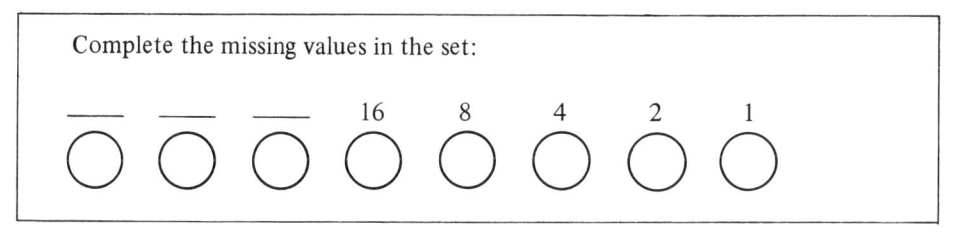

    Complete the missing values in the set:

    ___ ___ ___ 16   8   4   2   1
    ○   ○   ○   ○   ○   ○   ○   ○

— — — — — — — — — — — — — —

With no previous instruction, a relatively well-educated adult ought to be able to figure this out, I think. He might wonder why the circles were there, what kind of a set it is, and why the numbers went from right to left instead of in the normal direction, but he should be able to determine the rule for the series and apply it in the last three slots.

With all that figuring out and wondering, it would have to take him longer.

2.
> 1. Words are divided into classes. We call the largest class NOUNS. Nouns are a class of _____.
>
> 2. In English the class of words called NOUNS is larger than all the other _____ of words combined.
>
> 3. We call the largest class of English words _____.
>
> (*Programmed English,* Sullivan)

These are the first three items in this program. No previous learning is assumed. Yet students are expected to answer the third frame without having to copy the word. (They do, too.)

If the student looks back, he is copying, and the third frame is not, for him, prompted. For most students, however, a very strong prompt is operating in this frame. It is not a terminal frame for exactly that reason, although it resembles a terminal frame. What makes it highly likely that the student will respond correctly to frame 3?

— — — — — — — — — — — — — —

(In your own words.) He just read it, or it is the subject of discussion, or the context of the previous item makes the response obvious, etc.

3. If the stimulus that causes the correct response to be highly likely in frame 3 is a prompt (as we say it is), then it can be withdrawn as all other prompts can. How would you go about withdrawing this prompt to produce a real terminal frame?

— — — — — — — — — — — — — —

You could ask the same question out of context (or much later) when the subject was not being talked about.

4. For the purposes of this program, the prompt that operates from one frame to the next will be called a *sequence prompt.* In line with standard psychological terminology, we might have called it a "recency" prompt, or perhaps an "immediate memory" prompt.

Any of these names would suggest that a response to what looks like a terminal frame may not be a permanent part of the student's repertoire.

We can certainly assume that the sequence prompt varies in strength as a function of the amount of time or intermediate activity (either reading or different responses) that intervenes. It should therefore be a highly manipulable prompt.

In *Vectors,* the second section began in this fashion:

---

39. Things that have direction and magnitude are called vectors. Is displacement a vector?_____. Explain your answer.

— — — — — — — — — — — — — —

Yes. It has magnitude and direction.

---

40. A boy walks ten miles south and then six miles north. What distance has he walked?

— — — — — — — — — — — — — —

Sixteen miles.

---

41. What is a vector?

— — — — — — — — — — — — — —

A vector is a quantity that has magnitude and direction.

Suppose, as could happen (but didn't), students were making too many errors on frame 41. One way to repair a frame when students make errors is to increase the strength of the prompts. There are two ways to increase the sequence prompting in this situation. Name one (both, if you can).

— — — — — — — — — — — — — —

One way would be to make frame 41 frame 40, dropping the digression. Another would be to change the content of frame 40, making it about vectors. In the format of *Vectors* (through-the-book) the answer to frame 39 would appear next to frame 40. You can see, therefore, why the programers would not want to have 41 follow 39 directly—it would produce a kind of copying situation. (Note the similarity of the answers.)

114   THE BASIC ELEMENTS AND OPERATIONS

5. Would you class a sequence prompt as a [formal/thematic] prompt?

———————————————

You were asked what you would do. I would put it in the thematic category, since it is a function of the subject matter under discussion.

6.
> 1. All mammals give birth to live young and nurse their young. Since whales do this, whales are _____.
>
> 2. Birds are not _____.

The permissible grammatical categories are so broad in the second frame that we cannot say that even as weak a prompt as a syntax prompt is operating. (Some adverbs like "here," all adjectives, all nouns, and all past and gerund forms of most verbs fit!)

Yet in many programs students are responding correctly to frames such as frame 2. What would this lead you to say about the sequence prompt as compared to most other prompts?

———————————————

It is probably the strongest determiner of responses (short of a straight copying stimulus).

7. Several times previously, I've mentioned that "small steps" as a principle of programing led to many difficulties. The "Birds are not_____" frame (which I made up, but which is a type found in some programs) illustrates the difficulties beautifully. The subject of the frames is a concept, "mammal," a class which has widely varying members, such as whales, mice, dogs, men, and others, to which students should be able to generalize; and excludes a wide variety of non-members, such as robins and striped bass, which the student should be able to discriminate from members.

When we think of a "step" in a program as being defined by a short sentence and a small response, we end up with the difficulty illustrated in the sample frames—that is, defining a "step" by its form rather than its function. If, instead, we think of a frame as having a function, namely taking a step toward mastery of the concept, we would be more likely to write one having a behavioral function. In the case of a concept, this would be a frame requiring a discrimination or a generalization or both. For instance,

> All mammals give birth to live young and nurse their young. Whales do this, so they are mammals. Which of the following would be mammals?
>
> chicken   dog   goldfish   cow   frog

The function of this frame is
   A. Generalization
   B. Discrimination
   Both
   Neither

- - - - - - - - - - - - - - -

Both. Some of the animals are and some aren't mammals.

---

8. Take another look at the miserable pair of frames:

> 1. All mammals give birth to live young and nurse their young. Since whales do this, whales are _____.
> 2. Birds are not _____.

How do they rate in function? Do they require (a) generalization? (b) discrimination? Both? Neither?

Why do you say so?

- - - - - - - - - - - - - -

They require neither. The essential element "are—are not" is given to the student. All he does is learn to spell "mammal."

Note. Although the sequence prompt can be lumped with the other thematic prompts as part of the large class contrasting with formal prompts, sequence is such a strong and specific type of controlling stimulus that we will continue to label it as a separate prompt in discussing frames. Thus, when both word association within an item and recent exposure to the desired response are operating, we will say that the item has a thematic prompt (the word association) *and* a sequence prompt (the prior exposure).

9. | Since aardvarks find uncles indigestible, they eat _____ .
   | (Klaus)

Is there a sequence prompt operating in the above frame? [Yes/No/Cannot tell.] _____ .
Why?

— — — — — — — — — — — — — — —

Cannot tell. No previous frames are given, and this frame could possibly stand alone with no previous training (merely the assumption that the student knows that aardvarks are animals, not cannibals).

---

10. This pair of items occurred in *Vectors:*

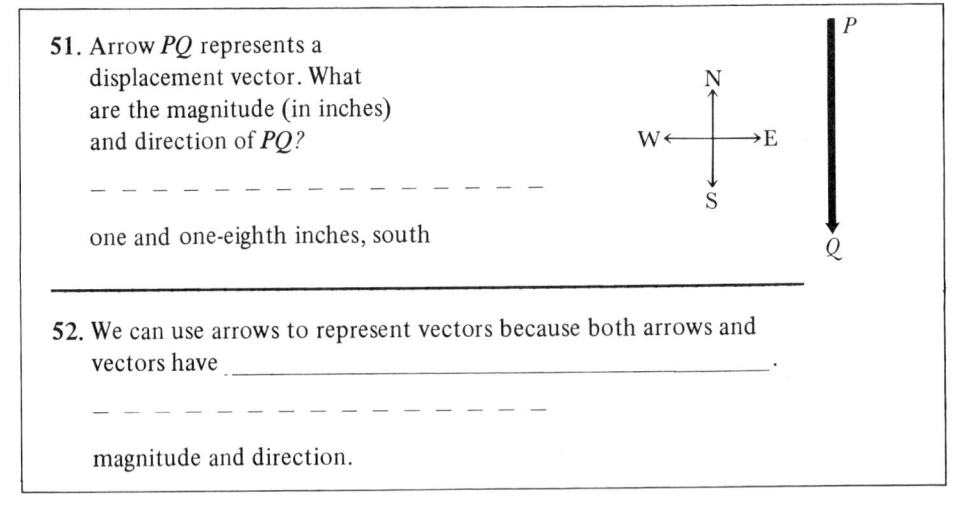

    51. Arrow *PQ* represents a displacement vector. What are the magnitude (in inches) and direction of *PQ?*

       — — — — — — — — — — — —

       one and one-eighth inches, south

    ---

    52. We can use arrows to represent vectors because both arrows and vectors have _____ .

       — — — — — — — — — — — —

       magnitude and direction.

A sequence prompt is based on recency of exposure to the content. Is a sequence prompt operating, then, in frame 52?

— — — — — — — — — — — — — —

Yes. In frame 51, "magnitude" and "direction" are part of the stimuli which control what observations and calculations the student makes. In frame 52, these former stimuli are now responses.

---

11. Obviously the sequence prompt as defined here operates within any program segment that has a logical sequence of frames. Making the sequence illogical to avoid it does not solve the issue! In fact, what seems to be required if the behavior being learned is to be thoroughly learned for long-term retention is to double the efforts to be logical in the sequential development across larger segments of the instruction. This is hardly news to people in curriculum development, who try to structure curricula so that what is learned in the early years will be required in later learning and therefore retained.

Programers in industry have fewer problems. Usually when a man has learned a job, he puts his new knowledge to work immediately. Retention is guaranteed by constant practice. Tripling the number of frames in an academic program to teach the student better something he will never use is not the solution! The problem of retention is part of the problem of relevance—a much-talked-of problem at the moment. This is not the place to digress on that subject!

All philosophical issues aside, the value to programers of knowing about the power of the sequence prompt lies in the jaundiced view it gives us about error rates and error data on the basis of which claims are made about how effective a program is. *The fact that students make no errors on a particular frame is no guarantee of the frame's value as a step forward in their learning.*

So, frames like

"Birds are not _____"
are [good/bad] frames
[in spite of/because of]
the fact that no student will miss them.

— — — — — — — — — — — — — —

bad in spite of (and to some people, that is heresy!).

Relevant Quote: Whatever the usefulness of error rates may be for purposes of program revision, the uncritical use of over-all error rates . . . is by now largely discounted as a validating measure of program effectiveness. (Lumsdaine, 1965.)

SECTION G. THE STRENGTH OF PROMPTS

INTRODUCTION

The following section has some value to those who will do research in factors that control verbal behavior. The "strength" of a prompt or type of prompt is one topic that could generate a good deal of research. The game is one of trying to predict the behavior of students by manipulating various aspects of frame design and then trying the various possibilities out to see if the predictions hold up. Part of the research described by Anderson (1967) is of this sort.

Most programers do not purposely do such research. Their main interest is in using techniques that have some promise and trying out their instructional designs on students with a view to improving those which fail. The research-and-development process of constructing a program differs in many ways from the basic research model. (Markle, 1967.)

If your primary interest is in the development of instructional materials, you may skip Section G. No crucial aspects of program construction depend on it.

1a. It is time to define the term "strength" as it is used in talking about prompts. There are two approaches to it, both of which are valid.

> The capital of France is _aris.

Only a single letter is required in the above frame. A student who has absolutely no idea of what the answer is has_____ chance in_____ of being correct if he guesses at random.

— — — — — — — — — — — — — —

one in twenty-six (we said nothing about English sequential dependencies—most students would not put in a *q* when no *u* follows the blank; but this would not be purely random behavior).

1b. > The capital of France is P_____ .

If the student knows absolutely nothing, are his chances better or worse in this item than his chances were in the first item?_____ .

— — — — — — — — — — — — — —

Much worse. Think of the number of plausible names that you could generate with the sole restriction that they begin with *P*.

THE STRENGTH OF PROMPTS 119

1c. | The capital of France is P_____. |

If we set to work those monkeys who are hypothetically producing the works of Shakespeare by typing randomly for thousands of years, we might get an answer to all three of these frames. Once in each 26 responses (on the average) the monkey would be correct in the first frame. Given random typing behavior, which frame would (on the average) be answered first: [the third one in which the behavior is typing any four letters in any sequence/the second, in which the behavior is typing any sequence of letters with the number unspecified]?

— — — — — — — — — — — — — — —

the third frame (the mathematics are pretty complex, but you could write a formula that would prove this for each of these cases).

---

2. We can define the "strength" of a prompt, then, by calculating the chances that a student has of being correct, giving purely random guessing. In order to do this, of course, we have to know the number of "reasonable" responses. As we add prompts, we can talk about restricting the number and increasing the student's chances of being correct.

| Pegasus had two _____. |

Prompt: Syntax
Number: All plural nouns

| Like a bird, Pegasus had two _____. |

Prompt: Category
Number: All plural nouns relevant to birds

| Pegasus had two ____ s. |

Prompt: Formal (number of letters)
Number: All plural nouns having four letters preceding the *s*.

| Like a bird, Pegasus had two ____ s. |

Logically, we have now restricted the response to . . . .

— — — — — — — — — — — — — —

All plural nouns having four letters preceding the *s* and relevant to birds.

120   THE BASIC ELEMENTS AND OPERATIONS

3. For visual thinkers, Venn diagrams come in handy. In the diagram below, the last frame above is represented by the letter _____ .

A = All plural nouns
B = Four-letter nouns
C = Nouns relevant to birds

- - - - - - - - - - - - - - -

In the Venn diagram, D represents the overlapping categories.

4. The effectiveness of a formal prompt obviously depends on self-editing. We assume that the student confronted with a blank that specifies the form of the response is behaving in a "rational" way. (We could program a computer to do the same.)

   (a) First he generates possible responses that fit other prompts. He limits himself to the subject matter under discussion in previous frames (thematic), in the frame at hand (thematic), and to the form class of the word wanted—nouns, verbs, etc. (formal); then

   (b) he tries out his possible responses for their fit in the restricted form given.

   Given the frame

   > Like a bird, Pegasus had two _____ s.

   the student has a fairly large store of nouns relevant to pairs of things that birds might have. Then what does he have to do?

- - - - - - - - - - - - - - -

He has to find such a four-letter noun.

5. The strength of a prompt has two different dimensions:
   (a) logical and
   (b) psychological.

   Consider this type of frame:

   > X's are always black, but Y's are always _____ .

From the logical point of view, with the prompt "but," is it certain that Y's are *not black?*
_____.

- - - - - - - - - - - - - - -

Yes. The sentence makes no sense in English (in all but very odd contexts) if the blank is filled by "black."

---

6. From a logical point of view, then, is it an adequate response to say that Y's are green? _____. (Is green nonblack?)

- - - - - - - - - - - - - - -

Yes. Any color (or shade of gray) is legitimate in that blank.

---

7. The psychological strength of a prompt depends, not on all the possible responses that are legitimate in a blank, but on the actual responses that students make. In other words, it is an empirical measure.
   You are a speaker of English and a member of the general culture. What would you predict that a student would be most likely to do in such a situation? Confronted with the stimulus [not black, but . . .], what is the most likely response?_____.

- - - - - - - - - - - - - - -

If you said "white," you agree with the measures of word association (which are psychological rather than logical measures of the association between various words).

---

8. Several years ago, I used the phrase "programing with blinders on" to describe the programer who expects every student to come up with the same associations to a particular word that the programer does.
   If the strength of a prompt is based on the probability that most students will associate "black" and "white," Frame 7 [is/is not] fair to the student with different word associations.

- - - - - - - - - - - - - - -

is not (there is no logical reason for assuming that he is wrong or stupid because he thinks of something different).

122 THE BASIC ELEMENTS AND OPERATIONS

9. The following is a frame from an early version of a vocabulary program (Markle):

> When you look forward to some event, what you see is the ___ spect of something happening.

There is only one word in English that fits the formal prompt. If the student produces an English word, then, what is the *logical* probability of his being correct?

— — — — — — — — — — — — — — — —

1 in 1, or 100%, or absolutely certain.

---

10. However, in the program students were being taught to construct words that they had never seen before by combining prefixes and roots. The *psychological* (what they may do) probability is [less than/equal to/greater than] the logical probability of a correct response.

— — — — — — — — — — — — — — — —

less than (they may make up a nonexistent word).

---

11. At this point in the program, the student had been taught the other three-letter prefixes *con-*, *dis-*, and *sub-*. The item above was the fourth in the training sequence on the prefix *pro-*. He also had been taught several other longer and shorter prefixes.

If the formal prompt works, he will reject all responses longer and shorter than three letters. With what we *know* that he knows, then, he has _____ chance in _____ of hitting the right three letters by random guessing among prefixes he "knows."

Even if the student ignores the oddness of what he constructs with one of his four prefixes, he has a much higher chance of selecting *pro-* than the other three. Why? (See the first paragraph.)

— — — — — — — — — — — — — — — —

one in four (data are never as clean as this logical analysis suggests, of course. Merely because the programer has not yet taught *pre-*, there is no guarantee that it will not turn up as a response in this item).

It was fourth in a training sequence; therefore, a strong sequence prompt would be operating.

12. | When you look forward to some event, what you see is the ___ spect of something happening.

According to our analysis of what students might do:

(a) the logical strength of the prompt "construct an English word having this form" is absolute certainty, but psychologically this prompt is not in operation, because of the nature of what students have been doing in the program.
(b) Given the prefixes that have been taught, the student has one chance in four of selecting the correct one, but a sequence prompt makes the correct one far more probable than it is logically.

If the formal prompt controls the student's behavior, there are then three "logical" errors—"conspect," "disspect," and "subspect"—and one correct response—"prospect." By pure and simple logic, we deduce that most students will be correct and that errors of intrusion will, because of the formal prompt, represent one of the three logical errors.

No such luck! The results obtained from many eighth graders led the author to coin the term "Procrustean response" to describe the students' efforts to make their preferred responses fit the required form. Most students were correct. The errors, however, were as follows: "*con*spect" (only once), "*sus*spect," "*ass*spect," "*asp*spect," "*exs*spect," and "*tran*spect" (only once).

How many times was the three-letter formal prompt violated? _____.
Would you call it a strong prompt or a weak prompt? _____. Why?

- - - - - - - - - - - - - -

only once (there are four letters in *tran*).

We could call it a strong prompt because only one student violated the requirement, and it also controlled the students' behavior to the extent of generating combinations of letters that they never would have thought of without it. We could call it a weak prompt, however, in terms of its controlling the correct response, which it did not do.

124 THE BASIC ELEMENTS AND OPERATIONS

13. | Like a bird, Pegasus had two_____. |

   Suppose we could specify the number of legitimate responses, and we find that there are *twenty* possible answers to this frame.

   (a) In terms of the probability that the student will be correct, how strong is the prompt *logically?*_____.

   Suppose that we try this frame on one hundred students, and we find that 90 of them say "wings," 5 of them say "legs," 2 of them say "kidneys," and 1 each respond "nests," "worms," and "eggs."

   (b) In terms of the probability of the student being correct, how strong is the prompt psychologically or empirically?_____.

   — — — — — — — — — — — — — — — —

   (a) Logically, he has 1 in 20 chances of being correct.
   (b) Psychologically, he has been shown to have 9 in 10 or 90 in 100 chances of being correct.

---

14. In my opinion, a programer should be fully aware of the logical strength of any prompts that he uses in designing a frame. This interesting intellectual exercise, however, should be tempered with a large dose of empiricism ("show me"). On the basis of the types of evidence shown in the last two frames (which you may reinspect, if you so desire), what two limitations of a purely logical analysis of your frame should be kept in mind?

   — — — — — — — — — — — — — — — —

   To put it succinctly, students do not behave in logical ways. (1) They come up with illogical answers and (2) they do not come up with possible logical answers. Or (1) a logically strong prompt may be empirically weak and (2) a logically weak prompt may be psychologically strong.

THE STRENGTH OF PROMPTS 125

15. | CANIS FAMILIARIS is man's best friend. CANIS FAMILIARIS is the technical name for "_____." |

Which kind of a prompt is "man's best friend"?_____.
Logically, how strong is this prompt? (What is the range of choices?)_____.

— — — — — — — — — — — — — — —

Thematic.

To the best of my knowledge, the student has one chance in one of getting this correct; according to the saying, man has only one best friend.

---

16. | The territory where Geronimo fought was the last to achieve statehood. The 48th and last continental state to be admitted to the Union was _____. |

The second sentence is the terminal stimulus. The first sentence is another one-to-one thematic prompt. If many students fail to answer this item, what do you know about the students?

— — — — — — — — — — — — — — —

They do not know where Geronimo fought or, perhaps, who he was (an unlikely situation in the day of the vast "Wasteland"!).

126   THE BASIC ELEMENTS AND OPERATIONS

17. | "The chair was broken." The word CHAIR is a _____. |

If the student fails to answer this, we do not know that he does not know any four-letter words. No doubt he does. We *do* know that his mastery of grammatical terminology is pretty weak. Either he knows "verb" and also knows that "chair" is not a verb, or he does not know whether "chair" is a noun or a verb. In any case, "noun" is at least a partial stranger to him.

Consider the following: If the term above were somewhere in the middle of a grammar program, the student might know both "subject" and "noun." Both of these words would be correct in the above item if no formal prompt were given. What important function does this suggest for formal prompts of the sort shown here?

— — — — — — — — — — — — — — —

Where more than one answer is absolutely correct, a formal prompt may hint to the student which answer the programer wants.

18. | Like a bird, Pegasus had two _____. |

The hypothetical data reported for this item showed: 90% of the students said "wings," 5% said "legs," 2% said "kidneys," and 1% each said "nests," "worms," and "eggs."

With *one* additional prompt, reduce the error rate to 1%. Rewrite the frame:

— — — — — — — — — — — — — — —

Like a bird, Pegasus had two w_____. (This eliminates everything but "worms." Four blanks would not eliminate "nests," which leaves you with an error rate of 2%–not bad either. If you wrote "w_ _ _ _," you did not follow the directions. That is two prompts.)

THE STRENGTH OF PROMPTS 127

19. By adding the formal prompt indicating the initial letter, we eliminated all the wrong answers except "worms." A further addition would eliminate that error too:

> Like a bird, Pegasus had two wi_____.

What is your opinion of the frame now? Is it good or bad? Why?

― ― ― ― ― ― ― ― ― ― ― ― ― ― ―

The question asked what you thought. I have no doubt about what I think! In the revisions in Frames 18 and 19, formal prompting is used to solve an error problem which would be solved more elegantly by manipulating thematic and sequence prompting. The resulting miserable frames defeat the programer's purpose of getting meaningful behavior from the student.

20. A copying frame will almost surely get a correct response. A strong sequence prompt in which the same word is required also makes repetition of previous answers likely. What other kind of prompt can also produce almost perfect responding?_____. Under what conditions?

― ― ― ― ― ― ― ― ― ― ― ― ― ― ―

Thematic, if it is a one-to-one kind of association.

21. > The galmsen is always grobal. In contrast, the bloober is always _____.

Is the thematic prompt in this frame logically strong or weak?_____.

― ― ― ― ― ― ― ― ― ― ― ― ― ― ―

Strong (the opposite of "grobal" is the most likely response, and if you knew what "grobal" meant, you could not miss. A prompt is a prompt even when it does not work!).

128 THE BASIC ELEMENTS AND OPERATIONS

22. > Reinforcement which consists of *presenting* stimuli (e.g., food) is called *positive* reinforcement. In contrast, reinforcement which consists of *terminating* stimuli (e.g., painful stimuli) is called _____ reinforcement.
    >
    > (*The Analysis of Behavior,* Holland and Skinner)

In this frame the authors elicit from students a technical term that the students have never seen before. Identify the strong prompts operating to produce a correct response.

Write.

_____
_____

— — — — — — — — — — — — — — —

The phrase "in contrast," combined with the contrast between "presenting" and "terminating" makes the opposite of "positive" likely. These prompts are all thematic. (The usual syntactical prompt—adjective required—could be mentioned, but it is a pretty weak prompt.)

---

23. The following paragraph (Meyer, 1960) describes data obtained from 58 above-average eighth-grade students:

    > A few items in the program were constructed in a manner intended to contrast two prefixes. In some cases the prefixes were opposites (e.g., *in* and *ex*), in others a difference in meaning of two words was in question (e.g., "export" and "deport"). One such item read:

    > If you *go against* a law, you _____ vene it; a group that is *going together* is _____ vening.

    > It occurred in the middle of a sequence on the prefix *contra* and constituted a review of *con*. The item elicited 26 pairs (the same response in both blanks), of which six were pairs incorrect in both blanks, three of these being nonexistent. Seven students wrote *con* in both blanks, 13 students wrote *contra* in both blanks, three wrote *inter,* one wrote *de,* one wrote *pre,* and one wrote *intra* in both blanks. The most successful item of this type explicitly stated the opposition involved; in the middle of a lesson on *dis,* this sentence appeared:

    > The opposite of consent is _____ sent.

    > Only four students wrote *con* in the blank!

    In the first frame above, clear signals that two different responses are required are missing. In the second frame, the signal is quite explicit. The data vary accordingly. Such

data should suggest to people programing for poorer readers and younger students that some standard frame designs which work at the college level may not work at lower levels.
In cases such as the above, has the logical strength of the prompt changed?_____.
What has changed?

———————————————

No. The number of sensible answers remains the same.

The psychological or empirical or actual working strength of the prompt. (Sophisticated prompts require sophisticated students.)

---

24. Programers run into two difficulties in utilizing thematic prompts as substitutes for copying frames. One is the very obvious difficulty of discovering in their own repertoires a thematic association that has a one-to-one relationship to the response that they want the student to give.
    What other difficulty makes the thematic prompt less likely to produce correct responses than a copying frame?

———————————————

The one-to-one association may not be in the student's repertoire.

Summary

The strength of a prompt, the probability that it will control the correct response, has two facets:

(a) The logical strength of a prompt can be calculated by asking how many responses in a sophisticated speaker's repertoire would make any sense in the item.
(b) The psychological strength of a prompt can be calculated from empirical measures of what students actually do in response to it.

The two types of "strength" do not necessarily overlap. We may find that a logically weak prompt (many possible responses make sense) produces only one or a limited number of the plausible alternatives. On the other hand, a logically strong prompt may be violated by "illogical" behavior on the part of students. The verbal sophistication of the students may have a great deal to do with the latter case.

SUMMARY: THE BASIC ELEMENTS A PROGRAMER WORKS WITH

In this chapter, frame design problems have been looked at from two functional points of view:

the behavior the frame intends to establish and characteristics of the design of the frame.

Although other categorizations and terminologies are possible, many programers use the four categories:

discrimination
generalization
concepts
chains.

Given an intended behavior, a frame may be:
priming it
prompting it (including sequence prompting)
testing it.

Introductory frames are typically primes or fairly heavily prompted. Terminal frames, in the true sense, must take account of sequence prompting.

A rationale was presented for avoiding one kind of prime, the copying frame, and for observing considerable caution in making use of one kind of prompt, the formal prompts. Exceptions to this caution lie in legitimate uses of multiple-choice and of other kinds of formal prompts when the behavior itself is "formal."

In the sense that visual layout aids the learner in grasping the structure of what is presented to him, the visual design of a frame may also be considered among the bag of prompting tricks the programer has to work with.

Chapter 3
Systematic Approaches to Design

INTRODUCTION

New programers would undoubtedly be delighted to learn that a set of rules for designing sequences had been developed and thoroughly researched. All that would be required, then, would be the mental effort to master the rules. The programer's task is, unfortunately, not so simple that a set of rules can easily be devised. In fact, the history of attempts to demonstrate the validity of certain practices shows otherwise.

> If there is one rule that seems to make intuitive and incontrovertible sense, it is that a subject matter should be sequenced in a logical order. Textbook authors, filmmakers, and curriculum designers of all sorts would agree with such a truism.

Yet attempts to demonstrate the rule have frequently failed. Programers have tried to show an inhibiting effect on learning by scrambling a "logical" sequence and have usually failed. (See Anderson, 1967, and Popham, 1969.) Students seem to learn when the sequences are shuffled. We may argue that the so-called "logical" order wasn't very logical after all, and this explains why it could be scrambled; or that the segment of subject matter used in the study has no inherent logical order. Or perhaps what was logical to the instructional designer is in no sense logical to the student. (See Mager, 1961.)

Programers have not been reticent about proposing systematic approaches, however. This chapter will examine several of these that go beyond the not-very-useful generalities that one should be logical, orderly, analytical, and systematic.

Relevant Quote: What is needed now is not more studies of scrambled versus ordered sequences, but constructive and creative research which will indicate when, how much, and in what way items may be sequenced. (Holland, 1965.)

SECTION A. MATRICES

Programers probably have no better memories than other people and can make good use of memory crutches of any sort. An old educational device for making sure that "everything" is covered is the *matrix*. It has proved useful to test designers in planning a test which covers the subject matter (listed on one axis) and kinds of questions or behaviors (listed on the other axis).

1. You have already explored one such matrix in programing, although you went at it backwards. This was the outline you made of the sequence on 'scalar' in Chapter 1 (on page 45.) A programer using such a matrix "forwards" would construct the matrix *before* writing the frames—you constructed it from the completed program.

    We can imagine a somewhat larger matrix for that section of *Vectors,* including all the subject matter in those first 73 frames. It would look something like this:

	Concepts				
Behaviors	Distance	Magnitude	Displacement	Vector	Scalar
(a) Given term, give definition					
(b) Given definition, give term					
(c) Given example, label it					
(d) Given term, give example					
(e) Given non-example, label it					

    This abbreviated matrix gives some idea of what a truly organized programer might go through to ensure that he has covered all the behaviors essential to understanding each of the concepts listed across the top. He has, in essence, a prescription for constructing 25 frames if he produces a frame for each cell in the matrix.

    When you outlined the published sequence teaching 'scalar,' you included two sets of frames that would not fit in the above matrix.

    One set was a couple of frames in which 'scalar' and 'vector' were contrasted.

    There is no room in the present matrix form to indicate frames of that type.

    All other key frame types are given in the matrix, though, and yet there were *more than five* frames on 'scalar'. What other set is missing in the matrix because there is no room to list it.

    _ _ _ _ _ _ _ _ _ _ _ _ _ _ _

    There is no room in the matrix for repetition of the same kind of frame. For any concept or principle that is complicated, you would probably want to have students identify several different examples (type c) or solve several somewhat different types of problems. And then, there is the business of making early frames easy by priming or prompting. There is no room on the matrix for indicating early items and late items of the same type. To include repetitions of this sort, you could, I guess, construct a *three*-dimensional matrix, but that might be a bit hard to work with!

2. The matrix in Frame 1 might be a help in designing a test—which should be no surprise, since it is the type of matrix that professional test makers might construct. If you wanted your test to reflect a sample of each TYPE of item and of each CONCEPT, how would you select *five* test questions from it to satisfy these two requirements?

- - - - - - - - - - - - - - -

The simplest way would be to write an item of type (a) on concept #1, type (b) on concept #2, and so on. In other words, go right across the diagonal. Of course, there is no reason for being so orderly, as long as there is one item drawn from each column and one from each row. Indeed, there might be a good reason for avoiding one kind of item with some concept. (For instance, it might be terribly hard to define in words, although students should be able to recognize examples of it.) In other words, your answer might look like:

	(1)	(2)	(3)	(4)	(5)
(a)	x				
(b)		x			
(c)			x		
(d)				x	
(e)					x

or

	(1)	(2)	(3)	(4)	(5)
(a)					x
(b)	x				
(c)			x		
(d)				x	
(e)		x			

134 SYSTEMATIC APPROACHES TO DESIGN

3. The use of matrices has been suggested for solving the difficult problem of "logical" ordering of a subject matter. (Thomas, Davies, Openshaw, & Bird, 1963.) Our first matrix, with its cells for behaviors and for concepts, left no space for a key part of subject matter analysis, namely, identifying *important relationships*. Although the system proposed by Thomas et al. is rather complicated, we can get a brief glimpse at it with the five simple terms from *Vectors*.

Here is how it is done:

The programer is supposed to list ALL the key concepts or principles or generalizations to be covered.

Our list has only five: vector, scalar, magnitude, distance, and displacement.

Then he constructs a matrix with each concept listed in the SAME order on the vertical and horizontal axis. The diagonal becomes the empty comparison of each concept with itself.

	V	S	M	Dt	Dp
V					
S					
M					

etc.

Then he puts a mark in each box which represents a key comparison. We are going to make two types of comparisons: one is CONTRAST (X_c) between terms that are opposites and the other is SUBSET (X_s) between terms one of which is the example of the other. (See markings for vector-scalar and scalar-distance)

	V	S	Dt	M	Dp
V		X_c			?
S	X_c		X_s		
Dt		X_s			

etc.

To check that you can see what is going on in the matrix, which symbol (X_c or X_s) would you put in the cell that has the ? in it?

Where, in the part of the matrix given you, would you indicate an X_c to show that distance and displacement should be contrasted?

- - - - - - - - - - - - - - -

Since 'displacement' is an example or subset of 'vector,' an X_s should go in the cell that has the ? in it. (If the whole matrix were there, as in the next frame, there would be two cells where the two concepts could be compared.)

In the part of the matrix given, distance is in the third row and displacement is in the fifth column, so the cell where they intersect (right hand edge, third down from the top) should get an X_c.

4. Now, according to the designers of this system,
    IF you have listed the concepts in a LOGICAL
    presentation order,
    THEN the cells marked for comparisons will
    CLUSTER AROUND THE DIAGONAL.

Take your time to process the two matrices below. Check the contrasts and subsets indicated.

(a) Which one is more orderly according to the rule?
(b) Something is out of place, apparently, even in the "more orderly" one. What concept would have to be moved to make the "more orderly" one even more orderly than it now is?

Matrix A.

	Vect.	Dist.	Magn.	Disp.	Scal.
Vector				X_s	X_c
Distance				X_c	X_s
Magnitude					
Displacement	X_s	X_c			
Scalar	X_c	X_s			

Matrix B.

	Dist.	Disp.	Magn.	Vect.	Scal.
Distance		X_c			X_s
Displacement	X_c			X_s	
Magnitude					
Vector		X_s			X_c
Scalar	X_s			X_c	

The second matrix is "more orderly" according to the rule that comparisons between items in the matrix should cluster around the diagonal. (Actually, Matrix A is a neater arrangement, but its orderliness violates the rule!) Matrix B is the actual order used in the program.

Even in the orderly matrix, the comparison of distance as a subset of scalar ends up in the far corners. Moving 'scalar' ought to help. (If you thought of moving 'distance' instead, that could help too.)

5. The notion of using a matrix to determine "logical" sequence is certainly intriguing. Had our 5 × 5 matrix been a 20 × 20 one, or even larger, we might be a bit suspicious of a comparison sitting off by itself in the corner, so far away from what the theory proposes is a logical order for introducing concepts that belong together.

If you constructed such a matrix for a set of concepts you were teaching and you found that one of your comparisons was hanging out in the corner, would you *have to* revise the sequence you had settled upon?

– – – – – – – – – – – – – – –

I hope you said "no". One of the objectives of this book is that you will, knowing full well what you are doing, do what appears best until data from students demonstrate otherwise. The determinant of what works will always be the student, not the theory. You can always justify having some concept out of sequence by pointing to the research results on logical order, mentioned at the beginning of the chapter!

Relevant Quote: There is, certainly, no one-to-one relationship between human decisions, including educational ones, and specific research findings. (Goodlad, 1968.)

6. *A Subtle Point.* In *Vectors,* the term 'vector' is introduced in frame 39 immediately after the term 'displacement' has been well practiced. Then there is the lengthy section about arrows as representations of vectors and displacements. The subject changes suddenly at frame 57 back to 'distance' to introduce the concept of 'scalar.'

(Check the sequencing in the program on pages 28-36, if you wish.)

Here are the two frames introducing the two concepts:

> **39.** Things that have direction and magnitude are called vectors. Is displacement a vector? _____ . Explain your answer.
>
> **57.** A distance has magnitude but not direction. Therefore distance is called a scalar. Quantities that have magnitude but not direction are called _____ .

Granted, neither frame is especially difficult. Which one is easier—on the basis of its design? Why did it have to be easier?

– – – – – – – – – – – – – – –

Frame 57, a copy frame, is definitely easier. (It could go anywhere in any program and a student who reads at the required level could answer it.) It doesn't require that the student remember the "magnitude-yes, direction-no" definition of distance.

This is a function of sequencing (if you said "sequence prompting," good). The programer knew that he was interrupting a sequence with a new term, understanding of which depends on material not recently practiced. Had he constructed a matrix of these terms, as you just went through, the X sitting off by itself would have suggested exactly this.

7. Suppose I wish to develop "real understanding" of schedules of reinforcement. There are five standard schedules, shown in the matrix below. (If this is not one of your areas of firm knowledge, don't panic.) On the vertical axis, I have identified ten terminal behaviors which could indicate mastery of each schedule, defining what I mean by "real understanding."

Behaviors

	Continuous	Fixed Ratio	Variable Ratio	Fixed Interval	Variable Interval
(a) Defines properties of sched.					
(b) Identifies standard example					
(c) Describes standard example					
(d) Rejects a non-example					
(e) Identifies cumulative curve					
(f) Draws typical curve					
(g) Identifies new example					
(h) Gives new example					
(i) Predicts effect on a response					
(j) Selects schedule to produce desired effect on response					

Schedules (column header)

There are fifty cells in the matrix—already quite a chunk of program if each cell were used to design a frame. Then, of course, the first instance of each cell would have to be a teaching frame and we could have fifty more to be terminal frames, not to mention the intermediate frames we might need. Even before the tryouts with students, which, as we showed in Chapter 1, are apt to increase the number of frames where more practice is needed, we already have a hundred or more frames.

Does a matrix such as this appear to you to solve the problem of what content belongs in a frame?

Does it appear to you to be helpful in deciding what content belongs in the program, no matter how the behaviors will be combined in various frames?

— — — — — — — — — — — — — — —

The questions asked how it appeared to you. From my point of view, that particular matrix fractionated the subject matter, breaking up certain interrelationships that would simplify the teaching problem. It would produce an impossibly long program if each cell were used to determine individual frame content. It could be useful, however, in checking whether all necessary content had been included and all key terminal behaviors asked for.

To Matrix or Not to Matrix. The answer depends on several factors. Programers, new or experienced, will vary in the "orderliness" of their thinking and program-constructing. If you suspect that your own thinking or planning is not very orderly, a matrix or two could certainly help. It can prevent you from overlooking certain key relationships, and many people have found it helpful for just this reason. An empty cell often suggests something that would not have occurred to you. It will not, however, solve that immense first problem of *locating all* the key concepts or principles that you want to include.

If you were constructing a language program, in which you were dealing with dozens of grammatical structures, hundreds of vocabulary words, and several behaviors (reading, writing, listening, and speaking, for instance), you would probably go crazy without some orderly way of remembering when a vocabulary item was last practiced or a structure used. Matrices and flow charts, like the outlines English teachers like to insist students write before writing a paper, can be a help when the subject is terribly complex. The problem is to get organized, whatever your preferred way.

Suggested Outside Exercise.

Take a chapter from a regular text in some subject teaching either a conceptual subject matter (any of the social sciences, for instance) or a sequential set of principles (mathematics, for instance) and design a content matrix like the one we designed for the five concepts in *Vectors*. If you can include more than five concepts (most chapters will), it will probably be more interesting. Given the order in which the author introduced the concepts or principles, how well does he rate on the matrix, in terms of "logical" (diagonal) order?

(You will have to know the subject matter yourself, obviously, in order to fill in the relationships or comparisons between each concept or principle.)

SECTION B. RULEG AND EGRUL

Matrices had been around in educational circles long before programing appeared. So had the basic elements in the next systematic approach we will consider. RULEG represents the first attempt to write a formula for writing frame sequences. The elements to be combined were:

RU's—rules (hence the RU) or principles or generalizations or definitions, and

EG's or examples (from e.g.).

The hope of the authors of the RULEG system was to produce a system which, once the programer had identified the content and split it into Rules and Examples, would give him a set sequence of frame types into which the content could be dropped like so many meatballs.

Although the precise formulas suggested by these authors are not often followed and are even rejected by some (the EGRUL programers), the language of RU and EG is a convenient terminology for describing almost all frames in verbal programs. It enables us to classify the content, whereas most other terminology in programing (prime, prompt, terminal frame, etc.) classifies the functional characteristics of a frame irrespective of content.

Segments of the original RULEG paper (1960) are presented below. As you read through it, keep the following questions in mind:

(a) The authors put forward a set of rules which imply a clear procedure (sort of a theory) for teaching subject matter. Do you find their approach compatible with the way you would like to handle your own subject?
(b) While the terminology of RU and EG relates, as we noted, to the content of the frame, the symbols also provide ways to handle functions of frames. Can you identify the way a copy frame is symbolized in this terminology? Primes? Terminal frames?
(c) As you read, imagine such frame types in subjects other than mathematics and science, from which all their illustrations are drawn. Would the system apply to the teaching of history? Of manipulative skills?

PANEL 3-1

Selections from "The RULEG system for the construction of programmed verbal learning sequences." J. L. Evans, R. Glaser, and L. E. Homme, 1960.

> The RULEG system is based on the premise that the verbal subject material which appears in a program can be classified into two classes of statements which we will call RU's (for "rules") and EG's (for "examples"). ... A RU may be a large number of things. It may be a definition, operational or otherwise. It may be a mathematical formula. It may be an empirical law. It may be a principle, axiom, postulate, or hypothesis from any area of knowledge. But the invariant feature of all RU's is that they are all statements of some *generality,* from which substitution-instances can be obtained. These substitution-instances are called EG's. An EG may be a large number of things. It may be a description of a physical event. It may be a theorem or deduction of any sort. It may be a statement of a relationship obtaining between specific objects, whether the objects are physical or conceptual. But the invariant feature of all EG's is that they are all statements of some *specificity,* derived from more generalized RU's.
>
> The clearest instance of RU's and their corresponding EG's comes from mathematics. For example, the algebraic "$a + b = b + a$" is a RU, which summarizes compactly an (infinite) number of substitution-instances, or EG's, such as "$7 + 2 = 2 + 7$" and "$3.4 + 8.6 = 8.6 + 3.4$." Again, the statement "Unsupported objects will fall toward the earth" is a RU, while

"If I release my pencil it will fall" would be an EG, as would "If I release my book it will fall." . . . Of course all these RU's (including the mathematical ones which are more precise) would need qualification to become acceptable, but the point should be clear that RU's involve some generality, while EG's involve specificity, albeit a relative specificity. That is, "3 + 2 = 2 + 3" is in turn a RU for such EG's as "3 stones + 2 stones = 2 stones + 3 stones" and "3 mammoths + 2 mammoths = 2 mammoths + 3 mammoths." Indeed, the early man who induced the "3 + 2 = 2 + 3" RU from these EG's for the first time was probably staggered at the profundity of his own insights. . . . It remained for a modern group theorist to produce that ultimate (?) RU "aob = boa" in which neither the objects nor the operator are specified, and in which "$a + b = b + a$" becomes a mere EG.

(At this point the authors describe the next step in preparing a program. The programer lists all the RU's he intends to cover and constructs a *RU-matrix*, parallel to the concept matrix we worked with on *Vectors* in Section A. He notes all the comparisons and contrasts for each RU. He also selects a large set of EG's for each RU. The system, as you will see, uses lots of EG's and these EG's have to be varied.)

To designate the incomplete RU's and EG's [where a response is required from the student] we add the symbol "∼" (tilde) over the symbols for rules and examples, like this: $\tilde{RU}$ (RU tilde) and $\tilde{EG}$ (EG tilde). . . .

Frame Types

1. RU + EG + $\tilde{EG}$. We have found this frame type to be the method par excellence for the economical introduction of a new RU. The RU + EG + $\tilde{EG}$ can have the student working an example of a brand new rule on the very first frame in which he is exposed to it. By giving him an explicitly stated RU, and one (or more) carefully chosen EG's before calling for a response by means of an $\tilde{EG}$, a powerful prompt is set up which makes an error in responding most unlikely. . . . It seems best not to introduce more than one RU at a time, or to introduce complex RU's too early, or to ignore consideration of the "simplest possible nontrivial example." . . .

Other combinations are certainly possible. For example, why not $\tilde{RU}$ + EG? We have found that one completely worked-out example is necessary to permit the working of the first EG with ease and efficiency. Why not EG + $\tilde{EG}$? This would be an *analogy* frame. The chief characteristic of an analogy is that one must induce the RU from the first EG and then apply it to the $\widetilde{EG}$. Rather than run the risk of having the student induce an incorrect RU, it seems preferable to state the RU for him explicitly. Incidentally, the same philosophy leads us to reject in general the inductive presentation which we might symbolize as $EG_1 + EG_2 + \ldots EG_n + \widetilde{RU}$. Here a large number of EG's are given and the student is asked to state the RU involved. Such a Socratic technique is inefficient. Humans, with their verbal and symbolic behavior, can be given a rule to follow and it is not necessary to make them guess at it. . . .

After the student can recognize and apply a RU with proficiency, then EG + $\widetilde{EG}$ frames are acceptable. But until that time, we feel that it is often hazardous and slow to "sneak up" on a RU through induction and incidental learning. We would prefer that the student adopt the expert programmer's carefully chosen statement of a RU rather than have the student use his own halting induction-derived statement. . . .

After initial introduction to a RU through the RU + EG + $\widetilde{EG}$ formula, a number of variations have proved useful for the subsequent frames. . . .

2. RU + $\widetilde{RU}$. RU's typically contain "technical vocabulary" words and terms, which we call TV words. These are words which may be quite new to a student, e.g., perigee in astronautics, or they are familiar words with new meanings to be attached, e.g., population in statistics. Students are often slow in adding such words to their active vocabulary. . . .

3. RU + $\widetilde{EG}$. In late frames stimulus support can start to be withdrawn by giving only the RU before giving the $\widetilde{EG}$. Likewise the previously mentioned "analogy" frame (EG + $\widetilde{EG}$) represented a weaker prompt for the $\widetilde{EG}$ than does RU + EG + $\widetilde{EG}$.

4. EG + $\widetilde{RU}$. An induction frame which can be used more safely when the student has the RU at some strength.

5. $\widetilde{RU}_1 + \widetilde{RU}_2$. Such frames can be used to compare and contrast two different RU's as part of the discrimination training involving the RU's.

6. $\widetilde{EG}_1 + \widetilde{EG}_2$. For comparing and contrasting examples of two different RU's, or for demonstrating how two RU's can be applied in turn. . . .

7. $\widetilde{EG}$. The terminal frame of a series in which criterion behavior is performed in the presence of minimal cues.

8. $\widetilde{RU}$. Although the EG frame is more basic, in the sense that to respond appropriately to an EG, the student must have command of the RU or RU's involved, on occasion we may wish to call for a statement of a specific RU. To exemplify: "What is the second law of thermodynamics"?

142 SYSTEMATIC APPROACHES TO DESIGN

(1) Terminological Issues

1. Match the following frames with the appropriate RU and EG terminology.

   (a) RU + EG + $\widetilde{EG}$ (b) RU + $\widetilde{EG}$ (c) EG + $\widetilde{RU}$ (d) EG + $\widetilde{EG}$

   _____ (1) When we multiply powers of numbers, we add exponents.
   $$a^6 \times a^{11} =$$

   _____ (2) $x^3 \cdot x^4 =$

   _____ (3) $(a+b)^2 (a+b)^3 = (a+b)^5$
   $(c+d)^4 (c+d)^5 =$

   _____ (4) $r^2 \cdot r^7 = r^9$
   When we multiply powers of numbers, we _____.

   _____ (5) When we multiply powers of numbers, we add exponents. For instance: $a^3 \cdot a^2 = a^5$
   $T^6 \cdot T^2 =$

- - - - - - - - - - - - - - - -

(1) is (b) RU + $\widetilde{EG}$; (2) is none of these; (3) is (d) EG + $\widetilde{EG}$; (4) is (c) EG + $\widetilde{RU}$; (5) is (a) RU + EG + $\widetilde{EG}$.

---

2. Which of the above frames would fit the definition of a *PRIME* (telling the student what to do)?

- - - - - - - - - - - - - - - -

Both (1) and (5) are primed (The RU primes solution of the incomplete $\widetilde{EG}$.)

3. Would you call the verbal material in this frame a RU? (Is it a rule, principle, generalization, or definition?)

> Calculate the mean of the following IQ scores:
> 101, 101, 98, 68, 106, 93, 123, 106, 134, 125.

Whenever a question asks "would you," your answer is correct. However, we will have to agree, for purposes of communicating. Let's say that directions to the student, telling him *what to do,* but NOT *how to do it,* is not what the authors meant by RU. The above direction, then, is not a RU.

4.
> Words beginning with the prefix *in-* meaning "into" DO NOT take the negative prefix *in-*.
> The negation of INCLUSIVE is _____INCLUSIVE.

There is a RU and there is an $\widetilde{EG}$. What is strange about the relationship of that RU to that $\widetilde{EG}$?
Does the RU prime the answer?_____.
Is the RU a prompt? (Does it help?)_____.

The RU does not tell the student what to do; it tells him what not to do.

No. (To prime it, we would have to give the positive RU—tell the student to use *un-*.)

Yes. (In fact, at that point in the program, the student had learned only two negative prefixes, *in-* and *un-*. If he attends to the RU, he can't miss. The frame is from *WORDS.*)

---

5. Not given you in the article is another set of symbols. The RULEG authors talk about the importance of including non-examples or noninstances of a concept when training in the concept. (You want to be sure that the student knows when *not* to apply the rule or what is *not* a "mammoth" as well as how to apply the rule and what the correct name is for a particular object.) These "negative instances" are called EG-bars and written $\overline{EG}$. In this notation, what would the RU above be?_____.

$\overline{RU}$ or RU-bar (not discussed in the article).

144   SYSTEMATIC APPROACHES TO DESIGN

6. A definition is a RU in the sense that it tells the student which examples to include in a concept and which are non-examples. This is only true, of course, if the definition is a clear one—many standard definitions are pretty bad RU's!

   The RULEG theorists make a very strong point about providing the student with the "expert programer's carefully chosen statement of a RU." Not all authors, however, define a term in a carefully chosen set of words. Some prefer to define a term by giving a long list of examples. A psychology programer might come up with something like this:

   > Lights, bells, puffs of air, the odor of onions, and electric shocks are all *potential* stimuli. Which of the following are also potential stimuli? (a short list would follow of energy sources, some of which, like radio waves, cannot be sensed by organisms and some of which can.)

   Would you call this a RU + $\widetilde{EG}$ frame or an EG + $\widetilde{EG}$ frame? (Ignore numbers of EG's in categorizing it.)

   – – – – – – – – – – – – – – – –

   Again, we have to come to some agreement. You expressed your opinion. I see no carefully chosen statement there. This seems more like the "analogy" frame—EG + $\widetilde{EG}$, even though it is, in another sense, a definition. Defining by giving examples is legal!

An Aside to Future Programers.   Textbook authors and the authors of professional papers, such as this one on RULEG, are not required to face the "borderline" case. Several times in this program, we have played games with such borderline cases, since programers, in trying to guarantee the full development of "understanding" of a concept, should enable students to make all the required discriminations at the edges of a concept. The borderline cases are the interesting ones—they stretch understanding to the limit. Even dictionaries may sometimes define by showing a picture—hardly a RU, certainly an EG. So the generalization (a RU!) that *all definitions are RU's* has its legitimate exceptions.

7. The RULEG terminology creaks badly when applied to manipulative skills. A science programer, for instance, might be priming the behavior of focusing a microscope with this frame:

   > Put slide #1 on the stage and turn the red knob gently in both a clockwise and a counterclockwise direction until you can see clearly what is on the slide. What is there to see?

   The student's behavior is controlled by a set of directions, equipment with knobs of appropriate color, and variables in his own eyesight, but we would be stretching the terminology to call this a RU. (A general principle of focusing by adjusting lens position could be a principle.) It is not at all clear what we could say was the "EG" in this situation—the student's response? the image on the slide? or what? (Focusing a microscope could be an EG of a general principle of adjusting lenses, I suppose. But that principle is not what such a program is teaching.)

What about this frame?

> All tape recorders plug into electric power. The illustration shows one location of the cord on a particular recorder. (Picture given.) Find the cord on your machine and plug it in to a wall socket.

Would you characterize that frame as a standard RU + EG + $\widetilde{EG}$?

— — — — — — — — — — — — — — —

Your choice. If you say "yes," then the first part of my frame is a $\overline{RU} + \overline{EG}$ (RU-bar + EG-bar). If you say "no," then you are considering this last EG as an "incomplete" EG of the generalization that RULEG terminology creaks badly in the area of manipulative skills. But note the title of the article mentions "verbal learning sequences"! In that last frame on tape recorders, we can identify a general principle, the illustration would be an example, and the student's own machine another example which he "completes."

---

8. A final semantic quibble. The authors talk about providing examples and non-examples and about having the student "complete" an example. This language works beautifully for mathematics programs where problems are to be completed. To extend the use of the terminology to other kinds of student responses, we will have to think of $\widetilde{EG}$'s (incomplete ones) as examples to which the student does "something"—whether or not we could call his response "completing the $\widetilde{EG}$."

Suppose we try this frame:

> When a word ends in a single vowel followed by a single consonant, you double the final consonant when you add a suffix beginning with a vowel. Which one of these words should have two *t*'s in front of *-ing:* TROT or TREAT?

(a) Does the question test the student's understanding of at least part of the rule?_____.

(b) Have we made the student actually misspell a word?_____.

(c) Does the student do at least *something* with an EG?_____.

— — — — — — — — — — — — — — —

Yes (the part about the single vowel followed by a single consonant, anyway).

No. He has not spelled anything.

Yes. He discriminates between two words, reporting which one is an EG and which is a non-EG. For our purposes, this will be classed as a kind of $\widetilde{EG}$ (incomplete EG) frame.

146 SYSTEMATIC APPROACHES TO DESIGN

(2) Sequencing Frames

9. The authors find one kind of frame to be "The method par excellence for the economical introduction of a new RU." What do you need to do to this frame to make it the "economical introduction to the RU"? *(Check frame type #1 if you've forgotten.)*

> When a word ends in a single vowel followed by a single consonant, you double the final consonant when adding a suffix beginning with a vowel.
>
> *(and then?)*

- - - - - - - - - - - - - - -

Add a completed example of the rule and provide another example (simple but nontrivial, of course) for the student to work. This gives you the standard RU + EG + ẼG introductory frame.

10. The RULEG authors state, "We find it best not to introduce more than one RU at a time." Consider:
    If you introduce two RU's and require the student to respond by completing an example of only one, has he learned the other one?_____.

- - - - - - - - - - - - - - -

No.

11. Programmers base the design of frames on three basic principles: active responding, errorless responding, and immediate knowledge of results. Which principle does a $RU_1 + RU_2 + EG_1 + \widetilde{EG}_1$ frame violate?_____.

- - - - - - - - - - - - - - -

Active responding (a student learns only what the frame leads him to do).

RULEG AND EGRUL 147

12. Might it be possible, however, to require the student to use two RU's in dealing with one $\widetilde{EG}$?_____.

Yes. Any procedure that takes two steps might be taught in one frame by giving the student directions (RU) to first do step 1, then do 2, then check his answer.

---

13. | When a one-syllable consonant-vowel-consonant word is followed by *-ing,* the final consonant is doubled. When *-ing* is added to a word ending in *-e,* the *e* is dropped. Thus, when you see PINING, you know that the simple form of the verb is PINE, and when you see PINNING, you know that the simple form of the verb is PIN. What are the simple forms of these verbs?

 1. MATTING:_____   2. MATING:_____

 3. SLOPING:_____   4. SLOPPING:_____ |

Demonstrate that the above frame satisfies the principle of active responding by outlining it in terms of RU's and EG's:

Write (it is too complex to hold in your head!).

_____
_____
_____

Check your answer. The frame has eight parts. Do you have eight symbols?

Sequentially, it goes: $RU_1, RU_2, EG_2, EG_1, \widetilde{EG}_1, \widetilde{EG}_2, \widetilde{EG}_2, \widetilde{EG}_1$.

If it can be said that we are demonstrating anything in the above frame, it is that a good idea may outlast its era. RULEG is typically connected with the small tell-'em and test-'em frames of early programing styles. That it applies equally to later larger-frame styles is what I had hoped to show. Much of instruction still boils down to the essentials of communicating valid generalizations and leading students to apply these to real examples of use in their lives.

14. The first frame in a RULEG program is a set design. Since this article is dated 1960, we may assume that steps are going to be small and repetitive, as was the fashion at that time. There is a strong emphasis on avoiding errors at all cost, and two important points are made about the EG in the first RU + EG + $\widetilde{EG}$ frame:

it should be the simplest possible nontrival example,

and, it is there to enable the student to handle the

incomplete $\widetilde{EG}$ with "ease and efficiency".

In other words, students should not suffer through lengthy and difficult calculations in order to apply a formula the first time, but the problem should not be completely trivial (such as getting a mean of two numbers!).

At that point in history, a programmer might have written a second or even a third frame of the same RU + EG + $\widetilde{EG}$ type before he began reducing the priming and prompting. (The word 'prime' was not in use then; both functions were called "prompting.")

When he finally gets around to the more difficult frame types, he has a choice, before terminal frames, of

$$RU + \widetilde{RU}, EG + \widetilde{EG}, RU + \widetilde{EG}, \text{ and } EG + \widetilde{RU}.$$

He wants to use the *easiest one* first and gradually reduce the amount of prompting. In what order would he use them?

Which of these frame types is NOT acceptable according to the principles taught in this book?

You may wish to reread the remarks about these frame types on pages 140-141 before answering.

— — — — — — — — — — — — — —

The arguments there indicate to me that the RU + $\widetilde{RU}$ is second in strength to the most powerful RU + EG + $\widetilde{EG}$. The authors suggest that "stimulus support can *start* to be withdrawn" by using a RU + $\widetilde{EG}$ frame. They also appear to argue that the weakest kind of prompt is the EG + $\widetilde{EG}$ type, so this would be the last kind of frame to use in a gradual reduction of prompting.

A RU + $\widetilde{RU}$ frame is a copy frame. There are several ways to get such technical vocabulary into the student's repertoire without using this frame design. (Chapter 5 will discuss them.)

15. You could write a "prescription" for a series of frames on a RU in which the frame type is never repeated and the prompting appears to decrease in a fairly orderly fashion. Omitting the out-of-favor RU + R̃U type, you'd have:

   (1)   RU + EG + ẼG
   (2)   RU + ẼG
   (3)   EG + R̃U
   (4)   EG + ẼG
   (5)   R̈U
   (6)   ËG

All you need now is a carefully chosen statement of the RU and a set of examples. With NO repetition of examples, how many examples would you need to write these six frames?

If the activity required of the student for each place we put an EG was that he discriminate between an example and a non-example, how many non-examples would be required to complete that sequence?

—————————————

If there is only one "carefully chosen example" at each point that either EG or ẼG occurs, you need seven.

If the activity is discrimination, you need four non-examples, one for each ẼG. (You might also want non-examples in the EG parts of course.)

16. In what sense is the E̋G in that sequence not really a terminal EG? How does it differ from our definition of a terminal frame?

—————————————

It is too close to the teaching sequence. Note that there is no listing in the RULEG notation for an ẼG by itself, in other words, an ẼG frame which is not terminal because of sequence prompting but which contains no other prompts. Nor is there any way to indicate a partial statement of a RU that you might want to use as a prompt.

Note. The RUs we've been using as illustrations (spelling rules and mathematical manipulations) provide hundreds of simple but nontrivial examples. But what happens to the teacher whose subject matter is drama and who wants to teach students the concept of "anti-climax"? Or the historian searching for examples of "direct democracy"? The problem of locating enough "simple but nontrivial" examples and non-examples to fill out such concepts is immense.

17. From the first paragraph of the article on the RULEG system, is a RU more abstract than an EG, or is an EG more abstract than a RU? _____'s are more abstract than _____'s.

- - - - - - - - - - - - - - - -

RU's are more abstract than EG's.

18. If a programer follows the RULEG formula, is he proceeding (a) from the concrete to the abstract or (b) from the abstract to the concrete?

- - - - - - - - - - - - - - - -

(b) abstract to concrete.

19. The RULEG system is a scheme for ordering the presentation of information to the student. If a programer follows its dictates, he will introduce the broad principles first and the details or specific examples second. Is there any other way of ordering the presentation of material to students? _____. Suggest one.

- - - - - - - - - - - - - - - -

Yes. See the next frame for one suggestion. You may have thought of another.

RULEG AND EGRUL 151

20. The RULEG system was one of the earliest attempts to formalize the production of frames and their sequencing according to some systematic rule. No matter what system a programer chooses to follow, he has to locate the generalizations in his subject matter and order them in some fashion. The analysis of verbal subject matters into RU's and EG's is a contribution that no one has contradicted.

    However, no sooner did the RULEG formula appear than a countermovement developed which, naturally, was tagged as the EGRUL approach. If the EGRUL programer does not question the classification on his subject matter into EG's and RU's, what is it that he questions? (What does he want to do differently?)

    — — — — — — — — — — — — — —

    The only thing that he can question is the order.

21. In Chapter 1 of this program, you were asked whether the *Vectors* program proceeded from the abstract to the concrete level or vice versa. The correct answer was that it proceeded from low-level EG's to higher-level concepts. Is *Vectors* a RULEG program or an EGRUL program? _____ .

    — — — — — — — — — — — — — —

    EGRUL (you would have a hard time finding a real RU + EG + $\widetilde{EG}$ frame in it, although there are a few).

152 SYSTEMATIC APPROACHES TO DESIGN

22.

> 47. The word ILLUMINATE has the definition "put light into." The root is *lumin*. What *form* does the prefix meaning "into" have? __.
>
> ---------------
>
> *Answer.* il.
>
> ---
>
> 48. The kind of informal speech that people use when they are "talking together" is called COLLOQUIAL speech. The root *loqu* means "talk." What form does the prefix meaning "together" have?____.
>
> ---------------
>
> *Answer.* col.
>
> ---
>
> 49. Acts that are not lawful are ILLEGAL. What form does the negative prefix have?_____.
>
> ---------------
>
> *Answer.* il.
>
> ---
>
> 50. The words ILLUMINATE, COLLOQUIAL, and ILLEGAL suggest that there is another spelling rule common to prefixes ending in *n*. It seems that they take a form ending in_____ when the root begins with_____.
>
> ---------------
>
> *Answer.* l, l.
>
> (*Words,* Markle)

This is a section teaching spelling variants of the prefixes, *in, con,* and *in*.
   Is this an EGRUL or a RULEG sequence?_____. Why do you say so?

EGRUL. The student works three examples before he completes the $\widetilde{RU}$.

23. Consider the following remark:

We would prefer that the student adopt the expert programer's carefully chosen statement of a RU rather than have the student use his own halting induction-derived statement.

Has the programer above allowed the student "his own halting induction-derived statement"?
_____.

- - - - - - - - - - - - - - - -

No. Only two key parts of the rule are missing.

24. At the beginning of their program, *Labor Relations for The Supervisor,* Yaney and Rummler provide this sample question:

> CASE A
>
> The company president told his managers that they must obey the law, but with a wink, and he said that there are always accidents in a busy plant which might injure union organizers. (unacceptable)
>
> CASE B
>
> One of the company managers told a plant guard to beat up a union organizer. (unacceptable)
>
> Based on what you observed in cases A and B, which of the two following cases illustrates an unacceptable action?
>
> _____(a) A company manager saw a plant guard beating up a union organizer but did nothing to stop it.
>
> _____(b) After work, two plant guards and a union organizer who were generally friendly got into a fight over a mutual girl friend.
>
> — — — — — — — — — — — — — — —
>
> (a) is not acceptable.

A later question goes like this:

> CASE A
>
> The company had allowed the local boy scouts to enter the plant during working hours to ask for money. When the XYZ Union asked to be admitted to the company premises for passing out literature, the management said this would disrupt production and the answer was no. (unacceptable)
>
> CASE B
>
> The very respectable International Union had asked permission to talk with the men during working hours. The company agreed. Next week when the National Union asked for the chance to talk with the men during working hours, the company said no. (unacceptable)
>
> (continued next page)

CASE C

The company policy as stated in the employee's handbook says that due to the dangerous nature of the work in the plant, no soliciting can be allowed. This rule was applied to church groups and to the organizers who wrote to the company president. (acceptable)

1. Which of the following statements seems to be acceptable?
   _____(a) The company owns the property and can invite or refuse anyone it sees fit.
   _____(b) The company can establish rules if they apply to everyone.
   _____(c) The company has a right to use special rules for controlling union organizers.

   _ _ _ _ _ _ _ _ _ _ _ _ _ _ _ _

(b) is acceptable.

How would you describe each of these frames in RU and EG terminology?
Do the programers lead the students to "use their own halting induction-derived statement" of the principles involved in these cases?

_ _ _ _ _ _ _ _ _ _ _ _ _ _ _ _

The first one is EG + $\widetilde{EG}$, basically. (If you wanted to get fancy, you could call it $\overline{EG}$ + $\overline{EG}$ + $\widetilde{EG}$—two non-examples, followed by a discrimination question!) The student is required to determine but not to state the principle involved in order to choose the correct answer.

The second is an EG + $\widetilde{RU}$, but the student selects rather than haltingly states the correct principle.

156   SYSTEMATIC APPROACHES TO DESIGN

25. The authors of *Labor Relations for the Supervisor* call the "style" of the program DISCRIMINATION PROGRAMING. The objectives call for supervisors to be able to discriminate between actions which are acceptable and those which are not. Being able to give lectures or write briefs on the principles are not among the objectives. For variety, however, a third frame from the same program takes this format:

CASE A

Several employees of the company who are active in the union movement were physically attacked by some company supervisors as they left the plant. (unacceptable)

CASE B

A supervisor told a group of employees, "If you guys don't stop flirting with the union, you'll be marking your ballot with a broken arm." Nothing ever happened to the men. (unacceptable)

1. How does case A differ from case B? (answer in one or two sentences.)

_____

_____

— — — — — — — — — — — — — — —

Case A is actual physical violence, while Case B is only a threat of violence. However, both are unacceptable.

Here the student is required to state the differences between the two cases—in a sense, a RU.

If the appropriate students couldn't make this relatively simple discrimination on the basis of reading these two cases, what might you do with the frame before giving up and telling the students? What other actions are there?

— — — — — — — — — — — — — — —

One possibility is to give two examples of each. Another is to try some other examples and see if there isn't some way to make the distinction obvious.

RULEG AND EGRUL   157

26.
> Look at these numerals: XIV. When a numeral comes between two larger numerals, you subtract the middle numeral from the numeral behind it:
>
> $(X) \; (IV) = 10 + 4 = 14$.
>
> Find the value of XIX.
>
> *(Introduction to Modern Mathematics,* TMI)

Is this an EGRUL or a RULEG frame?_____.

Is the RU clear to you?_____.

— — — — — — — — — — — — — — —

RULEG. The rule comes first, followed by an example, followed by an incomplete example. I think the RU could be improved!

---

27. Consider the following quotations:

> Difficult as programing is, it has its compensations. It is a salutary thing to try to guarantee a correct response at every step in the presentation of a subject. The programer will find that he has been accustomed to leaving much to the student, omitting essential steps, and neglecting relevant points. The responses made to his program may reveal surprising ambiguities. (Skinner.)
>
> By giving him an explicitly stated RU, and one (or more) carefully chosen EG's before calling for a response by means of an $\widetilde{EG}$, a powerful prompt is set up which makes an error in responding most unlikely.... Why not RU + $\widetilde{EG}$? We have found that one completely worked-out example is necessary to permit the working of the first EG with ease and efficiency. (Homme, Glaser, and Evans.)
>
> If a student cannot perform an operation, such as calculating the mean of a set of scores when he is given an "explicitly stated" RU, what might this suggest about the RU?

— — — — — — — — — — — — — — —

(In your own words.) In Skinner's terms, it might reveal some "surprising ambiguities" even in the expert programmer's carefully chosen statement!

158   SYSTEMATIC APPROACHES TO DESIGN

28. One of the most important functions of the student's response is feedback to the programer about the effectiveness of the teaching in the program. Clarity of expression is one of the absolute requirements for any kind of good teaching, programed or otherwise. From which kind of frame would a programer derive better feedback about the clarity of his "carefully chosen statement of a RU": a RU + ẼG frame or a RU + EG + ẼG frame? _____ .

— — — — — — — — — — — — — — —

A RU + ẼG frame may pinpoint an unseen ambiguity because the student does exactly what he thinks the programer told him to do.

Relevant Quote: Our student listens (or reads) and nods with every evidence of understanding. He is able to repeat the theory when we question him. [Then we ask him to perform what he has learned.] The student has missed the entire point of the subject-matter we were trying to teach him, even though he appeared to have such complete understanding. The lesson is clear: words are the most powerful and tricky stimuli man is subject to. (Gilbert, 1962a)

Summary: RULEG, EGRUL, and Middle Grounds

The RULEG system was one of the earliest attempts to formalize the design of sequences. Although no program that I know of follows the pat formula of the six frame types in their appropriate sequence (Frame 15 above), many programs reflect the thinking of the RULEG authors in the sense that

        general principles are stated first

and   examples are worked in great numbers.

The opposite approach to structuring subject matter, the EGRUL ordering, shares some of the same properties, but EGRUL programers prefer to start from the examples and lead up to the generalizations, using, of course, examples that the students can work from previous experience. In contrast with the now-popular "discovery learning" methodology, however, even EGRUL programers are not likely to permit the student to arrive at his own "halting, induction-derived statement" of the principles.

As far back as 1960, the RULEG authors insisted that the terminal EG frame was more basic than the terminal RU frame. Many programers, especially those who call their style "Discrimination programing," are carrying this to greater and greater lengths, putting almost no stress at all on verbal statements and putting greater and greater emphasis on the examples and non-examples—the keys to understanding and correct application. It is not difficult to teach a student to repeat a set of words. The challenge lies in making sure he knows what he means.

Possible Outside Exercise.

When discussing "communication," psychologists often used to ask one freshman student to instruct another one in the difficult task of putting on a sweater. The second student was to do exactly, literally, and with no interpretation, only what he was told to do. The results, if the second student was good at the game of words, were often hilarious and extremely edifying to those who assumed that communicating (or priming) a simple skill was a simple task.

In the early days of programing, many new programers cut their teeth on a relatively "simple" mathematical task—teaching a student to square in his head numbers ending in five (15^2, 25^2, etc.). With plenty of examples, most of the student programers' students mastered the task, whether the programer RULEGed or EGRULed it. The RU "multiply the left digit by one more than itself and put the product to the left of 25" (or other attempts at stating it "in carefully chosen words") rarely worked by itself. You might have some fun trying to state this rule (no EGs allowed) in such a way that a naive student, capable of getting the answer with a piece of paper but not wise to this gimmick, could produce the answer to his FIRST EG in something like one second. If he takes a long time on his first problem, he's probably using his "mental blackboard" and worrying through the carefully chosen words in which you stated the RU.

SECTION C. MATHETICS: A VERY SHORT COURSE

INTRODUCTION

The systematic procedures of mathetics were first described in 1962 in a pair of articles (Gilbert, 1962a, 1962b) in a journal that has since been discontinued. The terminology used in those articles differed considerably from that used by other programers and psychologists. The combination of a new set of words and unavailability of the source material may have something to do with the air of mystery that surrounded this new technology which was claimed to be superior to all other methods of programing. Many of its practices have blended into the mainstream of program design and others clearly parallel techniques advocated by people who do not call themselves matheticists. As far as possible, this description of the theory will avoid introducing new terminology. Hopefully this will not completely eliminate the flavor of Gilbert's original contributions.

A mathetics program begins, as does any other well-thought-out instructional plan, with a detailed analysis of what is to be taught. As other programers do, Gilbert emphasizes heavily that analysis must concentrate on student activity, not subject matter coverage.

> Matheticists are not the only programers who have discovered large chunks of irrelevant material in the typical content included in many training courses. Nor are they the only ones who have found that it is sometimes easier to change the procedures toward something more rational rather than training a man to handle ill-conceived procedures. (See, for instance, Rummler, Yaney, and Schrader, 1967.)

Whether these expected terminal behaviors are ways the student should be able to talk about the world (as in typical academic courses) or things he should be able to do (as in typical industrial job training), the analyst needs to have a complete description of what constitutes mastery. Gilbert dealt with three basic types of behavior: discriminations, generalizations, and chains (omitting which of the four categories mentioned in Chapter Two?). Primary emphasis was given to identifying the total range of stimuli which control the various responses or "operants," and to describing sequences of operants which constitute "chains."

Most of the examples in the original articles fall into one of these two categories—discriminations and chains.

(a) discriminations, such as the color code for electrical resistors—each of ten colors stands for a numerical value from 0 to 9, or rules of alphabetizing for file clerks. In these cases, there is a correct response for each stimulus situation, but no particular order in which these responses have to occur. The stimuli occur randomly on the job.

(b) chains, in which responses must occur in a fairly regular order. Each response produces some change in the stimulus situation that sets the occasion for the next response to occur. Examples are long division, the tying of shoes, and the settling of the day's accounts in a bank teller's cage.

One of the key concepts in mathetics is that of "operant span." The word 'response' as used by psychologists varies from such small events as the firing of a single neuron to immensely complicated and lengthy actions. An *operant* lies somewhere in the middle of the range. A typical example, illustrating a difference between the two terms "response" and "operant," is the operant "opening a door." Depending, of course, on the physical properties of the door, one may

> kick it open
> push through with one's shoulder
> back through it
> turn a knob with the right or left hand
> lift a latch
> etc.

At one level of investigation, it might be useful to consider each of these as different responses. At another level, however, we have, in response to the situation "door blocks further travel," an operant "opening the door" defined by the fact that, at the completion of whichever response is made, the door is open. The units into which a matheticist breaks a task for instructional purposes are of this sort—they are supposed to be unitary acts that result in a perceptible effect. The teaching exercise that the matheticist will construct will reflect the largest set of operants that the student can handle—his operant span.

> While the language may be new to you, the idea should not be, at this point. Several times in this book I have made nasty remarks about small steps or about fractionating the subject matter into steps that make no sense. Matheticists are not alone in their concern for step size which bears some relation to what is "meaningful" in the subject matter or skill.

In designing the first draft of an exercise, the programer is supposed to *over*estimate the operant span that students can manage. The experience of programers, matheticists or not, is pretty consistent here: *it is extremely difficult to get data which indicate clearly that steps are too small and relatively simple to discover when you have given the student more than he can handle.*

MATHETICS: A VERY SHORT COURSE 161

MATHETICAL EXERCISES

1. Taking a relatively large operant which is a step toward mastery, a matheticist designs a first step which "demonstrates" this operant to the student. The meaning of the term 'demonstrate' should be pretty obvious.

   If you are designing a first step in a program teaching *operation* of a tape recorder, your first step might be:

   _____explain the way the tape recorder reproduces sound from magnetic tape;

   _____show how to put a reel of tape onto the recorder;

   _____have the student memorize the names for all the buttons and operating parts.

   \- \- \- \- \- \- \- \- \- \- \- \- \- \- \- \-

   The second one is a demonstration relevant to operating a tape recorder.

2. The word "demonstrate," as shown by what matheticists *do*, is not always so obvious as in the above case of demonstrating how to operate a tape recorder. At times, a matheticist may "demonstrate" the *product* of an operation rather than the process. In other words, he may show what the result looks like rather than how you get to the result. Taking this into account, what would a "demonstration" of this operant look like?

   > the student will draw and label the circuitry
   > of a small transistor radio

   (Demonstrate the product, not the process.)

   \- \- \- \- \- \- \- \- \- \- \- \- \- \- \- \-

   If you said something like "show the student a completely labeled diagram", you have the meaning.

3. In the language of previous chapters of this book, the programer in each case above is [priming/prompting] the mastery response.

   \- \- \- \- \- \- \- \- \- \- \- \- \- \- \- \-

   priming. As far as I can determine, the word "demonstrate", as used by Gilbert, is absolutely synonymous with Skinner's newer term "prime."

162   SYSTEMATIC APPROACHES TO DESIGN

4. If "demonstrating" (priming) is the first step, will a mathetics program resemble a RULEG structure or an EGRUL structure most closely? Which?

— — — — — — — — — — — — — — —

Matheticists tend, like RULEG programers, to go directly to the point on the first frame rather than leading into it with a series of simple problems or examples.

---

5. Suppose your program is aiming at an operant of this sort:

> the student will draw an amoeba and label all its parts

and you assume that you do not have to "demonstrate" how to draw. What would your first frame look like if you assumed that the student could handle the largest possible operant span that could be used here?

— — — — — — — — — — — — — — —

You would demonstrate the "product," a completely labeled amoeba.

---

6. A frame from a mathetical program on just this subject was first presented in Chapter 1 (p. 9). Here it is again. Look at it with your new knowledge. ⇨
   (a) Is it the *first* frame in the program, according to the design principles of mathetics?
   (b) Is the operant span in this frame smaller or larger than the operant *label the parts (structure) of an ameba*?

   Check your frame design in frame 5 above. Is this real frame the same or different?

— — — — — — — — — — — — — — —

   (a) No, that is not a demonstration frame. (It's the second frame.)
   (b) The operant span is larger. Not only does the student work on the structure (the top of the frame) but also he grapples with the three functions.

The drawing below represents the STRUCTURE of the cell. In this case it is an AMEBA, a unicellular animal.

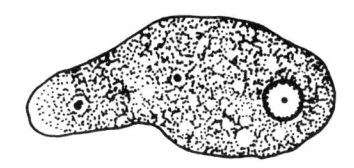

Using the following information, <u>you</u> draw arrows to and label the cell's STRUCTURES:

    NUCLEUS—the most prominent structure in the cell

    NUCLEAR MEMBRANE—the membrane surrounding the nucleus

    CELL WALL—the membrane surrounding the cell

    VACUOLE—cavity inside the cell

    CYTOPLASM (endoplasm, ectoplasm)—material inside the cell

The drawings below represent FUNCTIONS of the cell (ameba).

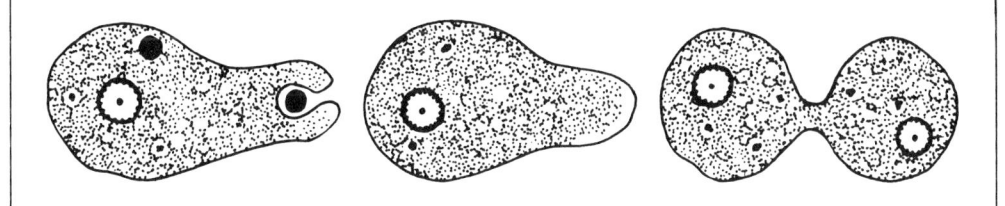

_____ _____ _____

Using the following information, <u>you</u> write in the FUNCTION represented by each drawing:

    FEEDING—by surrounding food with pseudopodia

    MOVEMENT—by thrusting of pseudopodia

    REPRODUCTION—by binary fission

7. On the facing page is the FIRST frame from the *Ameba* program (*Life Cycle: Entamoeba Histolytica,* Part 1). The target audience is public health medical personnel. The programer assumes that they know how to draw, that they can spell these words, and (as shown in student tryouts) that they can handle an operant span that includes BOTH structure and function.

   The frame is an excellent example of many mathetical characteristics. Note the visual devices used to control the student's attention to important details. Note the absence of lengthy explanations. Note, while you're noting, the amount of "noting" or observing the student does. While the activity is *covert* (no speaking or writing) in this particular frame, there is plenty of it.

   There are four exercises on this "structure-and-function" operant:

   (1) the demonstration you see here;
   (2) the prompted exercise you just inspected;
   (3) a third exercise;
   (4) the terminal exercise.

   The terminal exercise (which you should be able to predict at this point) looks like this:

   > Without looking back, represent both STRUCTURE and FUNCTION of an ameba with labeled drawings.

   The standard mathetical progression for an operant is:

   FIRST EXERCISE–*demonstrate*
   SECOND EXERCISE–*prompt*
   FINAL EXERCISE–*release* (Gilbert's term for an unprompted mastery exercise)

   In the *Ameba* program, there are two intermediate exercises between the first frame and the last. The first of these (on page 163) is heavily prompted. Given the terminal exercise above, what do you think the second intermediate exercise should look like? (It must be less prompted than the first but more prompted than the terminal one.)

   — — — — — — — — — — — — — —

   You could (a) remove the picture but suggest what labels should go on one, or (b) give a picture but not tell what labels to put on it. The actual third exercise is alternative (a).

At this point, you may wish to see the "whole program"–all four frames in order. Frame One is on the facing page. Frame Two is on page 163. Frame Three is in the middle of my frame 9 on page 166, and the terminal frame is immediately above in the middle of my frame 7.

CHARACTERISTICS OF AMEBAE

The CELL is the basic unit of life; each cell contains all of the characteristics necessary to sustain it. These may be classified according to STRUCTURE and FUNCTION.

Study <u>carefully</u> the characteristics, drawings, and labels shown below but <u>do not</u> try to memorize:

STRUCTURE characteristics⟶

Locate the
1. nucleus
2. nuclear membrane
3. cell wall
4. vacuole
5. cytoplasm
   a. endoplasm
   b. ectoplasm

FUNCTION characteristics⟶

1. FEEDING: note how the pseudopodia engulf the food

2. MOVEMENT: note how the cell is pulled forward by the extended pseudopodia

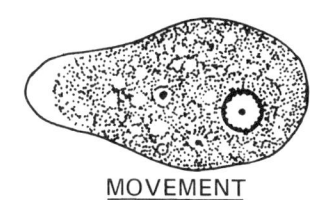

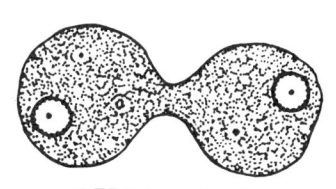

3. REPRODUCTION: note how the cell multiplies by binary fission

<u>Remember</u>:
all cells may be <u>characterized</u> by:
STRUCTURE & FUNCTION

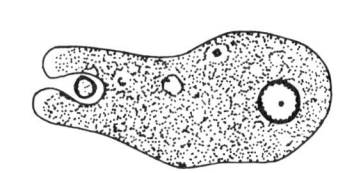

If you <u>already</u> knew the information contained on this page, you may skip to page 7—otherwise continue your study of the above material on the next page.

166 SYSTEMATIC APPROACHES TO DESIGN

8. Suppose we change the target population for the program from medical students and public health workers to students in freshman biology in high school. Though most people familiar with this latter population might not even try out so large an operant span as represented by the first frame in the *Ameba* program, suppose you were daring and did so. Suppose also that your tryout showed that this was too big a chunk. What would be the most logical way to divide this frame into two exercises?

— — — — — — — — — — — — — — —

I would think that a division along structure-function lines would be the next smaller step that would not fractionate the whole. Even that division might prove too large an operant span for below-average students.

Note. At some point in this division process, you would approach the "breaking point" where the "meaningful" chunk becomes fractionated into meaningless small steps. The technology of programing has no formula for calculating this "limit" at the moment. Perhaps someday, we will have more than common sense as a guide.

---

9. The third exercise in the *Ameba* program goes like this:

> Now you draw an ameba and label it according to STRUCTURE (nucleus, nuclear membrane, cell wall, vacuole, endoplasm, ectoplasm):
>
> *(Lots of white space for drawing)*
>
> Draw three amebae and label them according to FUNCTION (feeding, movement, reproduction):
>
> *(Lots more white space)*
>
> Turn back to page 1—check and correct your work.

The student has now seen these drawings four times (assuming he looks at his own). Suppose data from student tryouts indicated students were still not ready for the "release." Can you think of a possibility for designing an exercise to follow the one above for the operant on STRUCTURE? Is there any prompt intermediate to the orders to include the six labels as given to the student above?

Perhaps nothing occurred to you. But how about reminding the student that there are *six* labels to put on, without telling him what they are? Or giving him the initials of the labels? (Such formal prompting does occur elsewhere in the *Ameba* program.)

10. The operant on which the students are being instructed in the *Ameba* program segment is
    _____a chain (order is important)
    _____a set of discriminations.

----

a set of discriminations (no matter what order the student uses in giving the labels or listing the functions, he is right as long as he includes everything).

11. How does mathetics stand on the three basic principles of Skinnerian programing? In general, matheticists provide confirmation, although Gilbert theorized that a well-designed exercise should produce a mastery response so obviously adequate that a confident student would have no need of comparing his response with a model. Mathetical exercises are initially designed to overestimate student capacity in order to zero in on the most efficient operant span, but in student tryouts, each exercise is adjusted and readjusted until errors are eliminated.

   In the over-all mathetical sequence, *demonstrate, prompt, release,* there is strong emphasis on student activity. Consider, however, the problem of the first exercise, demonstrating the operant, when the student is instructed to "study carefully." Studying is certainly an active response, if the student does so, but it is covert. What indices would a mathetics programer have in tryouts to help him revise such a frame if it were inadequate. (Name two or three.)

Most students get a peculiar expression on their face if they don't understand. Facial expressions or restlessness might indicate poor design. If you are very observant, you might make use of eye movements indicating that a student was having difficulty locating what he was supposed to note. With proper encouragement, a student may volunteer his opinions about the amount of material or difficulty of finding something. Another key indication would be failure in the second exercise, indicating that something he was supposed to "study" escaped his notice.

168   SYSTEMATIC APPROACHES TO DESIGN

12. Not all demonstration frames in Gilbert's essays or in existing mathetics programs are of the "study carefully" type. Overt responses may be required. In demonstrating how to do long division, for instance, Gilbert's examples instruct the student in which operation to perform and where to put the result but require the student to perform the arithmetic.

    Below and on the facing page is an exercise from a program for fire-fighters. The objective of this section of the program is *correct interpretation of symbols used on maps of a fire area.*

    Inspect the diagrams on the facing page and the information in the frame below.

    (a) Is this a demonstration exercise (are the responses primed?) or is it a prompted exercise?
    (b) Given the subject matter in the diagrams and the objective *the student will read all the symbols on the map,* what would be the *largest operant span* the programer could have included in this exercise?

    SEE FACING PAGE (Figures 1 and 2)   ⇨

    Figure 1 illustrates a typical type of terrain in which forest fires are fought. Figure 2 illustrates the land features of the same terrain and certain other symbols, in map form.

    Comparing Figures 1 and 2, CHECK (☒) the appropriate box to identify the symbol that corresponds to each of the following features:

Feature (Figure 1)	Corresponding Symbol (Figure 2)
main fire area	☐ A ☐ B ☐ C ☐ D ☐ E ☐ F ☐ G ☐ H
road	☐ A ☐ B ☐ C ☐ D ☐ E ☐ F ☐ G ☐ H

    (a) Although it takes more looking around than the *Ameba* frame did, all the labels are there in Figure 1. So what each symbol stands for is primed. This is a demonstration frame.
    (b) There are eight symbols in the key (A-H), so the largest operant span would have the student working with all eight in the first exercise, before he gets any confirmation.

MATHETICS: A VERY SHORT COURSE 169

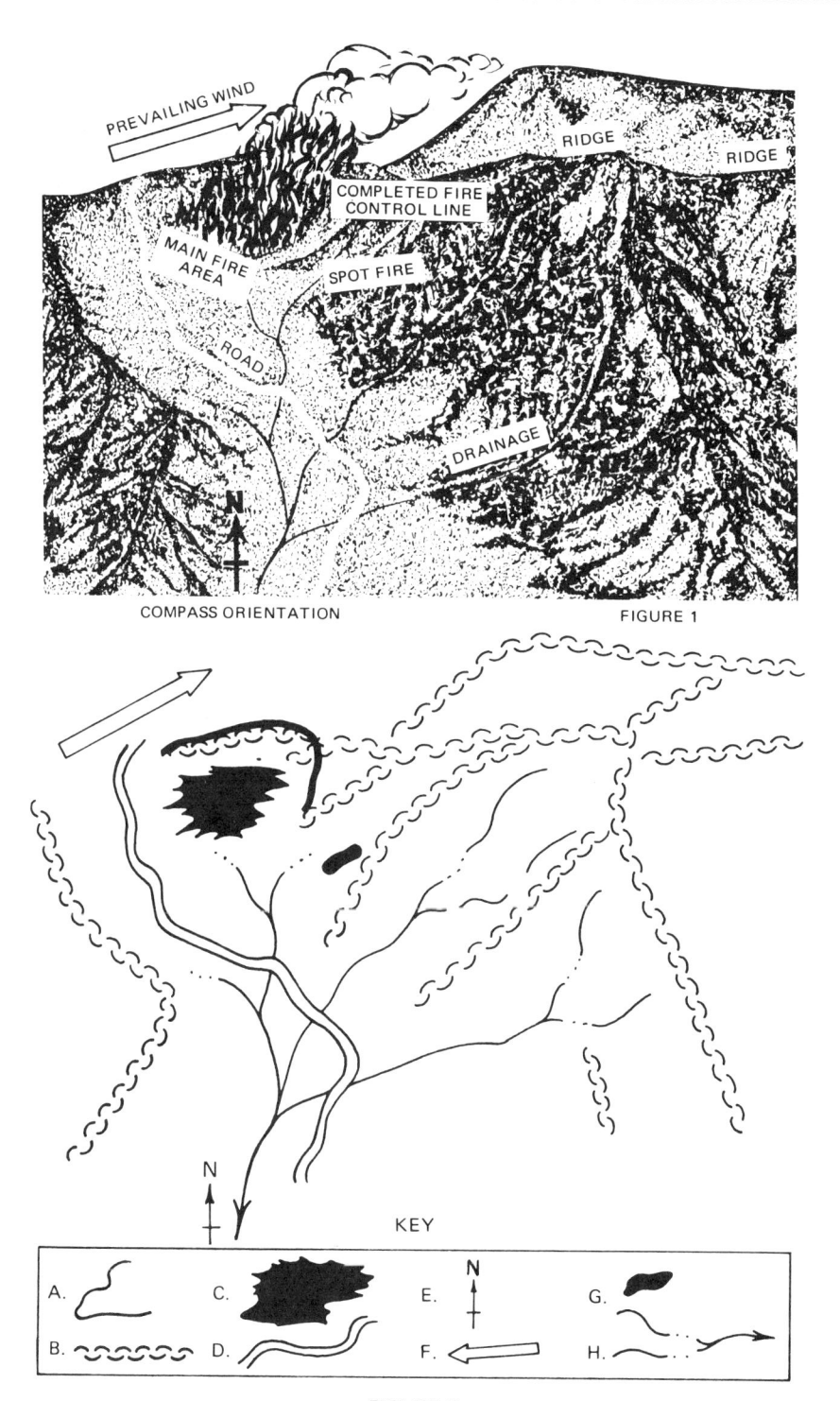

FIGURE 1

FIGURE 2

OTHER ISSUES

In his articles on mathetics, Gilbert noted that "motivation is not a variable in mathetics." He assumes that the student's own desire to learn or the desire of others (employers, teachers, or parents) to have him learn provides a spur to the student to exert the effort to learn, provided that the exercises are designed to enable him to do so efficiently. Motivational material like cartoons, pretty girls, anecdotes, and humor are generally lacking in mathetical exercises. They are not designed to "entertain." Perhaps you noticed that most of the verbal material in the *Ameba* program consisted of instructions and short phrases. Explanatory material was reduced to a minimum. Probably the most difficult part of the system for the average academic (like your author!) to swallow is the implicit instruction to stop talking! There are as yet few authentic mathetical programs in academic subjects, perhaps due to the academic propensity for talking at length.

One of the wisest and least mentioned principles of mathetics is hidden behind the terminology of "analytic repertory," "synthetic repertory," and "domain theory." Only *after* a complete analysis of the range of stimuli that a student must selectively respond to and the range of actions he must take, does the matheticist approach the difficult problem of finding a way to verbalize about these stimuli and responses—the "domain theory." The student will be taught to verbalize, if at all, only those rules or principles which relate directly to what he has to do. Terminology he does not need will be omitted. Does an electronics repairman need the language and the difficult concepts and principles of physics to perform his job? Does the parent need the language and all the fine discriminations of the research psychologist in order to apply basic principles to desired behavior changes in his child? These are the sorts of questions that Gilbert's procedures are intended to deal with. By building only the verbalizations that are obviously necessary, the programer avoids unnecessary "academic" subject matter of no use to the student.

In a sense we could say that Gilbert is advising that we construct the RUs only after surveying the EGs, rather than the typical RULEG procedures of listing all the principles in the subject matter and then selecting the EGs to go with them. In many training situations, the application of such a procedure has led to dramatic savings in training time. (Ofiesh, 1965.) What such a procedure might do for academic instruction, we can only conjecture!

If you have to stop soon, this would be a good place.

BACKWARD CHAINING

Perhaps the best-known aspect of mathetical procedures is the one derived from laboratory research, "backward" chaining. Consider the problem: you have a hungry rat and the task of training it to:

(a) climb a ladder to
(b) pull a chain which produces a marble which he
(c) carries down the ladder and deposits in a receptacle which turns on a light which
(d) signals that he should press a lever in order to get a pellet of food.

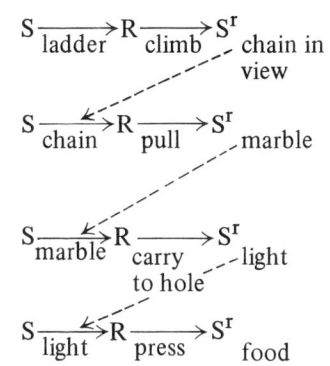

$$S_{\text{ladder}} \rightarrow R_{\text{climb}} \rightarrow S^r_{\text{chain in view}}$$

$$S_{\text{chain}} \rightarrow R_{\text{pull}} \rightarrow S^r_{\text{marble}}$$

$$S_{\text{marble}} \rightarrow R_{\text{carry to hole}} \rightarrow S^r_{\text{light}}$$

$$S_{\text{light}} \rightarrow R_{\text{press}} \rightarrow S^r_{\text{food}}$$

And then he starts over again through the chain, up the ladder, pull the chain, carry the marble, press the bar, eat, and head for the ladder. Everything must be done correctly and in order—if he presses the bar before putting the marble in the hole, no food.

Not even the brightest rats at Harvard have much chance of running through such a chain accidentally (discovery method of learning), and there is no possibility, with rats as students, of priming the chain by any set of directions, written or oral. Rats, however, will do anything for food. By starting with the last response (pressing the lever) which even unintelligent rats hit upon, the whole chain can be gradually built.

The experimenter *begins* instruction with the last response, the one that produces the food reinforcer. Then, by providing food only when the light is on, the light becomes a signal connected with food, and, according to most theorists, becomes somewhat of a reinforcer in its own right. At this point the experimenter is ready for the training on the next-to-last response which will turn on the light—he introduces the marble next to the hole where it is likely to be knocked in. When the rat gets the "marble-moving response" down pat, two elements of the chain are now in place, the last (press bar when light is on) and the next-to-last. Note that the response—putting the marble in the hole, *creates the stimulus*—light on—*for the next response.* This is a basic characteristic of true chains.

The experimenter gradually moves the marble away from the hole, toward the ladder, and up its rungs. There is, theoretically, a certain amount of reinforcement involved in "finding the marble," since it leads to light, which leads to an active lever, which produces the food. This procedure of gradually working back toward the first response is followed until the animal is running off the whole chain in order.

The account, of course, is oversimplified. The basic principle is rather simple, however. Since, to a rat, the whole chain is rather arbitrary, the only way to train him to take the steps in order is to start with the endpoint and always make each new element lead to this endpoint. The rat, you should notice, *never runs through the chain backwards. No matter where he starts, he gets to food.* It is only the TRAINING procedure to which the "backward" in "backward chaining" refers.

Gilbert, Mechner (1967), and others have seen applications of this basic training procedure to the teaching of complex chains to human students. Its basic advantage is that the student always completes the total chain and is reinforced by his success. At no time is he taking an arbitrary step which does not appear to him to lead anywhere.

---

13. One of the classic examples of a human chain is the one faced by all kindergarteners of getting their shoes tied. Tying a neat bow-knot which will hold through a day's activities is a rather difficult act.

    If you apply backward chaining to this procedure, where would you start?

    _____(a) The laces, untied, are put in the child's hands; the child attempts the first knot.
    _____(b) The bows are tied but are not pulled tight; the child pulls them tight.
    _____(c) The bows are tightly tied; the child unties them.

    – – – – – – – – – – – – – – – –

    You would start with the very last thing done when tying shoes, namely (b) tightening the bows.

---

14. If the shoes are now on and tightly tied, the chain is complete. According to the theory, this is reinforcing, since Junior can now go out and play. You now have:

    $$S \xrightarrow[\text{bows ready}]{} R \xrightarrow[\text{pull tight}]{} S^r \text{ shoes tied}$$

    The next operant you choose to teach must *produce the situation "bows ready"* in which tightening will produce the tied shoes. Suppose, for the next-to-last step, you decide that a reasonable operant is *making the bows.* You instruct the student in how to

    > make a bow on one lace and hold this in his left hand
    > and wrap the other lace around so a loop is available
    > and pull that loop through until both bows are the same size.

    He listens and watches and then tries it himself. Suppose the result of his efforts to imitate you is disastrous. What has happened? (Can you describe this in Gilbert's terminology?)

    – – – – – – – – – – – – – – – –

    You have exceeded the operant span or, in more ordinary terms, the step was too big.

make a bow on one lace and hold this in his left hand
and wrap the other lace around so a loop is available
and pull that loop through until both bows are the same size.

15. Given the above description of the operant *making the bows* (which turns out to be three separate acts), what would be the *smallest* next-to-last step you could require the child to take? (Try for a "meaningful" operant, one that starts with a clear cue and ends with a significant change in the state of the shoe.)

_ _ _ _ _ _ _ _ _ _ _ _ _ _ _

Pulling the loop through until the bows are equal suggests itself to me.

---

16. If you were developing a program in this subject, you might not want to try for the smallest operant. If you know from testing that *making the bows* is too large for the kindergartener's operant span, you might want to divide the "subject matter" into the next largest reasonable operant. What would you suggest for a reasonable operant smaller than *making the bows* but larger than *pulling the loop through to produce equal bows?*

_ _ _ _ _ _ _ _ _ _ _ _ _ _ _

How about "making the second bow"? This is the same kind of problem you faced before when you considered in Frame 8 above how to divide the *Ameba* frame into smaller units. The problem is how to decrease the operant span in an exercise without fractionating the reasonable operants (or sensible chunks) in the subject.

---

17. If the child can manipulate the second loop to produce equal bows, he is now ready for the last step, tightening the bows. Which, you will remember, is reinforcing—his shoes are now tied. His response *making the bows equal* created, in the manner of true chains, the stimulus situation in which the last response occurs. So we are underway in building a chain.

To produce a set of mathetical exercises for this chain, all you need to do at this point is to impose on this chain that you are building the standard mathetical exercise sequence: *demonstrate, prompt, release.*

174 SYSTEMATIC APPROACHES TO DESIGN

Your first frame provides a *demonstration* of how to pull the bows tight. The student imitates your demonstration.

"Frame" One

$$S \xrightarrow{\text{equal bows}} R \xrightarrow{\text{tighten}} S^r \text{ tied}$$

In your second frame, you *demonstrate* the next-to-last operant. The child imitates you, producing bows in a position to be pulled tight.

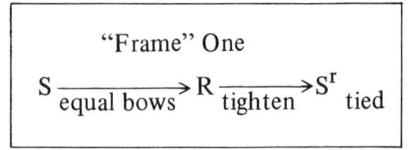

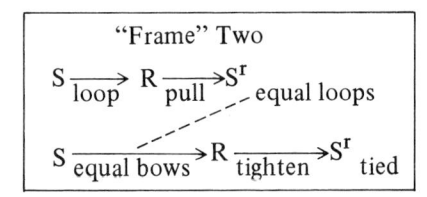

"Frame" Two

$$S \xrightarrow{\text{loop}} R \xrightarrow{\text{pull}} S^r \text{ equal loops}$$

$$S \xrightarrow{\text{equal bows}} R \xrightarrow{\text{tighten}} S^r \text{ tied}$$

What should you now do with the final response "pulling the bows tight"? Prompt it or release it?

— — — — — — — — — — — — — —

prompt it. For this age group, a reminder to tighten the bows could be the prompt. For an adult, who already knows how, it would be a prime, but the child didn't know how until he went through the first demonstration. Perhaps the word "tight" would be sufficient.

---

18. For the moment, we're ignoring the possibility that you might want to provide some practice on these two bits of the chain. Let's suppose you can move directly to the next operant and that *wrapping the second lace around the first one so that a loop is available* is within the operant span of our student.

    What do you do with this operant on the THIRD frame?

— — — — — — — — — — — — — —

demonstrate it. This is the first time out for this operant and the first frame on an operant is a demonstration.

19.

"Frame" Three	Procedure
$S \xrightarrow[\text{1st bow}]{} R \xrightarrow[\text{make 2nd bow}]{} S^r$ loop in place	DEMO
$S \xrightarrow[\text{loop}]{} R \xrightarrow[\text{make equal}]{} S^r$ equal bows	?
$S \xrightarrow[\text{equal bows}]{} R \xrightarrow[\text{pull tight}]{} S^r$ shoes tied	?

Once he has mimicked your demonstration of making the loop available, he is ready to pull it through to make equal bows—the next-to-last response. What do you do with this response in this frame?

When he has equal bows, what do you do about the final response (tightening them) in this frame?

— — — — — — — — — — — — — — —

You prompt the next-to-last response and let him make the last one with no help—that is, you release it. (It is legitimate to remind him to finish, but you should not have to remind him what to do in order to finish.)

---

20. There is the procedure (at least in the abstract) for backward chaining. Each step forward in the program adds a new element to the *beginning* of the sequence of responses the student will make. At each step, the student is moving through the sequence, as much as he knows of it, in the correct order and getting to the end, to a completed problem or a tied shoe or whatever the end result is. The design that you just created for a "shoe-tying program" was, of course, just that. Without a student to try it out on, we have no way of knowing whether we chose operants within the operant span of the intended student population. Nor does mathetical theory require that the *demonstrate-prompt-release* formula be applied rigidly.

In the Ameba program there were TWO prompted frames before the final release. With very young children, with slow learners, or perhaps with a very complicated operant that you didn't want to break down any further, the number of demonstrations might be increased. But these decisions are made on the basis of evidence from the actual students. The model provides only the design for the initial draft.

One of the standard examples of a chain in the academic curriculum is long division, a relatively rigid procedure which students learn when they have mastered all the subskills (adding, subtracting, multiplying, dividing simple numbers). Below are three frames (the first three) in a potential "program" based on mathetical procedures. The objectives are to divide a three-digit number by a one-digit number. *Note.* In order to have the student actually doing the steps, instead of just remembering the solution from the last frame, the problem is changed each time. This particular series of frames introduces another Gilbertian twist—what he calls the "observing stimulus" and what we might characterize as a running start on the chain, in other words, letting the student know the context in which the response you are demonstrating occurs. (A parent teaching shoe-tying might do the same thing, commenting verbally on some segment of the chain that precedes the one he is going to demonstrate to the child.)

Your job is to write the next frame. Get a fairly large sheet of paper. Advice from Gilbert: do it in pencil and keep an eraser handy—getting the steps in sequence and fitting them on the page in a readable order is work. If your arrows start crossing each other, try again! And, keep words to a minimum.

Frame One calls attention to the next-to-last operant (calculating the final product) and demonstrates the last operant (how to get the remainder).

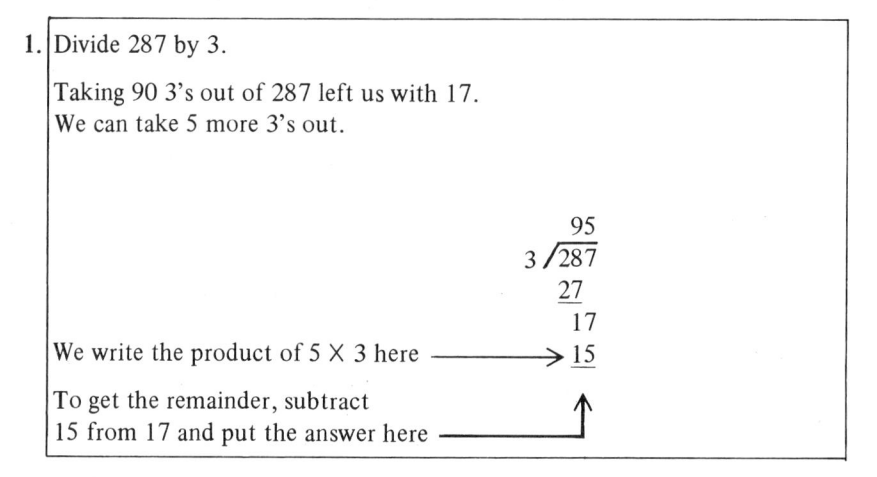

---

1. Divide 287 by 3.

    Taking 90 3's out of 287 left us with 17.
    We can take 5 more 3's out.

    $$\begin{array}{r} 95 \\ 3\,\overline{)287} \\ \underline{27} \\ 17 \end{array}$$

    We write the product of 5 × 3 here ⟶ $\underline{15}$

    To get the remainder, subtract
    15 from 17 and put the answer here ⟶

Operants in Frame 2: "where to write the multiplier," "calculating the final product," and "getting the remainder."

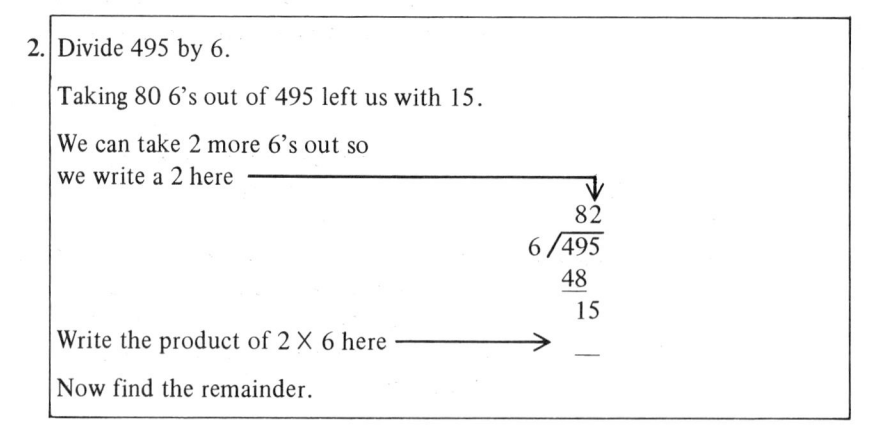

---

2. Divide 495 by 6.

    Taking 80 6's out of 495 left us with 15.

    We can take 2 more 6's out so
    we write a 2 here ⟶

    $$\begin{array}{r} 82 \\ 6\,\overline{)495} \\ \underline{48} \\ 15 \end{array}$$

    Write the product of 2 × 6 here ⟶ __

    Now find the remainder.

Here is the third frame.

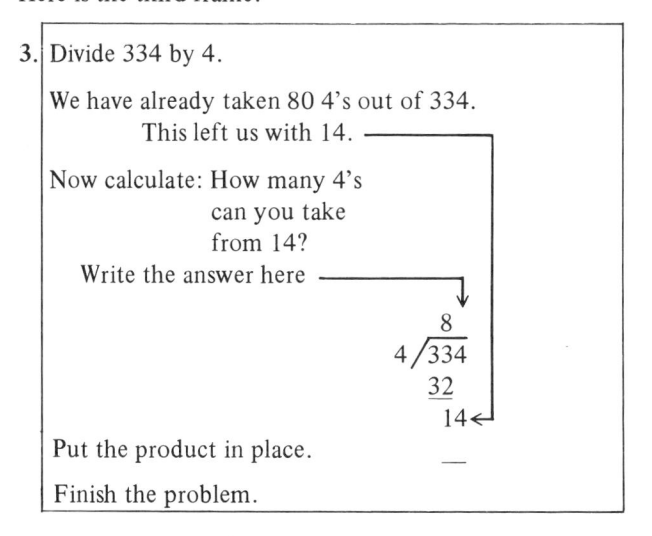

```
3. Divide 334 by 4.
   We have already taken 80 4's out of 334.
                     This left us with 14. ─────┐
   Now calculate: How many 4's                  │
                  can you take                  │
                  from 14?                      │
   Write the answer here ──────────────┐        │
                                    8  ↓        │
                                 4/334          │
                                   32           │
                                   14◄──────────┘
   Put the product in place.       ─
   Finish the problem.
```

Now *you* write the fourth frame.

Confirmation is provided on page 178 when you've completed the exercise.

─ ─ ─ ─ ─ ─ ─ ─ ─ ─ ─ ─ ─ ─ ─

Research Note. *Skip to end of section if not interested.*

Backward chaining, as a clear procedure differing significantly from the "normal" begin-at-the-beginning, has appealed to researchers almost as much as active responding and immediate confirmation as topics of studies. Several studies have been done comparing "backward chaining" with learning the same material in a forward direction. The results, to say the least, are ambiguous.

There seem to be at least two problems involved in the studies: first, is the operant being taught really a chain, pure and simple, and second, is the method of instruction really backward chaining? (That is why there are quotes around the words in the preceding paragraph.)

The most recent study (Hartley and Woods, 1968) is a good example of both problems. The subject to be learned was a four-verse poem. Each verse was taken as an operant (which could possibly mean some forward chaining within verses even if the verses were learned in reverse order). Poetry differs from long division in several ways. The whole poem has a "meaning" which could be a contributing factor to ease of learning it in any direction, or even in random order of verses. The steps in long division have no such "meaning." Also you can recite any line or couplet in a poem out of context; it is hard to see how you could calculate a remainder unless you had already calculated the product of the final quotient figure.

The procedural differences are almost as subtle as the differences in subject matter. In the "program" on long division, each problem began at the beginning and the student merely finished the remaining steps. In shoe-tying, you would have to go through the steps in the chain, in front of the child, getting his shoe ready each time for your demonstration and his response. In other words, in the "classic" examples, a great deal more demonstrating is going on than the theory calls for. The instructor begins at the beginning each time even if the student doesn't. The student's responses are always made in the context of a whole sequence. Perhaps this is a significant difference. In reading a poem once and then memorizing its last verse, the context (the preceding steps or the "running start") are not being demonstrated.

Mechner (1967) has suggested the application of the backward chaining technique to another kind of "chain"—that of playing a piece of music from memory. He stated that the learner should master the last phrase first, then the next-to-last leading into the end of the piece, and so on. Beginning at the beginning and breaking down in the middle happens to many a musical novice and Mechner noted that these breakdown points were the chief hurdles in playing a piece all the way through, especially if the student habitually returns to the beginning for another running start.

Thought Question: is there any way (given a person with appropriate musical skills, of course, or an accomplice—like the parent in shoe tying) to keep such learning in context? In other words, could we design a procedure for this "chain" which will parallel the procedure used in teaching shoe tying and long division? No one has actually tested such a procedure, as far as I know.

Relevant Quote: The first pitfall to avoid, then, in studying innovations, is the assumption that what is claimed in practice is, indeed, a reasonably accurate working model of the innovation being proclaimed. . . . Researchers must take any such claims with a grain of salt, coming to realize that labels can cover anything or nothing. . . . When one inquires, then, into the effects of an innovation, he frequently knows not what he studies, especially if he doesn't bother to examine it. (Goodlad, 1968.)

Confirmation of "mathetical exercise" on page 177.

CHECK: (a) Is the student dividing a one-digit number into a three-digit number?
(b) Is your problem a new one?
(c) Did you "release" the operant of where to write the product?
(d) Did you prompt but not prime the operant of calculating the final digit in the quotient and putting it in its place?
(e) What you chose to demonstrate may vary—either "bringing down the final digit from the dividend" or even getting the whole remainder of the first division process.
(f) Did you call the student's attention to some step that you would demonstrate on the next frame?
(g) Is your frame visually satisfactory to you? (Whether it is visually effective, of course, could be determined only by a student.)
(h) Do you feel that you have reduced verbiage to a minimum? (For some of us, that's pretty hard to do!)

Footnote for Scholars. In presenting my own interpretation of Gilbert, I have not only ducked as much terminology as possible, but have also on occasion used a technical term in its more common meaning. Gilbert's "operant," for instance, differs somewhat from the normal use and I have adopted the latter.

SECTION D. AN ESSAY ON CONCEPTS AND UNCOMMON SENSE

The objectives of this section are that you will become "familiar with" some of the problems that are continually turning up in the analysis of academic subject matters. Although you will, no doubt, become "familiar with" some of my own points of view on these matters, it is too early in programing history to impose anyone's point of view on the development of the technology. So this section is not programed. You may follow your own predilections!

Concepts. Most academic subject matters have two facets: they are ways of talking about the world and ways of dividing the "stream of reality" into manageable units. A psychologist, an anthropologist, a sociologist, and an economist can together observe the same chunk of reality and yet not attend to the same things. They can all say something meaningful to their colleagues who divide the world the same way and speak the same "language" and yet not communicate to each other. Each one speaks a different language about a different segment of reality. Students, until they become specialists, grope around in this morass confronted with the double problem of mastering several different conceptual models of the world and several different languages for talking about it.

Behavioral psychology and programing lore have something to contribute to the analysis of academic subject matters. All programers are advised to analyze the subject matter thoroughly to determine its relevant concepts and generalizations, the facts that must be known, the terms that must be mastered, the procedures that must be followed. *How* this is done is less clear. Everyone agrees that it is the roughest part of the programer's job. A textbook may be a compendium of knowledge of a subject, but it does not represent an analysis of how students who "know" its contents behave. Programing is something more than putting questions after paragraphs or putting holes in sentences in such existing sources.

A concept, as we have said before (Chapter 2) is a class or set of objects, events, or relationships which share certain properties and to which a subject matter expert makes a consistent response—often, but not always, naming. For example, "expansionist policies," "metaphor," "functional relationship," "one-half," "rationalize," "prompts," "faster than," "to reinforce," "compound interest," "mammal," "complex sentence," "above," "theory," "sportsmanlike," "equivalent," "enzyme," and "demonstrate" are all concepts. In other words, given lots of examples and non-examples and sufficient expertise, we could sort bits of reality into two piles—members of the class and non-members of the class. This is the basic stuff of "being able to see the world the same way a subject matter expert does," being able to "think like a psychologist," "make predictions like an economist," or "understand biological science."

In the terminology adopted in this book, there are two relevant behaviors:
> the expert *discriminates*—that is, he knows the difference between what is and what is not a member of the class as shown by his "sorting" behavior, and he *generalizes*, that is, given an example which he has never encountered before, he recognizes it as a member of the class.

Subject matter experts have another behavior relevant to concepts. They talk at length about them! This talking behavior should not, however, be confused with the significant signs of understanding—the way they discriminate and generalize.

The point has been made before but is worth emphasizing again: *the ability to spout a definition or state a principle is not a sign that a student sees the world as the expert does or can do as the expert does.* Verbal behavior is not synonymous with mastery behavior.

The pitfalls in concept teaching are many. Perhaps the most difficult is the selection of examples. *No concept is learned from a single example,* although inspection of many texts would lead you to think that many people thought so. We can think of a concept as a class, represented, as logicians do, by a circle. In the middle of the circle, we can put the "standard example"— the one frequently given in standard texts. If the student is given this standard example, will he generalize correctly to those "borderline" cases which an expert would include? Given a non-example, something outside the circle yet resembling members of the class in many ways, will he correctly discriminate? Anyone who has taught and tested is aware of the errors that students make along these lines, whatever the language we use to describe them. The student's concept may not go far enough—he rejects an example that experts would include in the class. Or his concept goes too far—he includes something the expert would reject. (Markle and Tiemann, 1969.)

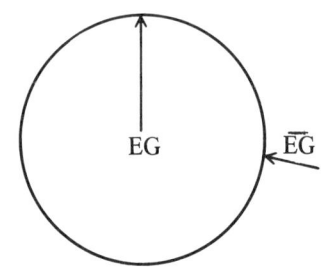

Dimensions. The solution to the problem of bringing the student's concept into line with that of the expert does not lie in simply piling example on top of example. The key is in choosing *a range of examples* which illustrate not only the central types but also the far-out, but still acceptable, members of the class.

In a psychology class, for instance, the concept of reinforcement is typically illustrated by a rat pressing a bar, receiving food, and therefore increasing its rate of bar pressing. Bravely piling on further examples of other lower organisms doing similar simple things for more food and drink does not produce students who can correctly generalize "reinforcement" to examples that occur in their own affluent environments.

The advice to use a range of examples is easier said than done, since thinking up a range of examples requires at least some elements of that mysterious skill called creativity. In some cases someone somewhere has listed all members of the class. This is true of "mammal" but not of "metaphor"; it may be true of "salts" but hardly of "sentences." From such a list you could prod your memory, making sure that your teaching of "mammal" included large ones and small ones, arboreal, terrestrial, and aquatic ones, and so forth. Without such a list, you search for the dimensions of the concept which enable you to generate widely differing examples.

Another way to get at it is by analysis of the standard case. What, in the typical example, is absolutely central to the concept (a defining attribute, that is) and what is "noise" or irrelevant material in the example. In the case of the rat, the lever, and the pellet of food, for instance, many irrelevant details are apparent. The organism is irrelevant. Cats, monkeys, or humans would do just as well, which provides ideas for the next example. The manipulation of a lever, or manipulatory behavior, is irrelevant. Verbal responses or observing responses would do just as well. Food is irrelevant. And so it goes. In each example, the irrelevant features can be changed, thereby extending the student's generalization to a wide range of differing examples.

No concept can be taught without a sufficient number of non-examples, carefully chosen to block incorrect generalizations. Luckily for programmers, this problem usually takes care of itself in structured subject matters. Concepts come in sets, and an example of one concept is a non-example of the other. We have, for instance, vectors and scalars, positive and negative numbers, complex and compound and simple sentences, primes and prompts and terminal frames, and many other such sets.

Non-examples can also be generated from analyzing the standard example or by manipulating the definition (if it is well defined). If something essential is changed, a non-example is generated. Often there are several kinds of non-examples. An example from this program is the two-dimensional concept "terminal frame," defined as being both unprompted and out of sequence. So two sets of non-examples are needed: (a) although out of sequence, the frame is prompted and (b) although unprompted, the frame is too close in sequence.

Understanding of a concept is tested by having the student deal with (identify or otherwise behave appropriately toward) a new example and, if possible, new non-examples. A programmer, like a classroom teacher, has a real advantage here over the designer of standardized or other widely used tests. He knows what is in the teaching sequence, so he can deal more effectively than the test constructor with the higher level processes mentioned by Bloom (1956) and others. If a programmer wants to test for generalization or application he can do so. A student cannot generalize if the example was used in the teaching sequence. He cannot analyze or synthesize or evaluate if the case has been thoroughly discussed during instruction. All these "higher" behaviors can be defined *only in relation to the instructional sequence.*

Problems in analyzing subject matter this way are immense and, at times, amusing. It is surprising (or is it?) how often within one discipline two people will use the same word for quite different phenomena or a different word for the same phenomenon. It is often frustrating to find that what appears to be a well-defined concept is actually extremely fuzzy and can cause all sorts of difficulty the minute the programmer gets beyond the standard examples. A programmer who takes the advice to reduce the verbiage and increase the number of examples can land in deep trouble in some subjects. It is hard to duck these issues when students are responding actively and erroneously, an experience textbook authors can conveniently avoid.

Conceptual hierarchies. In discussing matrices early in this chapter, one of the "relationships" that we built into a concept matrix was that of subset or example. Matrices are not the best devices for trying to get at the "structure" of a discipline. Structure, at the moment, is fashionable but not very well defined. One approach to it, a very difficult one, is a hierarchical classification diagram, beginning at the top with the most abstract or general concept and working downward through its subsets. A familiar example:

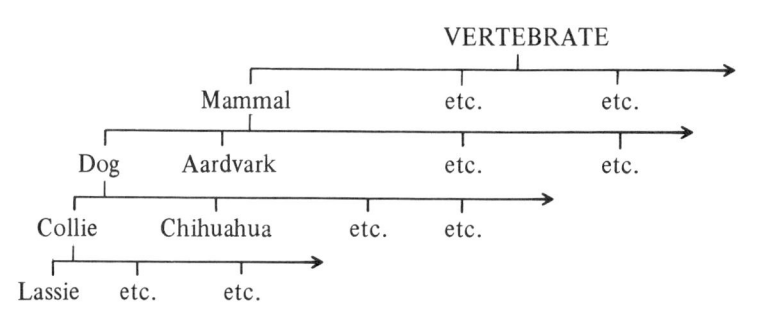

```
                              VERTEBRATE
                    ┌─────────────┬──────────┬──────────→
                 Mammal         etc.        etc.
            ┌───────┴───┬──────────┬──────────→
          Dog      Aardvark      etc.       etc.
       ┌───┴────┬──────────┬──────────→
     Collie  Chihuahua    etc.       etc.
    ┌──┴───┬──────────→
  Lassie  etc.      etc.
```

Starting with Vertebrate, it is relatively simple to present a neat hierarchical structure from the most inclusive class down to the least inclusive and therefore most concrete individual member of a particular breed of dog. Looking at this diagram, we can talk easily about "coordinate" concepts (the ones on the same line) and "subordinate" concepts (the ones which hang from a line above).

In analyzing any particular concept, such as "dog" or "mammal", we can use such a hierarchy. Among the attributes of all mammals is a backbone, by definition, as seen by their position on the hierarchy. Yet this attribute is useless in distinguishing mammals from other vertebrates, since it is shared with them. The hierarchy also suggests the most useful non-examples— those which are drawn from coordinate sets. The subordinate sets suggest a range of examples.

Attempts to produce such neatness in hierarchical structures may reveal some clues to the confusions that students feel when confronted with a mass of terms in a relatively technical but badly structured field. One of the prime examples is traditional grammar, which most students are exposed to and few learn. Try to put the following terms into a hierarchy of any sort and you may understand why: sentence, declarative sentence, interrogative sentence, independent clause, dependent clause, noun phrase, verb phrase, phrase, noun, verb, adjective, adverb. They cannot all be put in the same diagram in any way that prevents arrows (or relationships) from going up and sideways, as well as down. When students sense a jumble of terms, it may be because there is indeed a jumble of terms!

Is it of any use to try to determine such hierarchical structures? Perhaps. An EGRUL programer going from "concrete" to "abstract" is working with such relationships even if he never diagrams it. Typical advice to programers is to start with the "simple" and move to the "complex," or with the "familiar" and move to the "unfamiliar." The issue of what is "simple" or "concrete" or "familiar" is usually brushed over, leaving each programer to his own interpretation. "Dog" is really far more complex and abstract, because it includes such a wide range of examples, than "chihuahua" or "beagle," both of which are apt to be unfamiliar. A child is likely to be well-versed in "dog" before he learns its subsets. Whether this is of any use to determining whether to teach "vertebrate" before "mammal" or vice versa is dubious. Like a matrix, however, a hierarchy may organize a programer's thoughts and point out aspects of the subject which are difficult because there is no logical relationship underneath.

The answers to the questions about where to start in the hierarchy, what is simple, what is familiar, what is concrete, are not in. The frequent talk about logical structure, in other words, is just that—talk. What little work has been done (Gagné, 1966) tends to be in those areas in which most subject matter experts can agree structure exists—mathematics and the physical sciences. None of the systems we considered in this chapter provides quick answers to "Which RU should you begin with"? or "Which operant should you demonstrate first"?, except, of course, the limited case of backward chaining.

Principles. Principles (RUs) are, in the language of most behaviorists, statements of some relationship between sets of concepts. The most obvious examples, the key generalizations, such as $s = 1/2gt^2$ (or, if you're really literate, $e = mc^2$) state firm relationships (equality) between sets of well-defined concepts. The Law of Supply and Demand in economics may have less validity than the Second Law of Thermodynamics, but each relates one set of events (a concept) with another. "Applying a principle" would, then, mean the compounded kind of generalization that would result from having several concepts operating at once. The process is quite similar; generalization is the key as it is in the extension of single concepts. Everything we have said about the analysis of concepts applies equally in this field—the importance of many widely varying examples, the key role of non-examples, and the necessity to test "understanding" in new situations.

"The matheticist will attempt to exceed the student's probable operant span on the first draft of a demonstration frame" is a principle, relating several concepts you have just been grappling with. Your ability to apply such a generalization (to recognize examples or produce such an overestimation yourself) depends on your ability to generalize and discriminate the concepts involved. Note that I never attempted to teach the concept "exceed"—this was assumed. The behavior of any student applying principles, whether they are physical laws, spelling rules, statistical formulas, or whatever, depends on his grasp of *every* concept, including the "relators" themselves, in the principle.

Principles and definitions lend themselves to being verbalized. As anyone knows whose ear is to the ground in educational controversies these days, the battle over verbalization is still waging. There are some who believe that the only way to teach is to permit the child to manipulate objects or wade into problems without instruction until he himself discovers the principles and procedures involved. There are others, like the RULEG theorists (see also Ausubel, 1963), who insist on stating principles and definitions first and emphasize the difficulties and inefficiencies of analogy and discovery. The research goes on. The programer must decide now. If the research is not much help in being sure of yourself, it may perhaps suggest a flexible and non-dogmatic approach to the solutions you yourself are most comfortable with.

Definitions. Should you verbalize? The major pitfall in verbalizing is coming up with the right set of words. School textbooks are full of definitions that don't define and principles that can't be applied because it is impossible to figure out what they really mean. The solid learning that takes place turns out to be exactly what the proponents of verbalizing are hoping to avoid—analogy and induction.

One kind of error is defining something in terms that themselves have no meaning. My favorite example is the hoary old *"A sentence expresses a complete thought."* No one has ever bothered to define "complete thought" and even "expresses" is a wee bit wobbly. The definition is totally useless as an aid to discriminating a sentence from a non-sentence.

Another kind of error is defining a relatively simple, easily exemplified concept in terms far more abstract than the concept itself. See any dictionary definition of words learned at your mother's knee. A "door," for instance, is "a means of access." Try that one as a prime on a three-year-old! But we do this far more frequently than we should at higher educational levels. (See the textbooks in your own subject area.)

The emphasis on examples in the RULEG system is worth emulating. The attempt to make terms meaningful by leading up to them through concrete or simple or familiar examples in EGRUL is worth considering. Even more important is Gilbert's emphasis on deriving the principles (the "domain theory" or way of verbalizing) from inspection of mastery behavior rather than teaching behavior in classroom or text. And lastly, remember the discrimination programing style, de-emphasizing verbalization in favor of discriminations that are real. These are choices each programer faces.

A prefix, eighth graders told me from textbook learning, is a "couple of letters tacked on to the front of a word." Beginning with that RU and generating examples of it would have omitted four-fifths of the prefixing that goes on in the English language.

Relevant Quote: When the relationship between teaching and concept analysis is made explicit, the teaching sequence can be evaluated more precisely. We know that the goal of the program is to teach the structure of the concept. If the programer does not account for all facets of the concept structure, we don't have to run empirical tests to say that the program is inadequate. An examination of the program will disclose its inadequacies. (Englemann, 1969.)

SUMMARY. MAINSTREAM PROGRAMING: CHOICES THE PROGRAMER FACES

The majority of programers are terribly eclectic and feel free to borrow anybody's good ideas. The systems presented in this chapter have dealt with the standard problems faced by all programers: How do I discover what it is I want to teach? How do I organize it? How do I teach it? There are areas of common agreement in all of them and areas suggesting conflicts which confront each programer with the necessity for making decisions. There are areas of omission which leave room for "art."

The RULEG and EGRUL approaches sprang primarily from academic sources. The emphasis was on both verbalization and problem solving; the subject matter was analyzed into sets of concepts and principles to be learned and to be applied to examples. RULEG programers preferred a deductive or priming approach, in which generalizations were stated for the student to master and apply, whereas EGRUL programers favored a more inductive approach in which examples, whenever possible, were used to prompt the generalizations. Each programer still has to choose between the "essence" of these approaches. Perhaps the "teaching style" or personality of the programer is one variable in the choice. The eclectic programer should be able to follow either procedure, choosing on the basis of the nature of the objective he is teaching to, the population the program is designed for, and the nature of the subject itself.

Discrimination programing (an EGEG system?) arose in good time as industrial programers became restless with the emphasis on verbalization in the older system, an emphasis which sometimes produced trainees who could list all the components of a machine but could not find any of them. When the nature of the task to be learned was discrimination, the nature of the instruction should parallel the objectives. Each programer still faces the issue: when is verbalization called for and when is it an insignificant part of what ought to be taught? Again, the eclectic programer should be capable of handling cases on both sides.

In any sociogram of programing systems, mathetics might be off in a corner by itself because of its language problems! But the practices of good matheticists—the large well-organized exercises with their minimal verbiage and straight-to-the-point methods of approaching subject matter—have had a strong effect on the thinking and practices of other programers. The basic formula—demonstrate, prompt, release—is extremely useful in clear-cut tasks. In procedural chains, backward chaining is a technique of lesson design that offers a programer a clear formula for producing a sequence. In both cases, matheticists stress keeping as much of the total task together in a unit as the student can accept at one time.

The problem that remains with each of the systems is the determination of what to teach— which RU's, which operants, which concepts. Academically oriented RULEG programers were likely to raid all the teaching resources they could find (texts, syllabi, etc.) looking for all the RU's in the subject. In a clear sense, they determined what ought to be taught by determining what had been taught. Discrimination programers and matheticists tend to put heavy emphasis on an analysis of what the trainee must do on the job as the source of what ought to be taught. In most industrial programing efforts, then, the content of existing training courses is not likely to be used to determine the content of the program. In introducing some of the ideas in the essay section on Concepts, I hoped to suggest that some of the inefficiencies of academic instruction might be eliminated by similar attention to the "job" of seeing the world as the subject matter experts do and by critical examination of some of the verbalisms and typical examples in existing teaching materials.

All programing systems, by definition, have been concerned with effectiveness, as defined by student performance. In recent years, emphasis on efficiency equals that given to effectiveness. There is consensus on many points. Structural definitions of step-size (30 words or less) are dead, replaced by functional definitions such as Gilbert's operant span. Early attempts to design fool-proof frames on the first draft by manipulation of copy frames, formal prompts, and other techniques discussed in Chapter 2 have given way to almost 100% agreement on deliberately designing first drafts that overestimate the student's capacity. The $RU + EG + \widetilde{EG}$ design, for instance, is less efficient than a $RU + \widetilde{EG}$ design (p. 157). The programer learns most from the errors his students make. No one believes that much useful evidence can be gathered from "undesigned" or poorly designed instruction! The most efficient final product results from a deliberate first-draft program that overestimates step size, underestimates required practice, and stretches generalizations to the limits. The programer knows what he is looking for when he takes his design to the student.

Relevant Quote: Correct student answers, long sought by non-sadistic programers, are a reasonable goal for the final product. But confusion between the development process and program evaluation has led many to overlook the fact that correct answers provide no useful inputs to the development process. Highly frequent correct answers early in the development process do not unambiguously demonstrate that the job is done, but suggest that the job has been done inefficiently. (D. G. Markle, 1967.)

Chapter 4
Adaptive Programing and Individual Differences

INTRODUCTION

The first Henry Ford is reputed to have said that car purchasers could have any color car they wished, as long as it was black. More recent calculations suggest that, given the options, accessories, and so forth that a car buyer now confronts, each buyer could have a custom made car, unlike any other car. Education, despite the quantity of words produced about individualizing instruction, has barely progressed beyond the "black car" state of affairs.

A student in school takes a relatively fixed number of courses, which meet for a relatively fixed number of clock hours, in which identical assignments are made to all students, and in which a standard examination is given at the end to "see how far he got." The convenient administrative unit is time—course hours for giving credit to the students and student-contact hours for deciding how hard-working a teacher is. Certain mild adjustments to this "egg-crate" system have been introduced in most schools, in the interests of individualizing instruction (tracking systems for differences in ability, differences in curricula for college and non-college-bound students, and such) without disturbing the basic unit of accounting, time.

Programed instruction works on a different accounting system, *achievement.* Rather than standardize the instructional time and allow the achievement to vary, programers attempt to standardize the achievement and let other factors vary. Each student is supposed to attain mastery. Given the fact of student differences, something else has to vary. This was one of Skinner's earliest talking points: "One of the great sources of inefficiency in modern education is due to our effort to teach a group of students at the same rate." (From the article you read at the beginning of this book.)

In Chapter 1, Section A, the term "linear" was introduced at the same time as the term "Skinnerian." At this point, we should define "linear" without respect to any theory or system that might determine other aspects of frame construction. A pure linear program presents a fixed sequence of steps taken by every student who goes through the program. A linear matheticist might make those steps very large, a linear discrimination programer might use multiple-choice responses most of the time, and a linear eclectic programer might try a little of everything. The key characteristic that makes the program linear, however, is the fixed sequence. In some recent group-paced audiovisual programs (Popham, 1965; Tiemann, Paden, and McIntrye, 1966; Markle and Tiemann, 1967), the pace at which the student goes through instruction is controlled by the medium. In the majority of linear programs, whether presented in text form or on machine, the rate at which students go through the fixed sequence of frames is allowed to vary. This is the only way in which a linear program is *adaptive* to students, if by adaptive we mean *capable of treating individuals differently on some basis or other.* A linear program has been adapted to the group, as we saw in Chapter 1, by the programer's revisions of instruction that failed and by the inclusion of everything necessary for the slowest member of the target population to attain the goals. Is time the only variable? Are there other ways to vary the treatment given to individuals? Some approaches to this question are considered in this chapter.

Before going further in this section, make a list of all the ways you can think of in which students can be given differential treatment in instructional matters.

The rate at which they can go through instruction is one, the solution to individualization implicit in linear programing. How many others can you think of? (There will be no confirmation of this list of yours. To confirm would put me in the position of having to list them all myself, and it is quite likely that no one has thought of them *all.* If you have fewer than five, you might want to give it some more thought. Keep your list to see how many of your suggestions have been anticipated by other people or actually put into practice in cases covered in the rest of this chapter.)

SECTION A. THE RATIONALE OF INTRINSIC PROGRAMING

Although there were some rumbles about individual differences in the earliest discussions of programing (see Markle, 1964), the strongest early objector to the linear idea was Norman A. Crowder, whose writings launched the "intrinsic programing" style. An early paper presents his views.

Read it through with the following questions in mind:

    (a) What is necessary for learning to occur, according to Crowder?
    (b) What role is given to individual differences?
    (c) What is the attitude toward errors?
    (d) On the above points, how does Crowder's approach differ from Skinner's?

PANEL 4-1

INTRINSIC PROGRAMING

Norman A. Crowder
(distributed by U.S. Industries)

The basic structure of intrinsically programmed material is quite simple. In each program step, the student is given a "unit" of material to read, usually a paragraph of thirty to seventy words. This material is followed by a multiple-choice question. The student's answer choice determines directly and automatically what material he will see next. If he chooses the right answer to the question, he is automatically presented with the next paragraph of material and the next question. If he chooses an incorrect answer, he is automatically presented with material written specifically to correct the particular error he has just made. At the end of this correctional material the student will, in the simplest case, be directed to return to the original presentation to have a second try at the original question, having completed a *first order* branch. However, the material at which the student arrives by making an error may be the start of a "subprogram," or subsequence, of instructional material and questions in which the originally troublesome point is explained in smaller steps or with a different approach. Such an arrangement of material would be an example of *second order* branching.

The crucial and identifying feature of intrinsically programmed materials is the fact that the material presented to each student is continuously and directly controlled by the student's performance in answering questions. To permit this step-by-step control of the program by the student, the questions are put in multiple-choice form. The choice of an answer to a multiple-choice question can be directly translated into a distinct physical act (turning to a particular page or pushing a particular button on a machine) which can then bring the appropriate material into view.

... A program with multiple-choice questions is not an intrinsic program unless each separate answer choice in each question leads the student to material prepared especially for the student who has made that particular choice.

The rationale of intrinsic programming postulates that the basic learning takes place during the student's exposure to the new material on each page. The multiple-choice question is asked to find out whether the student has learned; it is not necessarily conceived as playing an active part in the primary learning process involved.

We have based our technique on the possibility of detecting and correcting errors because we think it both impractical and undesirable to attempt to eliminate errors. We think it is impractical to eliminate errors because of the inevitable individual differences, both in ability and information, that will occur among our students. We think it is undesirable to eliminate errors, because to do so we would have to present material in such small steps and ask such easy questions that we would not be serving the educational objectives we desire to serve.

---

1. Consider the following statement by Norman Crowder:

   The rationale of intrinsic programing postulates that the basic learning takes place during the student's exposure to the new material on each page.

   Skinner's approach to the variables that determine learning was quite explicit: the student must be active, he must make the correct response since he would learn the response he made, and he must be given immediate knowledge of results (reinforcement).

   Crowder, in the statement above, is less explicit. Does he say that the student *must* be active?_____. Does he say that the student *need not* be active?_____.

   — — — — — — — — — — — — — — —

   No. No.

---

2. A frame in an intrinsic program presents a paragraph or so of material followed by a multiple-choice question. Consider how you might deal with such a situation.

   (a) If you have read the paragraph too rapidly and find yourself unable to answer the question, what would you do to help yourself?

   — — — — — — — — — — — — — —

   Most would go back to the paragraph and read it again, perhaps more carefully.

(b) If you are reading a paragraph, knowing that you are going to be tested on it, do you attend to the materials and anticipate possible questions, or do you read passively (as when you read a novel for enjoyment)?

―――――――――――――――

Most people would study in preparation for the question.

(c) In both of the above cases, the learning is taking place while you are exposing yourself to the material. Are you being an active student?_____.

―――――――――――――――

Yes.

3. Suppose that in a program on trigonometry we tell the student what a tangent is, provide him with an example of how one calculates tangents, and present him with a problem in which he has to calculate the tangent of some angle, such as:

> The tangent of angle A is
>
> .60 .... go to page 19.
> .75 .... go to page 6.
> .80 .... go to page 12.

Does he have to understand what he has been told if he is to answer this question *without guessing?*_____.

―――――――――――――――

Yes.

4. If the student is given a definition of "tangent" (either in words or by formula) and an example of how one calculates tangents, and then is asked to calculate one himself in order to choose an answer, what general category of frame design does the frame fall into?
_____.

―――――――――――――――

RULEG or RU + EG + $\widetilde{EG}$ (the terminology is not used by most intrinsic programers, but it fits many intrinsic frames).

5. Classical linear programs employ the constructed-response format—the student must compose or write something. Classical intrinsic programs employ the multiple-choice response format—the student selects an answer from a limited number of alternatives provided for him. Program format and student information-processing behavior are not necessarily the same thing, however.

Inspect these two frames in terms of what the student must do to answer:

A. Forgetting and extinction are technical terms for different processes. The response is *emitted* without reinforcement only in the process called (1)_____. The response is *not emitted* in the process called (2)_____.

(*The Analysis of Behavior*, Holland and Skinner)

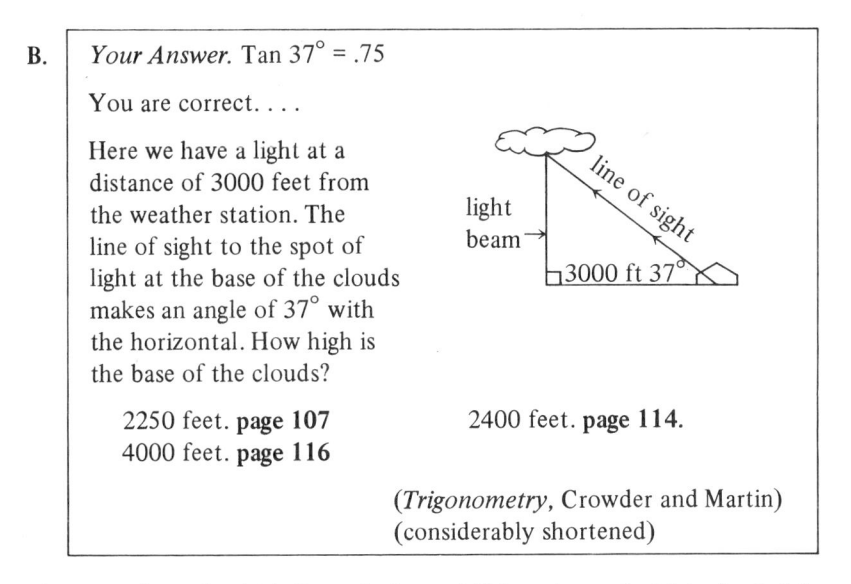

B. *Your Answer.* Tan 37° = .75

You are correct. . . .

Here we have a light at a distance of 3000 feet from the weather station. The line of sight to the spot of light at the base of the clouds makes an angle of 37° with the horizontal. How high is the base of the clouds?

2250 feet. **page 107** 2400 feet. **page 114**.
4000 feet. **page 116**

(*Trigonometry*, Crowder and Martin)
(considerably shortened)

There is no need to ask which frame is classical Skinnerian and which classical Crowderian programing! The authors are dead-giveaways.

In frame A, a student must [select/compose] one of two alternatives—"forgetting" or "extinction"—in order to [select/compose] his response.

In frame B, if we think of problem solving as a covert process of "composing" or arriving at an answer, a student must [select/compose] an answer to the problem in order to [select/compose] one of the alternatives.

— — — — — — — — — — — — —

Frame A: select (in order to) compose.

Frame B: compose (in order to) select.

6. In Frame 5 preceding, Example A was an *essentially* multiple-choice question in constructed-response format. The first sentence clearly directs the student to select one or the other word in order to fill in each of the blanks. The sequence prompt can also be used to make what *looks* like a constructed-response format into a multiple-choice type; e.g., the student knows that the answer has to be "vector" or "scalar," "prefix" or "suffix," etc., even though the programer has not provided the alternatives in the text of the item.

On the other hand, if the student is given a difficult enough problem to solve, we certainly would have to say that what he is going through could not be called "recognizing" the correct answer. In a program such as *Trigonometry,* students may be observed to be constructing the intermediate steps in the problem on their scratch pads before they select one of the alternatives.

In other words, for the majority of frames in a program,

(a) program format—multiple-choice or constructed-response—[does/does not] differentiate the two programing styles;

(b) student behavior in getting the answer—selecting or constructing an answer—[does/does not] differentiate the two programing styles.

(a) does

(b) does not

---

7. Crowder states that "the student's answer choice determines directly and automatically what material he will see next." The term INTRINSIC was adopted by Crowder to label this feature of his programing style. The *learner controls,* by the adequacy of his grasp of the material, the *exact sequence* that he will take from among the available tracks in the program.

Crowder often terms the linear style EXTRINSIC programing. What feature of linear programing does he mean when he uses the term "extrinsic"?

No matter what the student's response is, he goes on to the next item, or the programer controls the sequence.

8. Crowder states the following:

> In each program step, the student is given a "unit" of material to read . . . followed by a multiple-choice question. . . . If he chooses the right answer to the question, he is automatically presented with the next paragraph of material and the next question.

These units of material, which represent steps forward in mastering the subject matter, are termed the "mainstream" frames. Suppose a student is breezing along through the material, answering all the questions correctly. Does his progress resemble that of a student in a linear program? (Does the programer determine what he will see next?)_____.

Yes. The programer determines the order of mainstream frames just as a linear programer determines the order of his frames.

---

9. The sequence of mainstream frames, or steps forward, is linear in most intrinsic programs. However, the branching frames (remedial loops or first-order branches and subsequences or second-order branches) provide sidesteps for some students.

Suppose some students lack some information that is necessary for solving a problem in a program. An intrinsic programer might omit this information in his mainstream frame on the assumption that many of his students will know it. But he will provide an alternative to his question that will take those students who do not know the fact to a page where they will get the instruction they need.

If a *linear* programer finds, in testing his program, that some of his students do not know something that he thought they did, what does he do?

He writes a frame or several frames on the information they lack and puts these into his program. (Since the sequence arose from a problem requiring a remedy, we could call it a "remedial sequence." In the final draft, of course, it would be hard to identify which sequences arose this way. As far as the student is concerned, it would make no difference, since he would go through the frames whether we call them "remedial" or not and whether he needs this remediation or not.)

194 ADAPTIVE PROGRAMING AND INDIVIDUAL DIFFERENCES

10. Crowder stated that "we have based our technique on the possibility of detecting and correcting errors." The method of doing this is the provision of wrong alternatives to the multiple-choice question. Each incorrect alternative represents an error of some sort that a student might make.

    If you are programing the multiplication tables in the intrinsic style, you have a problem in designing your frames. In order to provide the extra help for each student who makes a particular kind of mistake, what do you need to know in order to determine what alternatives to provide for your question?

    You have to know what kinds of mistakes students make.

---

11. In a trigonometry problem, we might provide the following alternatives:

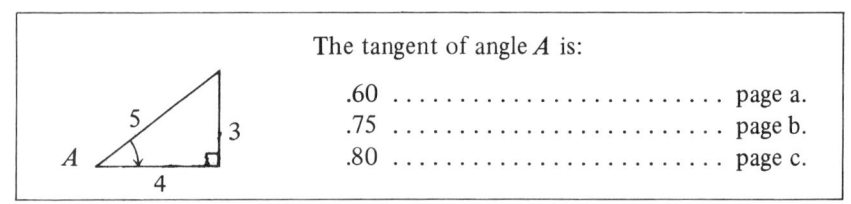

    > The tangent of angle A is:
    > .60 .... page a.
    > .75 .... page b.
    > .80 .... page c.

    (a) If the student thinks 3/5, he should arrive at .60. If he thinks 3/4, he should arrive at .75. If he thinks 4/5, he should arrive at .80. Given a correct answer of 3/4, what obvious alternative, which a student might construct, is missing?_____.

    4/3 would lead to 1.33 (getting the equation upside down would be an obvious kind of error).

    (b) If we give all four logical alternatives (only one of which is correct, of course), have we covered all errors that the student might make?_____.

    The assumption that the student's error is logical is only an assumption.

THE RATIONALE OF INTRINSIC PROGRAMING 195

12. Multiple choice, as a formal prompt, would operate in a fashion similar to giving the number of blanks in a word or one of its letters, etc. After the student has generated a response, he checks its fit.

    Suppose, in the problem above, that the student correctly says 3/4, then thinks that 3/4 is 70%. What happens to this response (.70) when he looks at the alternatives?

    — — — — — — — — — — — — — — — —

    Since it does not fit, he has to throw it out and find a better one. He could, of course, see which alternative is closest to his answer.

13. If the student taking an intrinsic program does not understand what is wrong with his incorrect answer, and if it does not match one of the alternatives, will he get the remedial instruction he needs?_____.

    — — — — — — — — — — — — — — — —

    No.

14. In a *linear* program, if the student makes an error, he finds it when he checks his answer with the correct answer (knowledge of results) provided. If this "linear" student does not understand why his answer is incorrect or why the correct answer is what it is, does he get the remedial help he needs from the program?_____.

    — — — — — — — — — — — — — — — —

    In most cases, no. Some programers provide discussion along with the correct answer.

15. In his description of linear programing, Skinner stated:

    > Like a good tutor, the machine insists that a given point be thoroughly understood, either frame by frame or set by set, before the student moves on.

    Unfortunately, by appropriate use of too many copying frames and too many prompts, this goal can easily be violated and never show up in the error data.

    Crowder describes intrinsic programing in equally glowing terms:

196 ADAPTIVE PROGRAMING AND INDIVIDUAL DIFFERENCES

> The crucial and identifying feature of intrinsically programmed materials is the fact that the material presented to each student is continuously and directly controlled by the student's performance in answering questions.

How can this goal be violated in the intrinsic format?

— — — — — — — — — — — — — — —

(One or more.) By asking too easy questions, by not providing all the alternatives that a student might choose, or by not questioning at all on something difficult.

---

16. Modern linear programers sometimes put their frames into the multiple-choice format. Does such a multiple-choice frame make that section of the linear program into an intrinsic section?_____. Why?
If you want a hint, drop down to the next line.

— — — — — — — — — — — — — — —

Hint. Crowder states:

> A program with multiple-choice questions is not an intrinsic program unless each separate answer choice in each question leads the student to material prepared especially for the student who has made that particular choice.

Why is a multiple-choice format not intrinsic in a linear program?

— — — — — — — — — — — — — — —

In a linear multiple-choice program, the student goes on to the next frame whether right or not.

SECTION B. A CLOSE LOOK AT A SEGMENT OF AN INTRINSIC PROGRAM

Intrinsic programs are typically presented in one of two ways: on a teaching machine or in a scrambled book. If the segment of the program you are to analyze were presented on a teaching machine, you would have no problem running through it. Each multiple-choice alternative

A CLOSE LOOK AT A SEGMENT OF AN INTRINSIC PROGRAM 197

would instruct you to press a button which would automatically advance you to the frame you chose. A scrambled book, however, is a rather complex invention. The pages are NOT read in order. The student (and the analyst) must follow directions very carefully. If he doesn't, he is likely to get a strong dose of the illogical sequencing we mentioned at the beginning of Chapter 3!

If you are familiar with the format of a scrambled book, take a brief look at the way we have "unscrambled" the book in the segment of program presented on pages 198-201, and then go directly to page 202 for further directions.

If you are NOT familiar with the format of a scrambled book, complete the following questions. They are all observation questions. Once you are looking in the right place, you should be certain of your answer. (If you wish to check your perceptions, the correct answers to these questions are given on page 210.)

Observe.

1. The segment contains several pages from a "scrambled book," the kind of book in which the student does not read one page and then the next. We have separated one page from another by dashed lines (– – – –). How many pages from the book are on the *second* page of the segment (i.e., p. 199 of this book)?
2. At the top right hand page of each of our "pages" (separated by – – – –) is the actual page number as in the book. The first page given here is page_____in the book.
3. The second page given is actually page_____in the book.
4. Next to the page number in the book, you will always find the number of the page [you came from/you are going to].
5. Each frame in this intrinsic program begins with the words "_____ _____."
6. At the bottom of the mainstream frame, page 21, there is a [multiple-choice/constructed-response] question.
7. How many alternatives are given?
8. If the student selects the ace of hearts as his answer to page 21's question, the directions tell him to turn to page_____in the book.
9. If the student turns to page 3, he is told [that he was wrong/why he was wrong].
10. When he has finished reading page 3, where does he go next?
11. Pages 3, 7, and 12 are all wrong-answer pages. If the student selects the correct answer, he goes to page 18. This is the next step forward in the program. Is this backwards or forwards in the *book that he is reading?*
12. In a scrambled book, the direction for the page that you turn to [is/is not] a clue to the correctness of the answer.

Figure This One Out.

13. You can get to a mainstream frame *only* by answering the previous mainstream frame correctly. The *first* mainstream frame is on page 1 of the book. Page 21 is the *third* mainstream frame. What is the page number of the *second* mainstream frame?

PANEL 4-2

SEGMENT OF AN INTRINSIC PROGRAM

Charles H. Goren, *The Elements of Bridge*
(Doubleday, 1960)

21 (from page 11)

Your Answer. Of the thirteen cards in any one suit, you would rather hold the Ace.

1. You are right, of course. The object in bridge, as in most other games, is to win. Since the highest-ranking card in a suit wins over, or captures, any of the lower-ranking cards in the same suit, it would be better to hold the Ace.
2. There are also times when any card of one of the four suits will beat any card of the other three. This is when that suit has been named "trumps."
3. We will explain later how a trump suit is named and when it is permissible to use trumps to capture cards of other suits. For now you should simply remember that any card in a trump suit—even Deuce or Trey—will capture any of the other three suits.
4. There is no suit that is always or usually trumps. In the course of several games, each of the suits will be trumps at some time or other. Depending upon the distribution of cards among the four players, any suit may be named trumps.

Now suppose Clubs have been named trumps and the four cards listed below have been legally played. Which will win?

| Ace of Hearts. | **page 3** | 10 of Hearts. | **page 7** |
| 5 of Clubs. | **page 12** | 7 of Clubs. | **page 18** |

A CLOSE LOOK AT A SEGMENT OF AN INTRINSIC PROGRAM 199

3 (from page 21)

Your Answer. The Ace of Hearts would win.

It would have won if it had not been "trumped." But two players played trump cards. Any card of a trump suit will take any card of another suit. Since Clubs have been named trump, the Ace of Hearts (or any other Heart) will lose to any Club.

Return to page 21 and look again at all the cards played. Then choose another answer.

----

7 (from page 21)

Your Answer. The 10 of Hearts would win.

It is suspected that you are not paying attention! Any one of the other three cards played would beat the 10 of Hearts in this situation.

Turn back to page 21 and review this whole question of the rank of cards within a suit.

----

12 (from page 21)

Your Answer. The 5 of Clubs would win.

It is true that the 5 of Clubs is a trump card, and any card of a trump suit will take any card of any other suit.

However, remember our discussion of the *rank* of cards within each suit. We pointed out that a card will win over every lower-ranking card in its own suit. This holds true in a trump suit.

The 5 of Clubs was *not* the highest trump card played. So it would not win in this case.

Please return to page 21 and select another answer.

----

18 (from page 21)

Your Answer. The 7 of Clubs will win over the others.

This is correct. Clubs are trumps and the 7 of Clubs is the highest trump played.

The suits have another order or rank which we might mention now. In choosing sides and in bidding, the suits are ranked in the following way, from highest to lowest: Spades, Hearts, Diamonds, Clubs.

This rank has little to do with play of the hand. A 10 of Hearts cannot be captured or taken by a 10 of Spades unless Spades happen to be trump that hand. But, as we will see later, the rank of suits has great importance in the bidding and in:

THE DRAW

Bridge is played by four players. They play in partnerships, each player seated across the table from his partner.

To choose partners, the deck is spread face down on the table, and each player draws a card. The player holding the highest-ranking card is the dealer, and also has the choice of seats. The player with the second-ranking card is his partner.

The other two players also play as partners and take the other two seats to the left and right of the dealer.

Any Ace drawn will rank higher than any King, of course, but if two Aces are drawn, the higher suit rank wins. For example, the Ace of Diamonds is higher than the Ace of Clubs. A card's rank in its own suit comes first, however. Thus the 5 of Clubs is higher than the 4 of Spades. The rank of the suits—Spades, Hearts, Diamonds, Clubs—is only used to break a tie.

If players draw as follows, who will be partners? Player No. 1: 10 of Spades; Player No. 2: 10 of Hearts; Player No. 3: Jack of Clubs; Player No. 4: Deuce of Diamonds.

Players 1 and 2 will be partners against 3 and 4.	**page 8**
Players 1 and 3 will be partners against 2 and 4.	**page 26**
Players 1 and 4 will be partners against 2 and 3.	**page 13**

26 (from page 18)

Your Answer. Players 1 and 3 will be partners.

You are correct. The 10 of Spades outranks the 10 of Hearts. The player who draws the 10 of Spades therefore teams up with the player who drew the highest-ranking card, the Jack of Clubs.

THE CUT AND DEAL

The draw for partners also determines who shall be the first *dealer.* The player drawing the highest-ranking card *deals,* or passes out, the cards for the first hand of bridge. In the preceding example, the Jack of Clubs was the highest ranking card drawn, and so the player who drew it became the first dealer.

If players draw the following cards, who becomes the first *dealer?* Ace of Diamonds, Queen of Spades, King of Hearts, Ace of Clubs.

>Ace of Diamonds. **page 5**
>Queen of Spades. **page 14**
>King of Hearts. **page 19**
>Ace of Clubs. **page 22**

The program segment contains the third, fourth, and fifth mainstream frames from the bridge program. It also contains the wrong-answer pages for the first of these frames. Read through the segment (including the wrong-answer pages) with the following study questions in mind:

(a) The multiple-choice question is supposed to test the student's understanding of the material. Do the questions require that the student attend to the material in the frame? (If he does not guess and does not already know the answer, do the questions *test* his acquisition of the material?).

(b) If the student has not understood, his error should lead him to the kind of help that he needs. Do the wrong-answer frames represent *different* content for students with *different* difficulties?

(c) Does the programer take into account all the logically possible mistakes that the student might make?

1. Since four people play bridge and each one plays a single card at any one time, only four cards may be played. Given the number of alternatives that the programer has employed in mainstream page 21, has he covered all possible answers to the question?

— — — — — — — — — — — — —

Yes. All four are there.

---

2. In a very clear sense, the multiple-choice question at the bottom of the page in an intrinsic program forces the student to interact with the materials in much the same way as a blank in a constructed-response frame does. He simply cannot get off the page without answering it.

Page 21 of the bridge program contains a considerable amount of material. Does the question provided there test the student's understanding of the *fourth* paragraph of the text? _____ .

— — — — — — — — — — — — —

No. A student could get through this page with the idea that clubs are always trumps and this misconception would not be corrected at this point.

---

3. We assume that reasonable programers will, of course, construct questions that are relevant to the material contained on the page. If learning takes place, as Crowder hypothesizes, "during the student's exposure to the new material on the page," is it necessary for the multiple-choice question to employ every bit of knowledge that the student has picked up? _____ .

— — — — — — — — — — — — —

I would think not, according to such a theory.

4. Locate at least one bit of information below the heading "The Draw" that is not covered by the question on page 18 of the bridge program._____.

— — — — — — — — — — — — — — —

Any of the following: who sits where, who deals, how the cards are placed for the draw.

---

5. Although a student is not supposed to be able to get through the "test" question without understanding the text, it is, of course, possible to do so in a multiple-choice format. What are the student's chances of being correct even if he does not read the material on page 21?_____.

— — — — — — — — — — — — — — —

One in four, or 25%.

---

6. A student who does not understand the material has one chance in four of being correct on his *first* guess. Can you think of another eventuality that would get him to the next mainstream frame even if he did not understand and made all sorts of mistakes?

— — — — — — — — — — — — — — —

Eventually, he is going to run out of wrong-answer choices, and he will have nowhere else to go.

---

7. Suppose such a thing happened to a student as he struggled with page 18. Having chosen page 8 and page 13, he ends up on page 26, still not sure why he is there. Is he given any help when he gets there?_____.

— — — — — — — — — — — — — — —

Yes. The situation is explained to him.

204 ADAPTIVE PROGRAMING AND INDIVIDUAL DIFFERENCES

8. In the glossary, the term *feedback* is defined as follows: "the sentence or paragraph which discusses why the answer the student chose is correct or incorrect."
Feedback therefore occurs [only on mainstream frames/only on wrong-answer pages/on both/on neither]._____.

– – – – – – – – – – – – – – – –

on both.

---

9. How does feedback differ from the confirmation or knowledge of results provided in a classical linear program?

– – – – – – – – – – – – – – – –

(In your own words.) Confirmation simply states what the answer should have been, whereas feedback tells why.

---

10. Could other programers employ the technique of providing feedback along with knowledge of results?_____.

– – – – – – – – – – – – – – – –

Why not? Throughout this book, you've been advised to adopt anything that looks useful from any system. That's being eclectic!

Historical Aside. More often than we like to think, historical accidents determine policy. Skinner's first teaching machine "caused" some of the conventions adopted by classical linear programers. In the machine, the amount of space provided for confirmation was extremely limited—it would not have been possible to discuss the reasons for the right answer. When linear programers moved to programed textbooks, they still behaved as if they were restricted by the old machine! Crowder's machine, on the other hand, provided a large amount of space for presenting frames, derived of course from his theory that large chunks of material should be presented at once. Since there was so much space, the programer could use some of it for feedback or discussion, repeating the main points of what he had just questioned the student on.

11. Wrong-answer pages come in two different styles, as Crowder noted in his article. One type, a remedial loop or "first-order branch," consists solely of feedback and returns the student to the page from whence he came, so that he can have another try at the question. A subsequence or "second-order branch" generally contains more extensive material than a remedial loop. Its distinguishing characteristic is that the student is asked a new question testing his grasp of the material that he has just read. Eventually, the student gets back to the mainstream of the program.

(a) Is page 3 of the bridge program a remedial loop or a subsequence? _____.
How do you know?

- - - - - - - - - - - - - - -

remedial loop (it sends the student back to page 21 with no question on the material he just read).

(b) How would you distinguish between a mainstream frame and the opening frame in a subsequence, if you had one of each to inspect?

Drop down one line for a hint, if you need it.

- - - - - - - - - - - - - - -

Hint. When the student chooses the correct answer, he is sent to the next mainstream frame, which repeats his answer, tells him that he is correct, and tells him why he is correct. How would this differ from a frame in a subsequence?

- - - - - - - - - - - - - - -

A subsequence would begin by telling the student why he was wrong, whereas a mainstream frame tells him why he is correct.

12. A standard mainstream frame in an intrinsic program contains six parts:

    (a) the answer the student chose in the last frame;
    (b) feedback, or discussion of why the answer is correct;
    (c) new information;
    (d) a question testing his comprehension of the new information;
    (e) two or more alternative answers to select from; and
    (f) a page number (or on a machine, a button designation) telling him where to go next for each alternative.

    A subsequence would resemble a mainstream frame except, as you just noted, it would tell the student why he was wrong. The new information would be something *he* needed but that other students, who had not chosen that answer, did not need. For instance, it might be a simpler explanation of a point that he had already read about but obviously had not mastered.

    Inspect the three remedial loops provided for the bridge program's frame 21. (They are all together on page 199.) Do these remedial loops consist solely of feedback (repetition of previously covered points) or do they contain new information the student has never seen before?

    _____ solely feedback
    _____ also new information

    _ _ _ _ _ _ _ _ _ _ _ _ _ _ _ _

    The wrong-answer pages consist solely of feedback. Two of them discuss the problem of rank and the third discusses trumping of high cards. Both of these subjects have already been presented in mainstream frames 11 and 21, respectively.

13. If the student has already been told about the rank of cards in a suit and about trumps, what is the cause of his error? In other words, why would a student pick one of the incorrect alternatives given on page 21 of the bridge program?

    _ _ _ _ _ _ _ _ _ _ _ _ _ _ _ _

    (In your own words.) He did not understand what he read or did not read carefully.

14. Crowder's position on errors was:

> We think it is impractical to eliminate errors because of the inevitable individual differences, both in *ability* and *information,* that will occur among our students.

When the writer of the bridge program designed the wrong-answer frames for the question on page 21, which cause of error was he attempting to remedy?_____.

Ability (either reading ability or ability to absorb information very fast).

---

15. The following frame begins a discussion of geometrical concepts:

> You should know that an angle is a geometric figure formed by two line segments drawn from the same point or vertex. Thus
>
> $$\angle \begin{array}{c} A \\ B C \end{array}$$
>
> An angle usually is designated by capital letters placed at the vertex and sides of the angle, as shown above. In this case, we might speak of the diagram as showing angle *ABC* (with the vertex letter in the middle), or as $\angle ABC$, or just as $\angle B$.
>
> Angles, as you know, are measured in degrees. A circle contains 360 degrees (360°).
>
> You should remember the answer to this question:
> How many degrees are there in a right angle?
>
>   45°. **page 29**   90°. **page 38**   100°. **page 42**
>
>   (*Trigonometry,* Crowder and Martin)

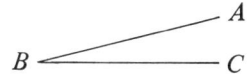

The phrases "you should know," "as you know," and "you should remember" are clear indications of the programer's assumptions about the nature of this frame and its purpose in the program. If the student selects an incorrect answer here, what is the source of his error according to Crowder's classification?_____.

Lack of information.

16. Lack of information, as a source of error, refers to assumed entering behavior—what the student already knows when he comes to the program. It is true that he may, in later frames, have forgotten information from early frames. Other programers would attribute this to insufficient practice, and, in Crowder's classification, we could put it with "lack of ability." The student is a slow learner in comparison with what is expected of him.

    If students were forgetting information from early frames, the linear programer will adjust his program in such a way that the concepts, facts, etc., are reviewed more frequently by additional questions on them that require active responses.

    How might an intrinsic programer review? Name one way that would not depend on the student making an error.

    Is this consistent with the theory of learning Crowder proposes? _____.

    — — — — — — — — — — — — — — —

    If students learn from exposure, the point could be mentioned now and then, where relevant, in order to keep it fresh. This would be perfectly consistent with Crowder's rationale.

17. From what you see in the three mainstream frames of the bridge program, will the programer have to review the concept of card ranks and suit ranks when the student correctly turns to page 5 from page 26? _____.

    — — — — — — — — — — — — — — —

    I would think not, since he has presented several problems. All these frames require knowledge of card ranks, and the last two test for suit ranks.

18. What important concept might he have to review the next time that he wants the students to remember it? (What did he introduce and then drop?) _____.

    — — — — — — — — — — — — — — —

    Trumps (two complex frames have come after the introduction of the concept).

A CLOSE LOOK AT A SEGMENT OF AN INTRINSIC PROGRAM 209

19. The answer to the question on page 26 depends on comprehension of two aspects of card ranks: (a) within-suit rank of cards and (b) rank of suits. As an exercise, outline the content that will have to be dealt with in each of the wrong-answer pages for that frame.

I would assume that page 14 would remind the student that the rank of the card comes first (since he picked the highest-ranking suit); that page 22 would remind him of the relative ranks of diamonds and clubs; and that page 19 would take up both points, since he has missed on both points.

20. On page 18, the relative ranking of four suits is given to the student, and he is required to use only two of these in solving the problem. What basic principle of programing would such a frame design violate? _____.

Active responding. He is not required to respond to half of the list.

21. On page 26 in the bridge program, the first paragraph deals with who teams up with whom, whereas the rest of the frame deals with the dealer. This apparent change of subject in the middle of a frame is a standard occurrence in an intrinsic frame. What causes the change in subject?

The first subject is feedback from the previous frame.

22. If you were analyzing how much of the material introduced in an intrinsic frame was tested by the question, would you include the feedback section among the material that should be tested by the question? _____ .

— — — — — — — — — — — — — — —

The question asked what you would do. Since feedback is a recapitulation of previous material, I would not expect it to be included necessarily in material to be tested by the question.

Summary: Sections A and B

In the majority of intrinsic programs, a sizable amount of text is presented to the student, followed by a multiple-choice question testing his comprehension of the material. The material that the student will see next depends on his selection of one of the alternatives. If his choice is incorrect, he is given some remedial instruction and (a) returned for another try at the question (remedial loop), or (b) given a new question on the remedial material (subsequence) and later returned to the mainstream. Intrinsic programers expect some errors, either as a function of variation in student ability or as a function of previous training.

The role of active responding is not central in intrinsic theory. Intrinsic programers offer less guidance to students as to what material in the frame is important.

Relevant Quote: There is face validity in the proposition that differences in individuals' past histories and innate abilities are best accommodated by programs which adjust to the performance of the individual. . . . Some programers make branching their principal tool. Other programers suggest that branching is rarely necessary. . . . The issue has become a red herring with debates regarding 'branching versus fixed sequence,' ignoring the need for analysis of difference among tasks and the related problems of diagnosing differences among subjects. (Holland, 1965.)

Answers to Observation Questions, page 197.

1. Three—3, 7, and 12.
2. Page 21.
3. Page 3.
4. You came from.
5. *Your Answer.*
6. Multiple-choice.
7. Four.
8. Page 3.
9. Why he is wrong.
10. Back to page 21.
11. Backwards (he is on page 21).
12. Is not.
13. Page 11 (that's where he came from in order to get onto page 21).

SECTION C: PROMPTING IN THE INTRINSIC FORMAT

INTRODUCTION

Although intrinsic programers rarely talk about prompting, the analysis of intrinsic frames in terms of their prompting structure and function as introductory, practice, and terminal frames is possible. There are problems with the intrinsic format in arriving at a frame in which the *only* prompt is the set of alternatives, a formal prompt that is always there. This section looks at the problems.

1.
> 49 (from page 62).
>
> *Your Answer.* $(7^2)(7^3) = 7^5$.
>
> You are correct. Very well, what is the product of $(b^3)(b^4)$?
>
> $(b^3)(b^4) = b^{12}$. **page 56**
>
> $(b^3)(b^4) = b^7$. **page 63**
>
> (*The Arithmetic of Computers,* Crowder)

The standard intrinsic frame includes six parts:

(a) the answer that the student chose in the last frame;
(b) feedback, or discussion of why the answer is correct;
(c) new information;
(d) a question testing his comprehension;
(e) two or more alternative answers to select from; and
(f) a page number (or button code) telling him where to go next for each alternative.

Inspect the frame above. It is missing two of the standard components. On the basis of the two that are missing, what is the function of this frame? In other words, does the question test new knowledge, does it practice previously learned material, or does it test previous (outside the program) knowledge in order to branch the uninformed student? _____

- - - - - - - - - - - - - - -

It is a practice frame (feedback and new instruction are missing and the problem in the frame is very similar to the one from the frame before, except that b has been substituted for a numeral and a new set of exponents used.)

212   ADAPTIVE PROGRAMING AND INDIVIDUAL DIFFERENCES

2.
> 3b (from 4a).
>
> Very good.
>
> $(8, -2, 3)$ is certainly a vector. It is an ordered group of three numbers written in the proper manner, that is, separated by commas and placed in curved brackets. The second number of the group, -2, is a negative number, but this is perfectly legitimate. *Any* numbers or even symbols representing numbers, may be members of the group.
>
> Is $(X, Y, 4, -1, 0)$ a vector?
>
> > Yes (page 15b).
> > No (page 17b).
>
> (*Vectors,* Carman)

This particular program has a space-saving device that we have not seen before in the previous frames. When two frames will fit on a page, the page has two levels—an *a* and a *b* level. Hence, the letters accompanying page numbers.

Although the format adopted by this author is different from Crowder's, his frames may be analyzed into the same six components: answer, feedback, information, question, alternatives, and directions for the next frame.

In the frame above, is everything included or is one or more of these six parts missing? _____. If you answered yes to the latter, which one or ones?

— — — — — — — — — — — — — — —

They are all there. (The answer is obvious although not set off—the first vector; the feedback in this case is the largest part of the item; new information is "even symbols," which is what the question tests; question, alternatives, and directions are obvious.)

3.
> 21
>
> You said that amplifying a microwave means to increase the size of the oscillations. Good! You are correct!
>
> Just to be sure you understand the two functions of a klystron see if you can answer one more question.
>
> Klystrons that generate microwaves are called:
>
> > (a) amplifiers .... page 23
> > (b) oscillators .... page 24
>
> (*Klystrons,* Kantor and Mager)

PROMPTING IN THE INTRINSIC FORMAT 213

Are all six parts of a standard frame included in the above frame?_____. If not, which one or ones are missing?

- - - - - - - - - - - - - - -

No. There is no feedback in the sense of discussion of why the answer is correct, and no new information.

4. Removing the feedback is one technique of reducing the amount of prompting in an intrinsic frame. In the above frame, the question tests learning that took place in an earlier frame, in fact, the preceding frame. If feedback had been given, the answer to this particular frame would probably have been given away, reducing this frame to a "copying" type of multiple-choice frame.

   The frame is prompted, however, and quite strongly so. Sequence prompting is at work. What else makes it highly unlikely that the student would equate "generate" with "amplifiers" and thereby choose to wrong alternative? Where is the prompt?

- - - - - - - - - - - - - - -

The previous answer, which is repeated, equates "amplify" with "increase the size," which is not the same as "generate." Therefore, "amplifiers" must be incorrect. The frame design parallels rather closely the $\overline{RU}$ (RU-bar, or instruction what NOT to do) discussed in Chapter 3 (page 143).

5. Would it be possible to allow the student to see the answer to a previous question, to be given feedback, and yet to have the multiple-choice question to a terminal question? _____. If so, how?

- - - - - - - - - - - - - - -

Yes. All that is necessary is that both the immediately preceding question for which the answer is repeated and the given feedback be on something different from the question that you want to be a terminal question.

6.
> 49 (from page 62).
>
> *Your Answer.* $(7^2)(7^3) = 7^5$.
>
> You are correct. Very well, what is the product of $(b^3)(b^4)$?
>
> $(b^3)(b^4) = b^{12}$. **page 56**
> $(b^3)(b^4) = b^7$. **page 63**
>
> (*The Arithmetic of Computers,* Crowder)

This frame lacks feedback and new information and, therefore, is a practice or review frame. It represents a step forward, however, since the student is now dealing with literal problems. Since these are tested, not taught, in this "transitional" frame, the student is expected to make the transition without instruction.

There is a strong prompt operating in the frame in conjunction with the formal prompt provided by the multiple-choice answer. What is the prompt?

- - - - - - - - - - - - - - -

The previous answer is an EG similar to the present problem and, therefore, a thematic prompt for addition. As before, the RULEG terminology fits nicely–this is an EG-ẼG frame.

7.
> 74
>
> You said that after the electrons are reflected they are returned to the cavity. Correct!
>
> Here's another question.
> Each time the bunches of _____ return to the cavity, they strengthen (increase the amplitude of oscillation of) the _____ in the cavity.
> The two missing words are
>
> (a) electrons, microwaves .... page 76
> (b) microwaves, microwaves .... page 77
> (c) microwaves, electrons .... page 78
>
> (*Klystrons,* Kantor & Mager)

Surprise! Although this is certainly an intrinsic program and the answer is certainly multiple-choice, it at least looks like a constructed-response frame.

How does this frame compare with the "forced choice" frame sometimes seen in linear programs? For example, this one:

> The word BOY is singular, but the word BOYS is [singular/plural].

Hint. Notice the parallel in the *Klystrons* frame between the answer that the student just chose and the opening part of the question that he is asked this time. Then look at the alternatives.

Answer the question: How do these two frames compare in terms of controlling the correct response?_____.

- - - - - - - - - - - - - - -

They are both forced choices—in both cases, the student is fed the answer. In both cases, then, the step forward is very small.

8.
> 40 (from page 46).
>
> *Your Answer.* A right triangle with one 60° angle in it is a 60° right triangle.
>
> You are correct. Very good. A 60° right triangle would have one 60° angle and, of course, one 90° angle. What would be the size, in degrees, of the third angle in such a triangle?
>
>   30°. **page 36**
>   40°. **page 48**
>   We can't find out without more information. **page 58**
>
>   (*Trigonometry,* Crowder and Martin)

In order to answer this frame for the right reasons rather than by guessing, the student must have in his repertoire a key fact about triangles—the sum of the angles is 180°. Is he told the information *in this* frame?_____.

Is this a practice frame? [Yes/No/Cannot tell.]

Is this a pretest frame for selecting students who need remedial information? [Yes/No/Cannot tell.]

- - - - - - - - - - - - - - -

No, the information is not in the frame.

You cannot tell what kind of frame this is.

9. By analyzing the information necessary to answer a question, it is easy to discriminate a mainstream frame, which imparts new information, from the other two, which are lacking essential information.

Where would you have to look in order to discriminate whether a frame such as the one above was a practice frame (testing information taught in the program) or a pretest frame (testing entering behavior)?

— — — — — — — — — — — — — — —

You would have to go back into earlier frames in the mainstream. If the information is there, this is a practice frame; if not, it is a pretest. (In this actual case, the frame is a pretest—the 180° information is given only in remedial loops.)

10.
> 13 (from page 18).
>
> *Your Answer.* If $ad = bc$, then $a = bcd$.
>
> No, it's not as easy as that. You can't just arbitrarily move letters from one side of the equals sign to the other.
>
> We have seen that to undo a division, as indicated by a fraction, we use multiplication. It follows then that to undo a multiplication, we will have to use division.
>
> (Solution of equation for a illustrated at length)
>
> And here we have the equation solved for a in terms of b, c, and d.
>
> Now suppose you were asked to solve the equation $ad = bc$ for c. What is c equal to in terms of a, b, and d?
>
> $c = \dfrac{b}{ad}$.   page 20
>
> $c = abd$.   page 28
>
> $c = \dfrac{ad}{b}$.   page 31
>
> (*Trigonometry*, Crowder and Martin)

Is this frame (a) a mainstream frame, (b) a remedial loop, (c) or a frame from a subsequence? _____. How do you know? What distinguishes one type from each of the other types of frames?

— — — — — — — — — — — — — —

(c) It is part of a subsequence, because it is arrived at only if the student makes an error on page 18 (which differentiates it from mainstream frames) and yet it contains a branching question (which differentiates it from remedial loops).

11. Page 18, the mainstream frame leading into this subsequence, asks the student to solve for a given the equation $ad = bc$. Frame 18 itself does not instruct him on how to do this. Therefore the question on page 18 was a [test of the student's understanding of the frame/ a pretest or selection device for remedial instruction].

— — — — — — — — — — — — — —

pretest (he is not told unless he makes an error).

218 ADAPTIVE PROGRAMING AND INDIVIDUAL DIFFERENCES

12.
> 13 (from page 18).
>
> *Your Answer.* If $ad = bc$, then $a = bcd$.
>
> No, it's not as easy as that . . . . etc.
>
> (Instruction on how to solve for one term, a.)
>
> Now suppose you were asked to solve the equation $ad = bc$ for c. What is c equal to in terms of a, b, and d?
>
> $c = \dfrac{b}{ad}.$ page 20
>
> $c = abd.$ page 28
>
> $c = \dfrac{ad}{b}.$ page 31   (*Trigonometry*, Crowder and Martin)

The question given on page 13 above is a [test of the student's understanding of the frame/a selection device or pretest for remedial instruction].

Notice that the student is allowed to make exactly the same mistake on frame 13 as he did on frame 18. The second alternative ($c = abd$) is exactly parallel to the wrong alternative that brought him *to* this frame. On the basis of your knowledge of human nature (programer's nature, that is), do you think that a student who turns to page 28 from 13 is going to get a subsubsequence or a remedial loop referring him back to 13? _____ .

— — — — — — — — — — — — — — —

test of understanding (of this frame).

Your choice, depending on how much punishment you think programers can take in generating more and more remedial material! The truth in this case is that he will get a remedial loop.

---

13. Think about this one:

At the beginning of paragraph two in his article, Crowder identifies the "crucial and identifying feature of intrinsically programed materials." Compare his statement with the reality exemplified by the remedial loops or first-order branches as shown in the Bridge program.

Does a first-order branch satisfy the theory of intrinsic programing? _____ .

— — — — — — — — — — — — — —

If you say "yes," describe why you think so and go to page 219.

If you say "no," describe why you think so and go to page 220.

You said "yes," a first-order branch satisfies the theory of intrinsic programing.

Crowder states that "the material presented to each student is continuously and directly controlled by the student's performance in answering questions."

Try this intrinsic sequence:

> Twas brillig and the slithy toves
> Did gyre and gimbel in the wabe.
>
> As everyone knows, a slithy tove is easier to gramlet than a winkle tove is. When you gramlet a winkle tove, you have to take the lamersary into account.
>
> Taking the lamersary into account, gramlet this winkle tove:
>
> ∞
>
> (a) I get a semi-ham (page x).
> (b) It becomes a demi-gob (page y).
> (c) I don't understand (page z).

Being honest and willing to learn, you pick page z and find:

> *Your Answer.* I don't understand.
>
> Well, let's see if we can clear up the difficulty. Perhaps you have forgotten about the globels that you studied in school. Remember that a globel is much like a tove, although it can't gyre. When you gramlet a globel, it looks like this:
>
> $\triangle \triangleright$
>
> With this in mind, return to frame Q and choose another answer.

On the basis of this demonstration (taken seriously), what can go wrong with a first-order branch?

— — — — — — — — — — — — — — — —

Answer is on page 220.

According to intrinsic theory (a) a student learns from reading, (b) the question is employed as a check on his understanding of what he read, and (c) depending on whether he lacked certain knowledge or misunderstood what he read, he is sent to different sets of materials.

A first-order branch or remedial loop contains no question and sends the student back to the mainstream whether or not he understood what was told him in the remedial instruction.

Problem for Consideration. There are obvious practical limitations to the number of remedial subsequences that can be inserted into an intrinsic program; first, they take time to write, and second, they take up space either in a scrambled book or in a filmed sequence for a machine. The programer wants to get on with the mainstream part of his program.

Can you think of ways to get around this difficulty?

— — — — — — — — — — — — — — —

There is no "right" answer. The question constitutes an excuse for discussion with your instructor, classmates, or colleagues. If you think the question sounds familiar, you are quite right. It first appeared in Chapter 1 under another guise. The question raised there was how far a programer should go in revising his program "downward" for the less able student.

SECTION D. THE PROBLEMS OF ADAPTIVE PROGRAMING

The objectives of this section, like the objectives of Section D in Chapter 3, are "familiarity" with the range of choices and the problems that confront programers in individualizing instruction. Instead of an essay, however, the approach in this section is rather "Socratic." Socrates, despite his reputation as a teacher, should be as famous for his teasing as for his teaching. You will often be asked to answer questions on the basis of common sense and creative leaps. I make full use of "Can you think of . . ?" and "Do you see . . ?"—a legitimate answer is "no."

When most people think of truly individualized instruction, they think of a single student who has at his command his own instructor. This instructor is, of course, infinitely patient, infinitely knowing, and completely versed in the arts of teaching. He knows what he wants to accomplish with his student, he knows the student, and he knows all the tricks of the teaching trade. It hardly bears saying that such an ideal situation does not exist. All instructional procedures represent a compromise and probably all are less than satisfactory to the real dreamers because of the compromises.

A programer of an eclectic bent is faced with three problems: How different are the different members of his intended student population? How much does he know about taking account of these differences? And, what are the practical limitations on doing so? We can look at the various problems and proposed solutions in terms of decisions the programer has to make and the alternatives available to him.

The first of these, so recently faced as to have relatively little firm research backing, is whether to take that first step toward individualization implicit in the original idea of linear programing, namely allowing each student to go at his own pace. Group-paced programs presented on film, filmstrip and audiotape, audiotape, videotape and other media, have been put through the research-and-development process and found successful in achieving their objectives. They qualify as programs.

In the research-and-development process, the group-paced program is adapt*ed* to the audience, but the final version is in no sense adapt*ive*. A student who daydreams can't go back over a point. A student who is slow to respond will have his feedback too soon. Once such a group-paced program is developed, it is relatively cheap to administer and, unlike any other form of programed instruction, easy to insert into the time-based school system. With greater cost and greater disruption of time schedules, such multi-media programs can be used in individually-paced modes, of course.

Linear programs presented in text form are in the majority at the moment. As we have noted before, a linear program is adapted to the population in its research stages and it does adapt in limited ways to student differences. Differences in reading and responding rates are its primary adaptive features. Also, if the program is not presented in a mechanical device that restricts the student to the programer's sequence, many students may "rewrite" the program closer to their own needs by rereading certain frames and sequences, thereby providing themselves with more practice or review than the programer built into his version.

Many people use the term "branching" as if it were synonymous with the relatively restricted intrinsic format. Because there are many ways to branch students, I will use "branching" as the broader term, including far more than the intrinsic technique. A branching program, then, is one that adapts at some point (not necessarily at every frame) somehow (not necessarily with a single multiple-choice question) to some aspect of student differences (not necessarily entering behavior or momentary comprehension). The decisions faced by each programer are: on what basis he might construct branches, when are branches needed, and how should he get students to the appropriate branch?

1. If a program is being designed for a broad audience, it certainly is reasonable to *assume* that there are going to be differences in entering behavior between students. Instead of thinking about the possibilities in your armchair, however, you could take an empirical approach. How would you go about getting information on potential differences in entering behavior?

    And when would you do so? (check one)

    _____before analyzing the subject to be taught.
    _____before constructing criterion measures.
    _____before producing first-draft teaching frames.
    _____before trying out the first draft with a student.

- - - - - - - - - - - - - - - -

You could test a sample of students on those skills and information that you want to assume they know. (Some general information, such as IQ scores and reading scores, might already be on file somewhere.)

The best point would be before writing frames. If your empirical determination is to be relevant to your program, you would have to have completed the analysis in order to know what to test for. Also, if your criterion items were already designed, you could check them out in the same test, making sure that students couldn't pass them.

Reminder: If you duck this step before preparing the first draft, you are going to learn the same things when you start testing your draft. Because of that, some programers do duck the step.

2. Trigonometry, usually taught late in high-school after geometry, is a typical example. The assumption normally made by trig instructors and programers is that students have "had" geometry. However, we know that in most classes students will get their credits for geometry with a range of understanding from A to D as reflected in their grades. Furthermore, there is no necessity for an A to mean complete mastery if, as is usually true, grades were given by rank-ordering students. So, suppose you give your prerequisites test to these "graduate geometers" and get the predicted results: they differ. You are faced with a decision.

One alternative is to do as the linear programer does: include everything anyone didn't know in your teaching sequence.

Another alternative is to do as the intrinsic programer does: when there is variability, you will produce a "pretest" question on that point keyed to a remedial sequence and put it into your mainstream where it is relevant to upcoming material.

There are other alternatives. What other ways might you handle such demonstrated differences in entering knowledge? (Name at least one.)

- - - - - - - - - - - - - - - -

You could have a pre-program (this has been done) in which all students failing specific items get remedial instruction *before* rather than during the main program.

Perhaps you're too much of a good guy to think of restricting the program to only those who meet the prerequisites!

---

3. Given a frame designed to be a "pretest" question from which the student will get remedial instruction *only* if he constructs or chooses an incorrect answer, and given the following sets of data:

(a) 100% of the students miss the question;
(b) 90% of the students miss the question;
(c) 50% of the students miss the question;
(d) 6% of the students miss the question;

would an intrinsic programer revise his pretest question under *any* of these sets of data? If so, which?

- - - - - - - - - - - - - - - -

Yes. A pretest question which is missed by all the students is obviously not a good pretest question, no matter what the programer's position on errors is. The remedial material obviously belongs in the mainstream.

If *you* were writing such a pretest question, would *you* include the remedial material in the mainstream if 90% of your students missed it?

— — — — — — — — — — — — — —

Your choice. This is one of those decisions a branching programer has to face. Is it practical to spend time writing remedial sequences so that 10% can save a minute or two?

---

4. A chance factor also enters into consideration when a multiple-choice question is used. Given 100 students responding to a four-choice alternative:
   (a) If they all know the answer, how many will get it correct?_____.
   (b) Taking chance into account, however, if the question is answered correctly by 100% of the students, can you assume that all the students knew the answer?_____.
   (c) If no student knows it and they all guess randomly, how many should be correct? _____.
   (d) If no one knows it and the question is constructed-response, how many will be correct? _____.

— — — — — — — — — — — — — —

(a) 100.
(b) No. Each student who does not has a one-in-four chance of getting the correct answer by random guessing.
(c) 25.
(d) Presumably none.

Relevant Quote: The available data suggest that branching procedures usually fail to teach better than fixed-sequence procedures, because, for one reason, any single item in a branching program is a fallible basis for branching decisions, often yielding false positives such that the student skips over the material he cannot afford to miss. When more elaborate and less error-prone procedures, such as those that presumably could be implemented with computer-assisted-instruction or by a teacher, are used to make branching decisions, then there may be an advantage to branching techniques, provided the instruction is competently prepared. (Anderson, 1967.)

(YOU WILL PLEASE NOTE THE LAST PHRASE FROM THAT QUOTE! No amount of branching can overcome poor instruction.)

5. Obtaining a test score is not the end of the decisions to be made in designing an adaptive system. Compare these two cases:

   (a) As a prerequisite for a program in long division, a student takes a multiplication test and gets 8 out of 10 answers correct. He is permitted to begin the program.
   (b) As a prerequisite for a program in fighting fires, a forest ranger takes a pretest on reading fire-map symbols and gets 8 out of 10 correct. He is branched to remedial instruction.

   What decision has each programer faced and answered in these two cases?

   — — — — — — — — — — — — — — — —

   There has to be a standard or cutting score. A little sloppiness in multiplication might not do too much damage to long division. In the case of the fire fighter, any error on his part could be disastrous. (A program on this subject, one frame of which you saw in Chapter 3, sets a 100% standard.)

So far, you have worked through some of the decision points that a programer faces when he contemplates branching on the basis of differing entry behaviors. You may collect data before writing frames or depend on developmental testing of the program to provide data on student differences. If students do differ, then you can adopt a linear solution or a branching solution. You face a practical problem of adopting a reasonable level of student differences for a branching decision—that is, what percentage of failures (10%? 25%?) lead you to branch rather than give the material to everyone? And there is, finally, the key problem of what constitutes enough evidence of knowledge or lack of it on which to base decisions about what each student needs. The faulty selection likely to result from basing a branching decision on a single multiple-choice question can be corrected in a number of ways:

(a) The element of chance lucky-choice can be reduced somewhat by making the test item constructed-response.
(b) The number of diagnostic items on the same objective may be increased. This solution is just as applicable to a single "frame" as to an outside test.
(c) A branching decision may be based on a larger sample of behavior than that in a single (even large) frame. In this case machinery, a computer for instance, can be a godsend. In the so-called "drill-and-practice mode" in computer-assisted-instruction, the student is presented, as the name suggests, with an extensive sample of practice materials. The computer can (not all do) keep score across many kinds of problems. In arithmetic, for instance, types of multiplication problems might be presented in a random order. The computer could be programed to "notice" that every time a zero occurs in a problem, the

THE PROBLEMS OF ADAPTIVE PROGRAMING   225

student gets a wrong answer. After three or four or some other set number of errors of this specific nature, the student could be branched to instruction on his individual problem. A student who made one careless error would not be subjected to the remedial instruction.

Sophisticated branching can be accomplished without a computer, as the next few frames will show. We will look at a complicated instructional system which includes three components: a series of short programs aimed at particular mathematical skills; precise diagnostic tests and a "flow chart" for deciding which student goes where; and a group of tutors who guide students through the decisions and also back up the programs when they fail to bring a student up to criterion. We will look at only one small part of the total system.

Before reading frame 6, inspect the flow-chart on page 226.

---

6. Let's follow a student through the system to see how it works. He enters either voluntarily or by assignment from a professor and begins with a total diagnostic test covering 18 mathematical topics needed in college work. If he makes an error on any of the test items that test his knowledge of negative numbers, his further progress depends on what is shown in the flow-chart on the next page. He is now at the top left-hand corner.

On the basis of *one error* on a broad test of many mathematical skills, would you be willing to say that a student does NOT know how to handle negative numbers?

— — — — — — — — — — — — — —

Your choice. That is pretty slim information for such a sweeping conclusion, even in a constructed-response test.

---

7. A single error gets the student into the flow chart, but this is not considered enough evidence to enable the tutors to insist that he spend a couple of hours going through the program on negative numbers. At the upper left is "Negatives A," a diagnostic pretest on all the sub-skills that make up "being able to handle negative numbers." When he has answered the 18 questions on the test, the arrow leads to a diamond-shaped box signifying a decision or choice point. *Check this, at the top left of the flow-chart.*

At the choice point, he bypasses this program if

_____he made no mistakes.
_____he made only one mistake.

— — — — — — — — — — — — — —

"All correct" means no mistakes. Note that the arrow marked "all correct" leads to the next program on Rational Numbers, where this branching process begins again.

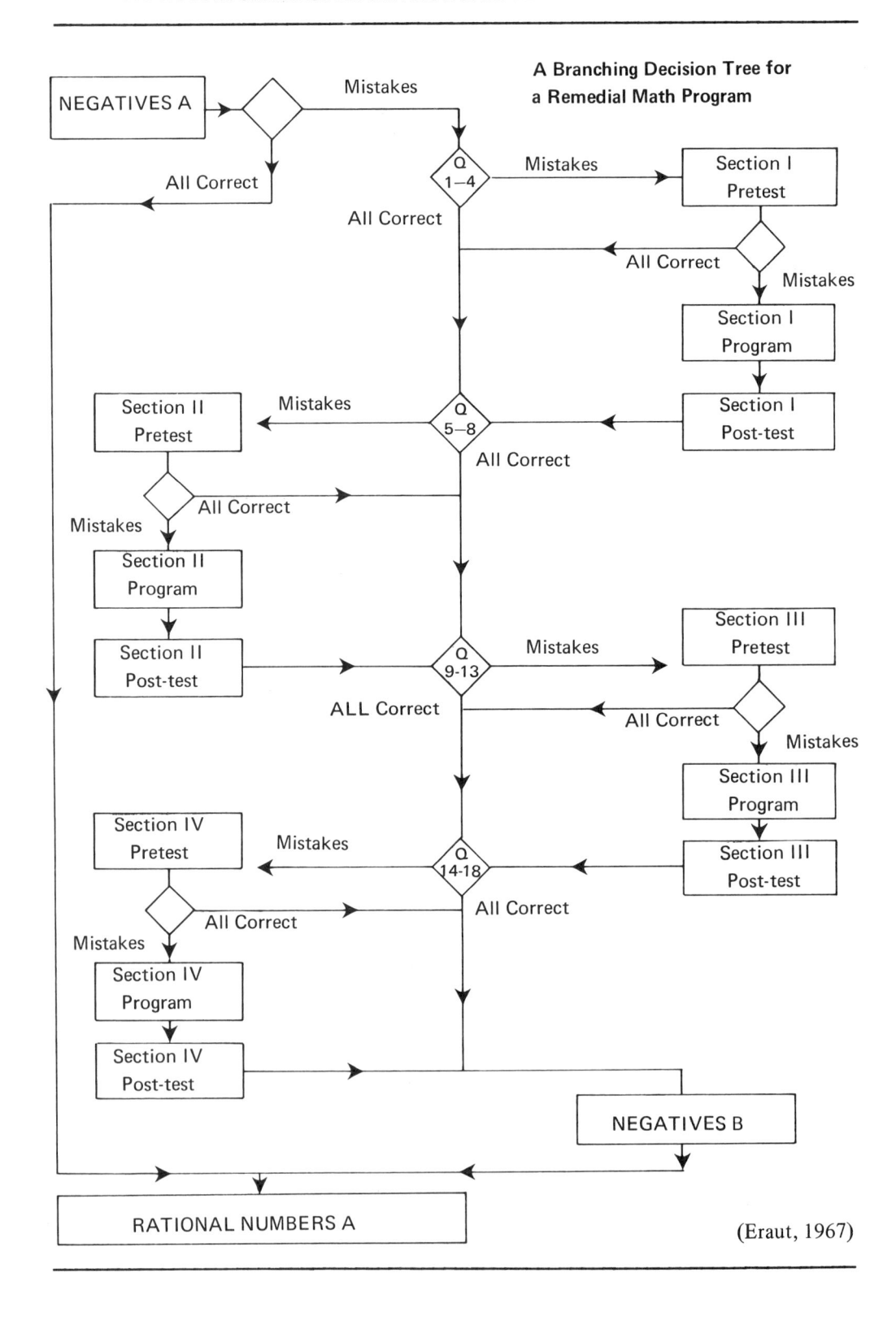

226 ADAPTIVE PROGRAMING AND INDIVIDUAL DIFFERENCES

A Branching Decision Tree for a Remedial Math Program

```
NEGATIVES A ──► ◇ ──Mistakes──► ◇ Q 1-4 ──Mistakes──► Section I Pretest
              │ All Correct         │ All Correct      │
              ▼                     ▼                  ◇ ──All Correct──►
                                                       │ Mistakes
                                                       ▼
                                                   Section I Program
                                                       │
                                                       ▼
              Section II Pretest ◄──Mistakes── ◇ Q 5-8 ◄── Section I Post-test
                   │                           │ All Correct
                   ◇ ──All Correct──►          ▼
                   │ Mistakes
                   ▼
              Section II Program
                   │
                   ▼
              Section II Post-test ──► ◇ Q 9-13 ──Mistakes──► Section III Pretest
                                       │ ALL Correct          │
                                       ▼                      ◇ ──All Correct──►
                                                              │ Mistakes
                                                              ▼
                                                          Section III Program
                                                              │
              Section IV Pretest ◄──Mistakes── ◇ Q 14-18 ◄── Section III Post-test
                   │                           │ All Correct
                   ◇ ──All Correct──►          │
                   │ Mistakes                  ▼
                   ▼                       NEGATIVES B
              Section IV Program               │
                   │                           ▼
                   ▼                       RATIONAL NUMBERS A
              Section IV Post-test ──►
```

(Eraut, 1967)

8. The program, Negative Numbers, is divided into four sections of about 20-25 frames each, on progressively more difficult skills. Now, we could send a student through the whole 100 frames on the basis of an error on the test "Negatives A." However, the programer (Eraut, 1967) reasoned that this was inefficient. The test is designed to pinpoint the difficulty more precisely.

Observe what happens to a student who made any mistakes on Test A. The arrow leads him into the center column of the flow-chart, where we see a new series of diamond-shaped boxes. The first one, labeled Q 1-4, is based on the first four test items and answers the question "Does he need section 1 of the program"? If he doesn't, he follows the arrow down the middle of the page to the next decision point.

What happens if he had made an error on one of these first four questions? The arrow labeled "Mistakes"

    _____sends him off to take Section 1 of the program.
    _____sends him off to take the pretest for Section 1.

— — — — — — — — — — — — — — — —

Decision point Q 1-4 sends him to a pretest.

---

9. The pretest for Section 1 contains seven questions exactly parallel to the first four of Negatives A. We are a long way, at this point, from the simple one-chance, multiple-choice question in an intrinsic program. The student has made at least two errors (one on the big diagnostic test and one on Negatives A) to get to this point. Still we give him another chance to demonstrate competence, since his previous errors may have resulted from "sloppiness." If he can pass this test, he can bypass the section of the program.

Look at it from another point of view, however. Tests, as all students know, can be punishing if you know you don't know how to answer the questions. If our student really doesn't know how to add and subtract negative numbers, he is likely to be pretty depressed at this point when faced with seven more questions. Can you suggest a way to prevent him from further depression when he is confronted with these seven new questions?

— — — — — — — — — — — — — — —

How about letting him skip the test and go directly to the section of the program if he knows he can't answer the test questions? Students can always take this option, of course, by failing to answer, but they feel better when given permission to go directly there without first failing!

10. If he makes a mistake or if he chooses to skip the test, he goes through a 22-frame linear program, Section 1, and takes its posttest. Check what happens to him then. Is there any provision for branching which depends on his performance on the POSTtest for that section? (Do you see any diamonds or more than one arrow leaving the "posttest" box?) *Check on page 226.*

No. Only one arrow leaves the box.

11. When a program has been researched until almost all students going through it can perform well on its posttest, the programer can feel pretty proud of himself. But what do you do with the one or two students who now and then turn up unable to handle the posttest adequately? What ideas occur to you?

Schools and colleges have two answers—flunk them or send them to remedial instruction. In this particular mathematical system, the alternative is the latter. The tutors are there to back up the program when it doesn't work.

12. Would it be *possible* for a student to lack some specific bit of information at an elementary level in a remedial situation like this and, once this difficulty is cleared up, be able to do everything else required to handle negative numbers?

Perhaps it is hard for you to imagine it, but it really has happened.

13. If it were possible for a student to remember everything he learned in high school about negative numbers except how to handle, say, $-(-x)$, then it [would/wouldn't] be an efficient use of his time to go through 100 frames to learn this item taught in the first 20.

---

wouldn't

14. Most programers who are dealing with first-time learning would not have to face the problem the programer of the remedial math system faced, since their students would know little about the subject being taught and branching would be used primarily to deal with prerequisites. In the case of remedial materials, however, a student may have some precise difficulty that, once cleared up, lets him proceed through all more complicated problems. For instance, a student who can't multiply by zero might be unable to get a good score on a long-division test. This would *not* mean that he should be taught the process of long division.

If the student in this math program lacked some elementary bit of information and landed in Section 1 of the program, it is likely that he made other errors on the Negatives A test. In other words, coming down that center line, he would be branched to other sections as well. Do you see how the flow-chart can permit him to bypass the rest of the sections? How could he prove that he can now handle the material in Sections II, III, and IV?

Check the flow-chart on page 226 again for this.

— — — — — — — — — — — — — — —

The reading of flow-charts is not a prerequisite for this program. However, if you didn't see, check this progression:

(a) Having taken the posttest for Section 1, the arrow leads to decisions about Q 5-8.
(b) With his elementary deficiency, he probably missed one of these. If he didn't, he proceeds to the next group.
(c) But, if he did miss one of these questions (or any in later sections), he still has a chance to bypass Section II by passing *its* pretest.

The objectives of the sequence you have just completed are neither that you will be able to recite the precise techniques employed by this particular programer nor that you will, in all programs you prepare, strive to branch at every possible occasion. Rather, long after you finish this program, as you delve in the literature (pro and con) about programs, programing, and computer-assisted-instruction and confront glittering generalities about "individualization" of instruction, you will be able to recall:

(a) that programs tailored at least in some respects to individual differences do indeed exist;
(b) that not all branching programs are intrinsic in design;
(c) that not all sophisticated branching techniques are found in computer-assisted-instruction.

Relevant Quote: Current educational talk is thus all for individualized instruction. But what does "individualization" mean? A case can be made for defining it as something like personalizing or customizing, namely taking a mass-produced object and stamping it with gold initials. . . . This is the sense in which current experimental computer programs greet you with 'Good morning, Johnny' by filling in the blank in 'Good morning,_____' with the name you had to give to identify yourself to the machine in the first place.... A loftier interpretation postulates that individualizing means giving full scope to idiosyncrasy, to the freedom to pursue whatever subject suits one's fancy in a manner entirely of one's own choosing. To current practitioners, individualization means much less than pure idiosyncrasy but usually more than golden initials. (Oettinger & Marks, 1968.)

Intermediate Summary

Varying levels of entry knowledge is perhaps the easiest type of student difference to handle. It has been handled by setting a criterion score on a prerequisites test or a test frame and:

(a) advising students not to take a program for which they are unprepared;
(b) suggesting some kind of remediation to enable the student to pass the entrance test;
(c) putting the remedial material at the beginning of the program, preceded by the test (often called "Express Stops" in this case), permitting students to bypass the first parts of the program if they pass;
(d) the intrinsic alternative of inserting it as a remedial sequence where relevant in the program (this may be done without other intrinsic devices, e.g., the test may be constructed-response, the branch may contain a linear sequence, and so forth.);
(e) the non-branching linear alternative of including it in everyone's sequence, hoping that the student who already knows will speed through it.

The more remedial material a programer chooses to include the more he has to prepare! There is a trade-off in efficiency between the programer's time in constructing branches and the time saved by the better-prepared student.

14. An argument can be made for allowing a frame with a very high error rate to remain in a program if it serves to sift those students in need of information from those that already know the answer. Even if only 10% of the students can answer a pretest type of question, the time of those 10% is being saved by enabling them to bypass instruction that they do not need.

How do you feel about a large percentage of errors that are a function of *reading or reasoning ability* rather than lack of information. If the following assumptions are satisfied:

(a) by logical analysis, it can be determined that all the information necessary to make the correct response has been given to the student and
(b) the student population on whom the program is being tested is a valid sample of the population for whom the program is intended,

do you believe that a frame eliciting a large percentage of errors (say 60%) caused by "ability" rather than by lack of information should be revised?

— — — — — — — — — — — — — — —

Yes. Go to page 231 A.
No. Go to page 231 B.

A. Your answer was "Yes." There is no right answer to this question. It is one of the toughest decisions to face in programing.

If 60% of the students gave wrong answers, then 40% of them were right.

Crowder reasoned: "We think it is undesirable to eliminate errors because to do so we would have to present material in such small steps and ask such easy questions that we would not be serving the educational objectives we desire to serve." Consider your reactions to this:

> In order to teach all of the students in a class, the material should be made simple enough for every student to experience success, even if this approach does not fully utilize the talents of the better ones.

Do you believe this to be the best approach? Can you think of a way around this problem of differential ability?

(Go on to page 232.)

B. Your answer was "No." There is no right answer to this question. It is one of the toughest decisions to face in programing.

If 60% of the students missed the item, there is still that 40% who answered correctly. If we assume that most of these students obtained the correct answer by careful reasoning or reading rather than purely by lucky guessing, then the item was within their reading and reasoning ability.

Crowder made *two* points about intrinsic methodology which are applicable to any kind of branching: not only should you *detect* errors, you should also *correct* them. In order to do so, you might find yourself teaching reading or reasoning in the middle of a program on bridge or on trigonometry.

Consider your reactions to this statement:

> In order to teach as much material as possible to the talented, it is necessary to proceed rapidly even if the less talented are left with incomplete understandings and inadequate mastery.

Do you believe this to be the best approach? Can you think of a way around this problem of of differential ability?

(Go on to page 232.)

(From page 231.) The idea of different programs or different tracks in a big program for students of different abilities will probably occur to most of you. The answer is a good one. It has been done. It raises many issues.

(a) One, of course, is how to do it. If the "operant of mastery" is "accurate long division," manipulating step size, amount of prompting, amount of priming, sequence effects, amount of practice, and all the other bits of the technology might give us dozens of different tracks fitting various levels of IQ. If the "operant of mastery" is proving geometric theorems, the problem may be quite different. At some point on any measure of ability, you would run into students to whom you would have to teach "thinking" (whatever that is) as well as geometry.

(b) Another is the nature of the measures themselves. Most ability measures are too general to be useful to programers. They rank students against each other instead of a criterion indicating precisely what skills they have and what skills they lack. (Glaser, 1965.)

(c) A third raises all the hoary issues of other tracking systems. A student slow in arithmetic is not necessarily slow in science or English. What is true of subjects could, at a more sensitive level of measurement, be true of parts of programs. Perhaps a student should start on a "slow" track and move out when ready to a "fast track" or start on a "fast track" and slow down when he runs into difficulty.

(d) What are the limits of practicality in creating different programs for different students? At some point we approach the dream state of a private tutor for each student.

---

16. The computer, as most educators know, has been offered as a solution to many of the problems posed by the demands of true individualization. CAI (computer-assisted-instruction) requires instructional materials (hopefully good ones), rules for deciding where a student goes next depending on what he has done in the past, and a mechanism for storing and retrieving materials to get them to the right student at the right time. Given a big enough storage area and a large number of options and extras, we could be permanently released from the "black car" era of instruction, mentioned in the Chapter introduction.

    Given a computer programer (CP) and an instructional programer (IP), who would make each of these decisions?

    IP/CP How much material can be presented on the computer interface at one time?
    IP/CP How much material is required in a frame to prime a certain operant?
    IP/CP What set of test items constitute an adequate sample for making a branching decision?
    IP/CP How many different alternatives can be handled by the machine efficiently at each point?
    IP/CP What kind of feedback should be given to the student if he gives a particular answer?

- - - - - - - - - - - - - - -

The computer programer decides (or knows) the limits of his machine—the first and fourth questions. All the other questions land in the instructional programer's lap.

17. A computer with a typewriter input from the student can permit students to construct responses on the basis of which it makes the branching decisions by comparing each response with its stored set of responses. Do you see a problem for the instructional programer in this comparison procedure? If so, what?

— — — — — — — — — — — — — — —

A major problem, identified by computer buffs, is getting *all* potential answers into the computer. Beyond that is the problem of storing a sufficient number of branches. In order to do so, you have to know what each student needs who came up with a different answer. (And those are questions the computers don't have the answers to!)

18. One strong area for individualization is adapting a program to the amount of practice needed by each student. CAI has had considerable success in "drill-and-practice" in reading and arithmetic (Atkinson and Wilson, 1968). The instructional programing is not too difficult, in this case, nor is it difficult to set appropriate criterion standards. Also, the computer is an ideal data-collector. Sorting responses into two piles (right and wrong) it can keep providing more examples until the student reaches the criterion, for instance 10 correct responses in a row.

Consider: given a paper program with as many exercises as could possibly be needed by any student, and given the ten-in-a-row standard to be reached, how would you get a student to stop when he had reached the criterion?

— — — — — — — — — — — — — — —

I can think of two ways—have the teacher score papers, which is a solution all teachers would reject, or have the student himself keep a running count on his progress. Such bookwork might distract him if it didn't also depress him. Some branching techniques are difficult to implement with paper programs. Machinery can be helpful!

19. The amount of practice a student needs is only one facet of "general ability." Suggestions abound for adapting instruction to other facets. How about "learning style"? An "inductive thinker" might do better with an EGRUL program, while a "deductive thinker" might prefer a RULEG approach. A "visualizer" might want a lot of pictures and diagrams, while an "abstract thinker" would prefer words and symbols.

    Would any of these adaptations require a computer?

    ─ ─ ─ ─ ─ ─ ─ ─ ─ ─ ─ ─ ─ ─ ─

    No. They do require different programs, though. And a way to get the right program into the hands of the right student.

20. So far, we have been talking about diagnosis on the basis of test results or errors during a program as ways of differentiating the sequence a student might get.

    Can you think of a way to get a student into a remedial sequence he needs without requiring him to demonstrate his ignorance by making an error?

    ─ ─ ─ ─ ─ ─ ─ ─ ─ ─ ─ ─ ─ ─ ─

    Perhaps you thought of the idea of asking the student. Especially at higher levels, students are often capable of making this decision themselves.

21. Student option branches have been around for quite awhile. All that is required is that the test be exhibited and the student allowed to make a choice. Intrinsic programers sometimes use an alternative "I don't understand" or "I don't know" as a way of branching into a remedial sequence without errors. Some computers have a HELP! button for students to use when they're stuck.

    Although "paper teaching machines" (like the one you're working on) can use this device, there is a serious problem involved. Students are not always wise about how much they know. There is an inefficiency in opting for instruction if the student does not require it. There is a worse problem in NOT choosing remediation when he does need it. In the usual programed text, he will try the question he is not ready for and then compare his answer with the confirmation provided.

Can you now give him help so that he can solve the same problem more accurately?

Could a computer help in this situation?

- - - - - - - - - - - - - - -

No. A student is not "solving" a problem if he already has seen the answer to it.

Yes. A computer, or some other kind of machine could block his progress, branching him without showing him the right answer.

Aside. Again, in mathematics, the situation is not much of a problem. You simply make up another example. In using a student-option branch in Chapter 2 (p. 88), I was in a somewhat different position. There are very few frames known to me that are as complex as the famous Aardvark one. To test "everything" with the same question required a very special case.

Now, check the list you made at the beginning of this chapter. Did you include student options among the ways you listed there to individualize instruction? At this point, how many other ways can you add to your list that would permit the student to have a say in what happens to him?

22. Here, from *Klystrons,* is a rare type of branch constructed by Kantor and Mager.
On what is the student allowed his option in this frame? What difficulties do you see in trying to emulate this?

> Although you could see from the pictures on the previous page that the klystron looks a good bit different from a radio tube (and we will see why this is so as we go on), the klystron does the same sort of things a radio tube does, only it does them at microwave frequencies.
> Now, what would you like to know next?
>
> Tell me something about what you mean
> by microwave frequencies .... turn to page 11.
>
> Why is anyone interested in microwave
> frequencies .... turn to page 7.
>
> (Whichever alternative you choose, you will have a chance to choose the other later on.)

- - - - - - - - - - - - - - -

Sequence or order. This could only be done if the subject matter lends itself to teaching the material in either order. Most programs, whether their order is truly logical or not, build on previous sequences in such a way that the student cannot dabble in the program the way he might in a book of readings.

Final Tidbits. Among the ideas used in some programs to adapt to student's desires or needs is what is sometimes called the "nice-to-know" objective. If the objective is not critical for everyone, students may be given the option of skipping material of no use or of no interest to them. In previous chapters of this program, some "Research Notes" fell into this category. Unprogramed material, anything that the student does not have to use, also falls into this category, but the programer is using his own option if he puts it in without suggesting students skip it. (This section is a good example of that. There is no suggestion that you ignore this material at your option.) The logical extreme of the "nice-to-know" objective is putting all objectives in that category and allowing students to pick and choose among instructional goals, tailoring their education to their own needs and desires.

Another intriguing suggestion offered by Lewis and Pask (1965) is adapting to the student's preferred error rate, a feat of instructional engineering that has rarely been accomplished. They noted that individuals differ in the amount of punishment they find acceptable. Very bright students may feel they are not learning if they are not making mistakes. Certainly they are not being challenged. The programer would have to know what the student was capable of and arrange to provide him with a sufficient number of problems slightly beyond his capacity to maintain his preferred degree of challenge.

Personality is a variable that is both hard to measure and rarely taken into account in creating instructional materials. Frase (1963) created separate feedback content for "dependent" and "aggressive" students. The "dependent" ones were praised generously when they succeeded and treated gently when they failed. The "aggressive" students, on the other hand, were treated to very casual acknowledgement of successful answers and to not-too-subtle insinuations about their intelligence when they failed. Both groups liked the treatment matched to their personalities.

Need we mention "cultural" adaptation?

SUMMARY

The intrinsic style of programing was a step toward individualization beyond the first step, individual pacing, taken by the linear style. Programers are moving into increasingly complex adaptive designs, with the major progress being adaptation to prerequisite knowledge and progress through the program, as measured by increasingly sensitive tests. Increasing sophistication can be expected as sophisticated hardware, such as the computer, provides greater flexibility in the options open to the programer.

It is well to remind ourselves that the existence of a couple of clever examples of the many good suggestions for individualization does not mean that there are enough examples of thoroughly researched flexible programs to put the ideas into practice on any large scale. This has been the finding of several projects that have adopted individual progress plans. (Lindvall and Bolvin, 1967; Esbensen, 1968.)

Relevant Quote: A few of the reports about CAI are based on substantial experience and research, but the majority are vague speculations and conjectures with little if any data or real experience to back them up. . . . The problem for someone trying to evaluate developments in the field is to distinguish between those reports that are based on fact and those that are disguised forms of science fiction. (Atkinson, 1968.)

Chapter 5
Editing

INTRODUCTION

The assumption behind this chapter may not be valid for all writers. Few people write so well that no revision is required when the first draft is completed. Programers should not expect to be different. I, for one, generate frames as fast as I can type them out and then return to the sequence to analyze and edit what I have written. I am assuming that you, the student, will write in somewhat the same fashion and that instruction in editing will not produce a "mental block" when you are confronted with clean white paper. Do not let that happen. Get down in sequence what you want to teach as rapidly as you can write. Your first draft should be for you alone. It presents an opportunity to analyze and revise. The basic purpose of this chapter is to provide you with some of the tools with which to do so.

Most people are aware that publication of a book does not guarantee that the book is either true or well written. The same is true of a program. Editorial behavior, either by the programer himself or by a colleague, should begin with the truth, clarity, and facility of expression embodied in the program. Student data will never, of course, provide the programer with feedback about the validity of his subject matter, although complete confusion may be noticed by students. (See D. Markle, 1962). Pompous over-stuffed language is likely to get its comeuppance, but its opposite—the "Dick and Jane style"(see *A Guide for Wiley Authors,* 1967) of simplified, dull, stereotyped prose—is not the answer either.

There is nothing in the technique of programing that requires dull writing! I recommend to every programer a critical reader (spouse, friend, or other) who will inspect the frames with a jaundiced eye, trying to spot ambiguities, pomposities, and other inelegances, before any student sees the program.

The rest of the editing falls into two classes of judgments: *Is this frame necessary? Where is that necessary frame?*

We assume that the programer has some idea of the capabilities of the students for whom the program is intended. This "initial" or "entering" behavior will determine what reading level is employed, what sorts of assumptions about previous learning are made, and what kinds of examples might be appropriate. In testing developmental editions of programs, even master teachers are in for some surprises, but the programer has to start with some assumptions.

We assume also that the programer has a clear idea of the terminal behavior toward which he is heading. From his analysis of it, he has constructed terminal (criterion) frames for the program. If an outside test is desired, this also has been constructed.

From bitter experience, I can advise on the importance of taking this step first. With a complex transfer (application) objective, and the program already written, I could find only one example that fit the criterion! Be warned. It could happen to you. This is especially true in those sensitive areas of the higher objectives, where you wish to test the student's ability to generalize the concept, to apply a principle, to analyze a situation and the criterion must be a new but realistic example. Specify it first and save it for testing.

We assume that, having both end points (the initial behavior and the terminal behavior) the programer is interested in getting from the beginning to the end in the most efficient manner.

The fastest way to cover the distance between these two points is to eliminate anything the students can be expected to know (or you know they know) and to make the steps as large as they can possibly take, even a bit larger. Data from students will flesh out a lean program. Programs, like people, find it hard to reduce.

The basic purpose of a frame is the *elicitation of significant behavior from the student.* A student learns what he has been led to do. The programer's task is relatively simple to describe, difficult as it may be to put into effect. All he has to do is to provide the context in which the behavior will occur.

The first drafts produced by many experienced programers and almost all neophyte programers in hot pursuit of a logical teaching sequence contain errors of the following sorts: copy frames, irrelevant responses asked for, irrelevant frames, overloaded frames or "lectures," too many prompts, incomplete discrimination sequences, overemphasis on the sentence-completion model, and, when a multiple-choice format is used, poor selection of questions and/or alternatives. These errors can easily be edited out before the manuscript is submitted to "trial by student." For most writers, concentration on these details while trying to structure the sequence may result in loss of the overall idea. The first step is to write; the second is to edit; and the third, of course, is to test the sequence, which leads you back to step one on at least some frames and sequences.

Most of the errors listed above will *not* be pinpointed by errors made by students on the frames containing the faulty design. Almost every one of them produces a frame that is too *easy* to be missed. The fact that erroneous frames of these types exist in the program will only be determined by noting that students cannot answer the terminal frames or posttest despite having made few errors. They seem to have been successful and busy, and yet they have not learned. The temptation to double the number of teaching frames when students do not learn should be resisted until all inefficient frames have been made as efficient as possible.

SECTION A: RELEVANCE

1. When material is presented on a panel or display, questions may be asked that require the student to observe what is on the panel.

    The panel is a poem. Which of these questions forces the student to look at the panel?

    > In "Stopping by Woods on a Snowy Evening" there are _____ sections or stanzas, with _____ lines in each stanza.
    >
    > *(Poetry: A Closer Look,* Reid)
    >
    > In "Stopping by Woods on a Snowy Evening" there are four sections or stanzas, with four lines in each _____.

- - - - - - - - - - - - - -

The first one.

2. *Rule.* The response elicited from the student should be relevant to the teaching purpose of the frame.

If observation of something is what is wanted, the student who has not observed it should be unable to answer the frame.

The purpose is to require the student to observe the method of representing electrons around a nucleus:

> Electrons are particles that move around the nucleus. In the drawing below, two electrons are moving around the _____.
>
> (diagram of nucleus with two electrons e⁻)

The response in this frame is [relevant/irrelevant].

— — — — — — — — — — — — — — —

If you said "relevant," go to Level A, item 3.
If you said "irrelevant," go to Level B, item 3.

---

3. Level A. The purpose is to require the student to observe the method of representing electrons around a nucleus.

> Electrons are particles that move around the nucleus. In the drawing below, two electrons are moving around the _____.

The purpose of the frame is to make the student look at the picture. We have removed the picture. Could a student still answer the frame? _____ .

— — — — — — — — — — — — — — —

Yes. Go to Level B.

Level B. A response is relevant if it requires the student to do what the frame is trying to make him do.

> Electrons are particles that move around the nucleus. In the drawing below, two electrons are moving around the _____.
>
> (diagram of nucleus with two electrons e⁻)

The stated purpose of the frame was to require the student to observe the method of representing electrons. Rewrite the frame so that he has to look at the drawing in order to answer.

Write.

Electrons are particles that move around the nucleus. In the drawing below,_____

———————————————

The most obvious revision is to require him to count the electrons, which he can do only by looking at the picture. Or, he may be asked to describe the path (a bunch of dots). Removing any other word such as "electron" or "around" still leaves a copying frame. These deletions are not satisfactory revisions.

---

4. Where the response required of the student is irrelevant to the teaching purpose of the frame, the answer to the question "Is this frame necessary?" is "no." The programer is left with the question "Where is the necessary frame?" If, as in the past examples, the purpose of the frame is to require observation of something in order for the student to have something to talk about later, the programer is going to have to write another frame. Programs can get pretty long if this happens very often.

Frames with irrelevant responses usually tell the student what it is that the programer wants him to know. Fresh young programers often wonder why they have to tell the student the same thing so many times. If the response is irrelevant, however, the programer *may be* distracting the student from important information and definitely *is not* arranging the conditions under which the student learns. (See Holland, 1965.) What basic principle does the irrelevant response violate?

———————————————

(In your own words.) The student learns what he has been led to do—often called the "activity" principle or principle of active responding. [Evidence that irrelevant responses are indeed distracting is provided in Anderson's survey (1967).]

242 **EDITING**

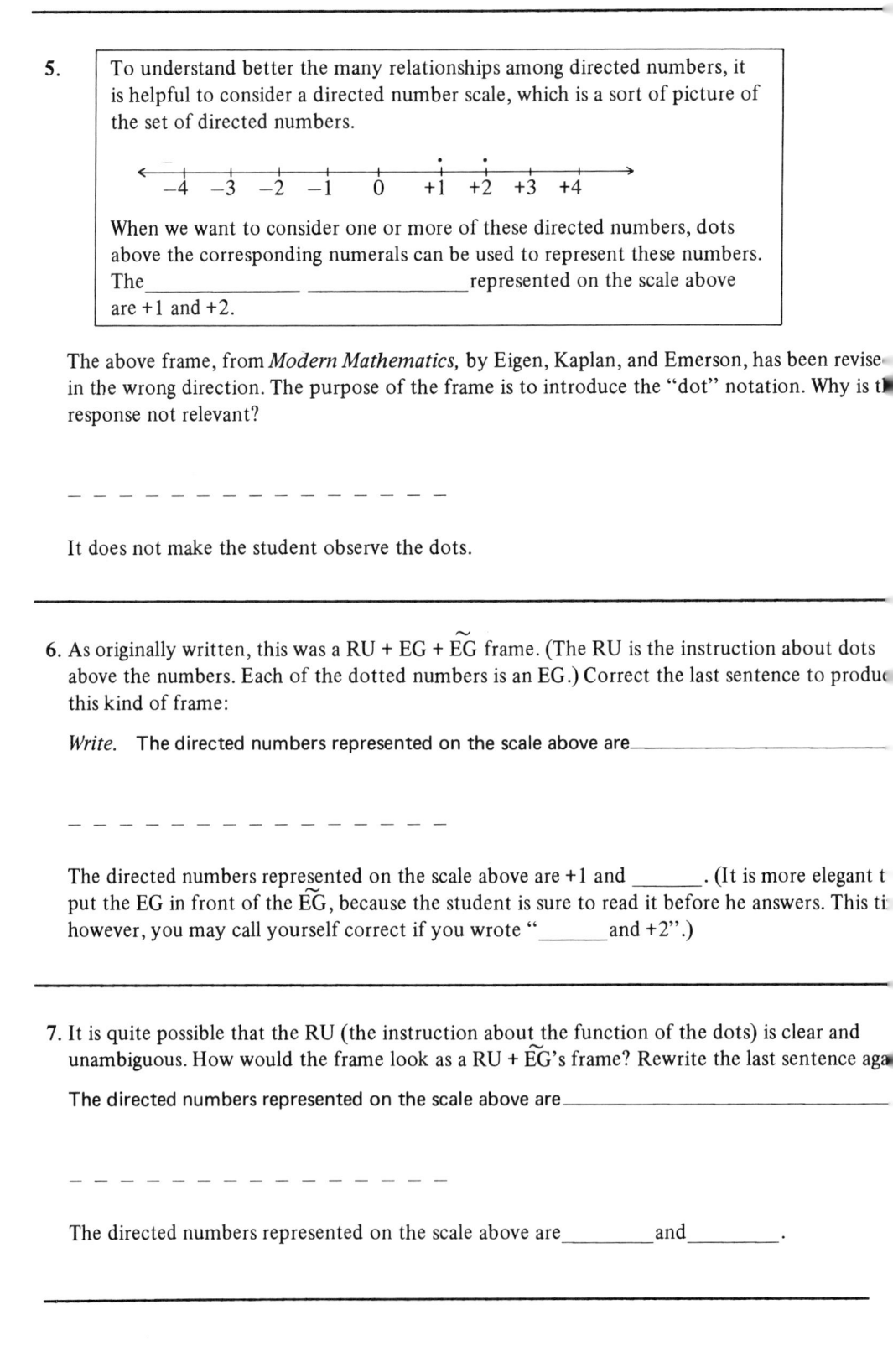

5.
> To understand better the many relationships among directed numbers, it is helpful to consider a directed number scale, which is a sort of picture of the set of directed numbers.
>
> ```
> ←——+——+——+——+——+——•——•——+——+——→
>    -4  -3  -2  -1   0  +1  +2  +3  +4
> ```
>
> When we want to consider one or more of these directed numbers, dots above the corresponding numerals can be used to represent these numbers. The _____ _____ represented on the scale above are +1 and +2.

The above frame, from *Modern Mathematics*, by Eigen, Kaplan, and Emerson, has been revised in the wrong direction. The purpose of the frame is to introduce the "dot" notation. Why is the response not relevant?

— — — — — — — — — — — — — —

It does not make the student observe the dots.

---

6. As originally written, this was a RU + EG + $\widetilde{EG}$ frame. (The RU is the instruction about dots above the numbers. Each of the dotted numbers is an EG.) Correct the last sentence to produce this kind of frame:

   Write. The directed numbers represented on the scale above are _____

— — — — — — — — — — — — — —

The directed numbers represented on the scale above are +1 and _____ . (It is more elegant to put the EG in front of the $\widetilde{EG}$, because the student is sure to read it before he answers. This time, however, you may call yourself correct if you wrote "_____ and +2".)

---

7. It is quite possible that the RU (the instruction about the function of the dots) is clear and unambiguous. How would the frame look as a RU + $\widetilde{EG}$'s frame? Rewrite the last sentence again.

   The directed numbers represented on the scale above are _____

— — — — — — — — — — — — — —

The directed numbers represented on the scale above are _____ and _____ .

8. In a geography program you might have reason to teach students which South American countries are on the Pacific Ocean side of the continent.

> Name the South American countries that touch the Pacific Ocean.

This makes an adequate terminal item. But it could be used as an introductory frame. How would you go about arranging for the student to answer this item correctly the first time he sees it?_____. (If you want a hint, drop down one line.)

— — — — — — — — — — — — — —

Hint. Unless you are a geography teacher or student, you probably do not have the answer to that terminal frame at your fingertips. If you had to know the answer, where would *you* go to find out? Could a student go to the same source?

— — — — — — — — — — — — — —

A map is the most obvious source (or atlas, etc.)

---

9. While the student has the map in front of him, he obviously has not achieved the terminal objective of the item given above—namely, being able, unprompted, to list the countries. Of course, it might be possible to elicit the response "Chile" (misspelled) by prompting, but any formal or thematic prompt that could produce "Ecuador" is really hard to imagine. If the programer does not permit the student to pull the information off the map, what other way of teaching is left to him? How will he have to inform the student?_____.

— — — — — — — — — — — — — —

Tell him—in so many words.

10.
> The three states that border the Pacific Ocean are California, Washington, and Oregon. California borders on Mexico, whereas Washington borders on Canada.
>
> _____, in the middle, is south of _____ and north of _____.

(a) If only the first sentence were given and then the student were asked to list the Pacific states, the frame [would/would not] be a copying frame.
(b) The above question [is/is not] a copying frame.

— — — — — — — — — — — — — —

(a) would.
(b) is not.

244 EDITING

11. There is no information in the verbal frame in Frame 10 that could not be found out by a student who had a map to look at. But, in order to avoid writing a copying frame, the programer had to make the step [larger/smaller] than he would have, had he used an "observing" response.

    Check the frame. Do you also see an assumption about entering behavior that would not have to be made if the student could look at a map?_____. If you say "yes," what is it?

    _ _ _ _ _ _ _ _ _ _ _ _ _ _ _

    The step is larger—not only the names, but the relations between them are asked for.

    The above frame assumes that the student knows where Canada and Mexico are in relation to the U.S. (This could be ducked, of course, by saying "Mexico to the south," etc., but such an addition might lead to confusion.)

12. Can you think of any way to get the naive student to give the list of states on the basis of the first sentence alone if you may not write a copying frame?_____.

    _ _ _ _ _ _ _ _ _ _ _ _ _ _ _

    I can't. Pictures, maps, and other diagrams are great helps in providing contexts within which relevant responses can be elicited.

13. > Here is an important word: "numeral" (NEW-mer-ul).
    >
    > The number of the correct spelling of the new word is:
    >
    > (1) nemural. (2) numeral. (3) neither of these. (4) both of these.
    >
    > *(Modern Mathematics,* TMI)

    What is the purpose of this frame?_____. Does it achieve its purpose?_____. Why do you say so?

    _ _ _ _ _ _ _ _ _ _ _ _ _ _ _

    It requires the student to observe (recognize, look at) the spelling of the word.

    Yes, it does. This BABOON design (page 101) forces attention to both alternatives, because of the "neither of these".

Note. The programers of the above frame have taken the position that students in mathematics should not be given the opportunity to misspell the terms in that discipline. English teachers will applaud this approach. The programers have found, as I have, that a complicated model (a long word) does not reliably produce correct copying from students at the junior high level or below. There is a step that precedes copying, and that step is taking a good look at the word. Oversimplified as this frame may appear to sophisticated copiers, it is necessary for poor readers. In a linear program, frames necessary for poor readers turn up frequently.

Here is a real teaser for class discussion: In order to allow good readers to bypass frames of this type, the first idea that should occur to you is the provision of a remedial sequence which a student takes only if he misspells a word. This could be done by telling him in the answer space "If this is not the way you spelled the word, do items a-e." A difficulty arises, however. If he is unable to copy the word in the first place, he is almost certain to be unable to see that he has copied it incorrectly. (See Meyer, 1960 and Knight, 1964 for evidence.) He will not know that he should take the remedial branch. Is there any way out of this dilemma?

14.
> A teaching machine is a device that presents material to a student, requires a response to the material from the student, and provides knowledge of results. Since a film, as ordinarily used, does not require a response from the student, it is not a _____ _____.

The frame begins with a RU—a definition of the three characteristics of a teaching machine. If the student is to learn these, he should do something about them or with them, or at least with one of them. That establishes the purpose of the frame.

Is the response relevant to the purpose of the frame? _____.

— — — — — — — — — — — — — —

No. The spelling of the words is not the purpose.

---

15. A relevant response to the above frame would require some sort of response to one or more of the listed properties of teaching machines. Suggest a repair that would require attention to, but not copying of, one or more of the properties, given the material that you have to work with in that frame.

— — — — — — — — — — — — — —

You might ask what property a film shares with a teaching machine, or what properties it does not share, or whether a film *is* a teaching machine.

246 EDITING

16. A response is relevant if you, the programer, know that the student has had to observe something, follow a procedure, or read some material in the way you want him to before he can respond correctly. In the following frame, which you are to construct, the word to be discovered is actually irrelevant—any word would do, although this one "fits" the situation.

    Context of the frame: the student has been led to put slides into place in a microscope. So far, the microscope, as prearranged by the programer, has been in focus. In the immediately preceding frame, the student has switched lenses and the microscope is now out of focus.

    Purpose of the frame: get the student to focus the microscope.

    Equipment available: a microscope with the focusing knob painted red (other knobs are painted other colors); a slide with the number three (3) legible, and a word (the word is "focused") illegible except when seen through the microscope.

    Assume that you have a picture in your frame, with an arrow indicating that the red knob may be turned either clockwise or counterclockwise. The microscope is beside the student and the slide is the next one in order in his box of slides. (You hope.)

    Design a frame that will require the student to focus the microscope.

    Write.

    Your frame should include the following:

    (a) Instructions to put slide No. 3 into place.
    (b) Instructions to manipulate the red knob.
    (c) A question that asks what is on the slide. This question should be worded in such a way that the grammar does not give the word away; i.e.,
    Wrong. "When you have the microscope in focus, you can read the word which tells you that the microscope is _____ " will not do.
    Right. Something like "What do you see on the slide?" is fine, and so is "What word is written on the slide?"

17. Each frame in a program should be checked against the overall objective of the program. Here are two objectives:

   A. Given a map with any of ten symbols in any combination on it, the student will be able to identify what each one stands for.
   B. Given an aerial photo of a rough terrain, the student will produce a map indicating roads, ridges, peaks, and watersheds in proper scale.

   Inspect this frame for its relevance to each of the objectives.

   > Show on the sketch how you would indicate a stream beginning at the top of the mountain and flowing eastward into the gulley.

   This frame is relevant to Program A _____
                                 Program B _____
                                 Both   _____
                                 Neither   _____

   Program B. The student in that program is expected to attain mastery of map drawing. This is part of the skill, even though the photo is not present. Producing maps is not the behavior specified for Program A.

Underlying the discussion of the relevance of the response to the purpose of the frame is an assumption: the frame *has* a purpose. The next question follows naturally. Is the purpose of the frame relevant to the purpose of the program? Having constructed his posttest first, as the rule books tell him he should, the programer can check each frame against the objectives that he has set up.

In an elaborate system like Gilbert's, a complete "prescription" for a frame would be prepared before any writing was done. The more organization of this sort you can introduce, the less likely you are to find you have written a frame which does not match your overall objective, even though it has a purpose of its own and would go well in another program. If you do not work from such an outline specifying what each frame is meant to accomplish, check each one when you edit your first approximation to the testable first draft. A highly recommended object in a programer's immediate environment is a wastebasket. A big one.

248 EDITING

18. *Frames That Belong in the Wastebasket*

(a) In this category are the first ten frames leading into the program, based on the way a lecturer introduces his subject. These first ten frames will tell the student what he is going to study in this program and how important it is to know this subject.

> *Logic* is the study of the way sentences are put together. Logicians are interested in the study of l_____ thinking. (*Answer:* logical)

Standard characteristics of these frames are (1) parroting of undefined terms (and you do not know what the student thinks that you mean), and (2) formal prompts of the first-letter type if the frame escapes from the realm of pure copying frames. This is *not* to say that motivational or organizational material does not belong in a program. How might you present to a student a brief description of logic and its utility before he plunges into the frame-by-frame approach to mastering it?

— — — — — — — — — — — — — —

This program has, on student demand, tried the "introduction" approach. You may have thought of other ways. *Not all the material contained in a program has to require a response from the student. Introductions, asides, notes, etc., ARE NOT programed, even when they occur within a program, however.*

(b) In programs aiming to teach the students to talk about, recognize, discriminate, or judge procedures (such as judging whether an experimenter utilized appropriate statistical procedures), all frames in which the student has to solve long and complicated problems that adding machines could do more accurately belong in the wastebasket. If you feel (or find) that going through the steps of solving a problem increases "appreciation," what kind of problem would be relevant in such a program?

— — — — — — — — — — — — — —

A simple one illustrating the steps but not requiring complicated calculations.

(c) In programs aiming to teach a skill or procedure, all frames in which the student is taught to verbalize lengthy procedures or state long lists of rules should be thrown out. In a program teaching the student how to write an organized paragraph, for instance, the programer can waste considerable time teaching the student to answer the following question—time more usefully put to the task of practicing how to organize paragraphs.

> Name the ten characteristics of a good paragraph.

Checklists may, of course, be helpful mnemonic devices, but they may become part of the student's repertoire without rote drill, if they are part of the teaching of discriminations and operations. If the student can successfully list the ten characteristics above, what do we *not* know about his competence with paragraphs?

We do not know whether he can discriminate the presence or absence of any of them or whether he can use them in his own writing. The *choice* is the programer's. What he is choosing here is *which* objectives he considers worth achieving. There are some who would not agree with the strong stand taken in this program that objectives of the type "The student will list the six principles of . . ." are not worth the effort on either the student's or the programer's part. The important objectives (I think) are "The student will be able to identify new examples of . . ." and "The student will be able to apply the six principles to a new case of . . ."

Relevant Quote: Programed instruction was certainly not the first field to become concerned with instructional objectives, but it was the first to be helpless without them. (Deterline, 1968.)

An Aside on Asides.

Should programs include humorous asides, not-quite-necessary stories, and momentary digressions from the subject matter? The only answer, of course, is "It depends." The key factor is the audience for whom the program is intended. Highly motivated industrial trainees may suffer through dullness gladly in order to be promoted. (This is not a justification for boring programs. However, creativity takes time and the programer's time may be limited.) In the classroom, high motivation does not always exist. The word "boring" rings in many a programer's ear. Gotkin (1964) reported widely different reactions to the same program from the upper and the lower part of the ability range in one school. In this case (unusual to hear) it was the lower part that found the program boring. As Gotkin quipped, "One man's humor is another man's wisecrack." He concluded:

> I am advocating that the style of the programer needs to be matched with individual learning styles. It is time to give up the notion that a single sequence is the optimal sequence for all learners, a notion often attributed to but not shared by Skinner.

One source of data for the programer is, of course, the first few students with whom he is in close contact. If the not-so-necessary story becomes a source of distraction, it might be worthwhile to eliminate it. If a humorous aside elicits a groan instead of a grin, it might be worthwhile to drop it. But what if one student guffaws and the other groans? This will happen. No one has yet suggested branching students in and out of various types of humor or digressions, as their interests dictate. Someone should suggest it.

SECTION B: HOW TO AVOID THE COPYING FRAME

1. *Rule.* Unless you are teaching only the spelling of a term, drop all copying frames!
   This is a pretty drastic rule, and some programers will disagree with it. It is, however, based on the following points.

   (a) As has been demonstrated by means of nonsense frames earlier in this program, a copying frame can represent absolutely no progress in the student's understanding of what is being talked about; such a frame can be answered on the basis of the structure of English. *(Chapter 2.)*
   (b) A frame should represent a step forward in the student's acquisition of the subject matter, and if the programer is being efficient, it should represent as large a step as the student is capable of taking. *(Chapter 3.)*
   (c) The behavior that we want from a student (that we judge will demonstrate his understanding of a term) includes defining it, giving an example of it, correctly labeling examples of it, recognizing when something is not an example of it, etc. If we are talking about RU's instead of terms, then the list is similar—stating it, being able to use it, knowing when not to use it, etc. Not included in this list of terminal objectives is the ability to copy the word when asked to.
   (d) One function of responses given by students is feedback to the programer. As we have tried to point out before, the ability to copy a word is not much of an indication to the programer that the student has learned anything.

   In an introductory frame on a new term, which of these combinations are acceptable and why are they acceptable or unacceptable?

We present a new term and define it "in the programer's carefully chosen words." Then:
- (a) We ask a student whether *x* is an example of this term or not. Is this acceptable or not?_____. Why?
- *or* (b) We ask him to define the term. Is this acceptable or not?_____. Why?
- *or* (c) We give him three things and ask him to pick out the *x*. Is this acceptable or not?_____. Why?

- - - - - - - - - - - - - -

- (a) Yes. It will test both the adequacy of the programer's statement (if too many students cannot do this, revise the definition) and the student's comprehension of the definition.
- (b) No. The programer just defined it. That makes a copying frame again, even if the student is not copying the term!
- (c) Yes (at least if the examples are well-chosen). It forces the student to respond to the definition.

2.
> Programed instruction is a technology of teaching that depends upon the empirical testing of a set of teaching materials. When we use any set of materials, such as a film or a set of frames, which has been carefully tested and revised until it produces the desired behavior, we are using _____ _____.

Make a discrimination frame out of that copying frame.

Write.
Programed instruction is a technology of teaching that depends upon the empirical testing of a set of teaching materials._____

- - - - - - - - - - - - - -

There is considerable latitude for your answer. You may have picked one EG or one non-EG and asked for a *yes-no* answer or an *is-is not* answer about your example. You may have asked the student to label one of two or three EG's. (EG's should be concrete examples such as a tested film, a workbook to accompany a reader, etc.)

252 EDITING

3. *Advice to the New Programer.* The most prevalent cause of copying frames and frames with irrelevant responses in them is what we might call the "lecture approach" to frame writing. If a programer thinks of a frame as a way of telling the student something, that is exactly what the frame will do. Having told the student something, the programer (since he wants to follow the rules) is now caught with the problem of finding a response after the fact.

> The ticket attached to each article of clothing must include: the price, the size, the material, and the model number of the article.

Having given this little lecture, the programer is stuck. In order to get the student *to respond to the four bits* of information that should be on a sales ticket, the first question that comes to mind, of course, is

> List the four things that must be included on a sales ticket.

or

> A sales ticket must include the _____, the _____, the _____, and the _____ _____ of the article.

Rejecting these as copying responses, the next thing that comes to mind is

> How many things must be listed on the sales ticket?

That is pretty elementary and does not get the student to notice *what* they are, only how many they are.

Where should the programer have started? (Drop down one line for a hint.)

Hint. The programer above started with the *stimulus* and had difficulty finding an appropriate *response*.

— — — — — — — — — — — — — — —

He should start with the behavior he wants to get and look for an adequate stimulus.

Suggest a way of getting the student to say what the programer wants him to say in the above situation.

— — — — — — — — — — — — — — —

If he wants to get a list of four things out of the student, one obvious solution is to have the student tell what he sees on a real sales ticket or a picture of one.

HOW TO AVOID THE COPYING FRAME 253

4. All dogmatic rules, of course, should be accepted with a grain of salt. The injunction against copying frames is a dogmatic rule. It is also difficult to set the precise point at which a frame stops being a frame that asks the student to observe something and shades into asking him simply to copy something.

> A pentagon is a closed figure with five sides. A five-sided polygon is called a _____.

The frame above is a copying frame. We have required the student to observe and reproduce the spelling of the word. That is all.

Suppose we try this:

> A pentagon is a closed figure with five sides. Which of these is a pentagon? _____.
>
> A   B

Now we have a response to "fiveness" in the presence of the stimulus "pentagon." That is progress.

Can you suggest a way in which the above frame can be redesigned so that it combines the functions of both frames? Get the student to respond both to "fiveness" and to the spelling of "pentagon." Finish the frame.

Write.
A pentagon is a closed figure with five sides.

_____
_____
_____
_____
_____
_____
_____
_____
_____
_____
_____

— — — — — — — — — — — — — —

If you gave him two or more pictures and asked him to label the pentagon, you have done both.

254 EDITING

5. Providing a model, which Skinner called *priming* and Gilbert called *demonstrating,* is sometimes an obvious first step to bypass tedious small-step shaping of discriminations. The copying frames to which the dogmatic rule is directed are those all too frequent ones in which students copy words which they can perfectly well spell or at least could learn to spell in conjunction with some more meaningful activity.

The frame below is for junior high-school students. An outside text, the Supplement, presents the Greek numerals for 1-9, 10, 20, 30, 100, 200, etc. The Greek numeral for 3 is $\overline{\Gamma}$, for 4 is $\overline{\Delta}$, and so forth.

> The Greeks used the letters of their alphabet as their numerals. To distinguish numerals from letters, a line or bar was placed over each numeral. Look at the Supplement and copy the Greek numerals for:
> 4_____, 30_____, 9_____, 500_____.
>
> (*Introduction to Modern Mathematics,* TMI)

Would you object to this way of controlling their observations of at least some of the numerals?

— — — — — — — — — — — — — — — —

Your choice. If the objective is to have the students be able to construct Greek numbers using these numerals, this approach would seem to be as legitimate as showing a child how to make a bow in his shoelace. (The real objective of the program would probably be more satisfying to most teachers—the students only went through enough of this copying and constructing to "appreciate" the economy of the decimal number system.)

---

6. Chapter 3 presented several systems of program construction some of which advocated the rule: *Get as much out of the student at each step as you can.* (Most of the big-frame systems were developed by programers who dealt with adult students. Even they would not produce frames like the Ameba frames for junior high-school students!)

Here's a tricky kind of item.

> *Animate* objects are alive. *Inanimate* objects are not alive. Is a rock an animate object?_____.

This is a simple enough frame. It introduces two "technical terms" and asks a question that requires the student to interact with the terms by discriminating whether an EG is a member of at least one of the classes.
What could you do to make him interact with both terms?

— — — — — — — — — — — — — — —

Ask two questions, one on each class.

---

7. The frame you just edited must have assumed that students could already discriminate what is "alive" and what is "not alive"—at least in the examples given. The programer, then, must be more interested in correct application of the technical terms than in the underlying discrimination. The student is going to have to spell these words *and* use them correctly eventually. So why not start with a frame that combines *both*
      the response to meaning (alive-not alive)
    and the response to form (the spelling).
Redesign the frame so that the student writes both terms in response to EGs of each.

Write.
Animate objects are alive. *Inanimate* objects are not alive.

_____
_____ _____

— — — — — — — — — — — — — — —

There are several ways of doing it. Among them,
    A rock is an _____ object (or your example).
    A (man) is an _____ object (or your example).
 or Is a rock animate or inanimate? Which?_____.
    etc.

Now you have increased the relevance, increased the size of the step, and still avoided a RU + R̃U frame design.

8. A RULEG or EGRUL frame is an obvious way around telling the student something and having him repeat it after the teacher. In their article (page 140) the originators of the system pointed out that a RULEG frame can "have the student working an example of a brand new rule the first time he sees it." Discriminating whether something is or is not an example is another possible interaction with a new rule. Classifying three or four things makes the step a little larger.

One of the reasons for RU + $\widetilde{RU}$ frames given in the article was that students are slow to add certain technical terms to their active vocabularies. (The slowness with which students learn to "use the correct word" comes as a surprise to many instructors who have always assumed that, given their carefully chosen definition of a term, their students now "know" the word.) How does a programer get around this problem? One way is the labeling type of frame.

There are two prompting techniques which might be used when the term that you want correctly spelled is not itself in the text or stimulus portion of the frame.

(a) One kind of formal prompt works well with a "which-kind-of-thing-is-this" type of frame. Assuming that the student has a limited number of technical terms that apply, how can you increase his knowledge of the subject and control his spelling at the same time?

If you want a hint, drop down one line.

— — — — — — — — — — — — — — —

Hint. In the frame below, the student who has gone through preceding frames in the program has a choice between *prefix, suffix,* and *root* in this frame. The frame requires him to label an example. The programer knows that the label is going to be misspelled if the student is not given a model. Give him one without giving the answer.

| In "disintegrate," *dis-* is a _____ . |

— — — — — — — — — — — — — — —

Make it a multiple-choice among all the reasonable terms. Here are two formulas that ask the student to copy the right word:

| In "disintegrate," *dis-* is a [prefix/suffix/root]. Which?_____ . |

or

| In "disintegrate," *dis-* is a _____ . |
| [prefix/suffix/root] |

(b) Where spelling is not one of the problems, a special prompt (one of the thematic prompts) is often sufficient. College students do not have to be taught how to spell "reinforce" or "negative reinforcement." The programer teaches them *when* to use the words, not how to spell them. What prompt can you use to increase the likelihood of a student's producing the correct technical term the first time that he is asked to in an EG + $\widetilde{RU}$ frame?_____. (Hint given below.)

HOW TO AVOID THE COPYING FRAME 257

Hint. Most of us *pick up* important terms in fields that we study without copying the terms. Studying implies active reading, of course, in which we are paying attention. Having studied, we can use the word later. What kind of prompt does this "learning by assimilation" suggest?

— — — — — — — — — — — — — —

The sequence prompt. If the word is used frequently in contexts where the student is "actively responding" to it (even though he is not writing it) it is likely to appear when he is asked to give it. If it does not, try some other format.

---

9. electrons
    nucleus

    Here is a picture of an atom. The center of the atom is called the nucleus and the particles that move around the nucleus are called electrons. _____ move around the _____ .

If the picture were not there, we could not call the response irrelevant, but in this case it ignores the picture. As it stands, this is not a very good frame. There are two ways of rewriting it in order to relate the text and the picture. In both cases, the frame will be a step forward in teaching the spelling of the terms too.

Revise the frame in two ways. Be sure that the responses get at the relationship being taught in the frame and utilize the illustration.

Write.
Here is a picture of an atom.
_____
_____
_____

and

Here is a picture of an atom.
_____
_____
_____

— — — — — — — — — — — — — —

(Either order.) In one frame, the picture should be labeled and the student completes the description in the text; e.g., "The center of an atom is called the _____ and the particles that move around it are called _____ ."

In the other, the text is complete and the student is asked to label the picture.

258 EDITING

SECTION C:
THE "LECTURE" FRAME AND WHAT TO DO WITH IT

1. > There are four kinds of sentences: declarative, imperative, interrogative, and exclamatory. Declarative sentences make a statement and are punctuated with a period. Imperative sentences give a command and are punctuated with a period. Interrogative sentences ask a question and are punctuated with a question mark. Exclamatory sentences express an emotion and are punctuated with an exclamation point.
   >
   > "Robert is here." This is a _____ sentence because it makes a statement and is punctuated with a period.

   What *two* obvious things are wrong with this frame? (Answer the question only in terms of frame design. There is a good deal wrong with the subject matter!)

   — — — — — — — — — — — — — — —

   There are two ways of describing one of the errors: either it does not require the student to respond to all the information in the frame (too narrow a response) or it provides too much material for the student to digest at once (too broad a stimulus). Also, the response required is a straight copying response, since the whole definition is repeated. The student does not even have to look at the example to answer the question.

---

2. Frames of the type presented in the last frame have been given many disparaging names, such as "lecture frame" and "overstuffed frame." The key to the difficulty is not the number of words. Many times, a programmer may need to write whole paragraphs in order to get complex points across. In a "lecture" frame, however, a programmer is not trying to get across *one* complex point. Frames of this type contain *too many* points with a response to only one of them.

   This should suggest two possible repairs, one that might work with sophisticated students and one that would be necessary for slower students. What two repairs might you make?

   — — — — — — — — — — — — — — —

   (a) Require more responses from the sophisticates (or a response that requires them to relate the bits of information in some way).
   (b) Break the item up into smaller steps for slower learners.

THE "LECTURE" FRAME AND WHAT TO DO WITH IT   259

3. | (4p⁺) 2e⁻ 2e⁻ | Generally speaking, atoms with 3 or less electrons in the outer level tend to lose electrons when ionizing, and atoms with 5 or more electrons in the outer level tend to gain electrons when ionizing. In the light of this, how might each of the atoms shown ionize to attain the structure of an inert gas?

(17p⁺) 2e⁻ 8e⁻ 7e⁻

(13p⁺) 2e⁻ 8e⁻ 3e⁻

(*Chemistry 1*, Basic Systems)

How many "bits" of information are introduced in this frame? _____. (The students have already been exposed to "electrons in the outer level" and "ionizing.")

Are the students required to respond to each bit? _____.

— — — — — — — — — — — — —

Two (even if you do not understand the item, the facts about 3 and 5 electrons should be apparent to you).

Yes. There is an example of each type and a third example thrown in, which reduces the "multiple-choiceness" that might occur if there were only two examples (bright students would expect one of each—and would only have to figure out one, if there were just two.)

---

4. Suppose that the programer has a good reason for keeping quite a large chunk of information together. He does not want to break it up, but he knows his students cannot swallow it all at once. What technique can he use to keep the information together and still require small-step responses? The answer, which has not been "taught," should be obvious. If you wish a hint, it is given below. If not, what technique can he use? _____.

— — — — — — — — — — — — —

Hint. We found it impossible to present in one frame enough illustrations of each type of program to give students of programing an example of how a lengthy sequence of frames is put together. In order to keep the lengthy sequence of frames together, so that they could be inspected at leisure for the answer to many different types of questions, we resorted to a standard technique in programing. How did we present the whole section of a program in Chapter 1? _____. Would this work for a "lecture" frame?

— — — — — — — — — — — — —

A supplement or outside text, traditionally called "panels." It could help with "lecture" frames.

260 EDITING

SECTION D: TAKE THE HOLES OUT OF THE SWISS CHEESE

1.
   | A reinforcer is a _____ which _____ a _____ and _____ the _____ of the _____ or _____ the _____ of the _____ . |

   This type of frame, which appears all too often in programs, has been given the name "Swiss cheese" frame (Markle, 1966)–the more holes it has the better it is. Is it a terminal frame?_____. Why?

   – – – – – – – – – – – – – – –

   No. It is full of fairly strong formal prompts.

2.
   | A reinforcer is a _____ which _____ a _____ and _____ the _____ of the _____ or _____ the _____ of the _____ . |

   Take the holes out of the Swiss cheese. Make a terminal frame of it.

   – – – – – – – – – – – – – – –

   "Define reinforcer" or "What is a reinforcer?" are good answers.

3. Frames of the Swiss cheese type are a temptation when the programer wants the student to give a precise and inclusive definition. Although there are many occasions for responding "in your own words," there are other occasions that require producing the exact set of words. With discouraging frequency (no more so than is seen in other forms of teaching, however) students omit half of an important definition or use a set of their own words which sophisticated readers realize does not sufficiently limit the area being defined or limits it too much.

   For instance, in my experience, the majority of eighth graders will define a prefix as "a couple of letters that go in front of a word," a definition which (taken literally) leaves out a great many longer prefixes and all cases in which the prefix is put in front of a unit that is not a word. College students trained to talk about reinforcers in terms of their effect on

TAKE THE HOLES OUT OF THE SWISS CHEESE 261

the rate of pecking seen in a pigeon or bar pressing seen in a rat tend to omit the part of the definition having to do with the probability of recurrence of a response when the situation recurs.

The repair of the terminal frame by indicating the number of blanks to be filled defeats the purpose, of course. By definition, it is not a terminal frame. What kind of repair could be made if the students' responses were imprecise on terminal items?

— — — — — — — — — — — — — —

When students are not precise, the answer is that they have not been trained to be precise, and the logical repair of the program is to provide sufficient training by increasing the number of items on the definition, making clear, of course, why precision is required. At the back of your mind should always be some question about the legitimacy of the objective which requires such precise spouting. There are times, however, when the world, especially the academic world, requires it.

---

4. The caveat against "Swiss cheese" is a relative matter. When carried to its extreme, as in the illustrative frame on "reinforcer," the use of formal prompts prohibits even legitimate variations in grammar and poses a kind of puzzle in rote learning for the student. In the middle of a sequence in which a definition is being taught, a certain amount (to be undefined except by common sense!) of formal prompting is an aid to the programer. The following frame appeared in the *Vectors* program:

All vectors and all arrows have _____ and _____ .
(*Vectors*, Basic Systems.)

This is one way to tell the student that he is supposed to give two properties that both of these things have. In what other way could you write the frame in order to insure that the student does not give one but two properties?

Write.

— — — — — — — — — — — — — —

Any question or statement including the word "two" will do. "Name two properties that both vectors and arrows have" or "What two things are true of both arrows and vectors?", etc.

SECTION E: THE ROLE OF THE FORMAL PROMPT

You have come quite a distance since formal prompts were introduced. If you feel rusty in this area, you might wish to review the concept, either by rereading the summary on page 94 or by working through the short sequence on pages 89 and 90.

1. > A doctor taps your knee (patellar tendon) with a rubber hammer to test your re_____s.
   >
   > If your reflexes are normal, your leg r_____s to the tap on the knee with a slight kick (the so-called knee jerk).
   >
   > In the knee jerk or patellar-tendon reflex, the kick of the leg is the r_____ to the tap on the knee.

   The above sequence represents a change for the worse in the first few items of *The Analysis of Behavior,* by Holland and Skinner.

   Would you say that the items were (a) overprompted; (b) adequately prompted; or (c) underprompted? (To answer this question, consider whether a normal college student could have answered these items without the formal prompts, would need the formal prompts, or would need more prompts.) (a), (b), or (c)? _____ .

   — — — — — — — — — — — — — —

   If you said (a), you agree with Holland and Skinner. The formal prompts are not used in the published version of this program.

2. *Rule.* Formal prompts have two important functions:

   (a) to control the spelling of words where spelling mistakes are frequent and
   (b) to eliminate alternate answers where the students are known to have two absolutely correct alternatives, one of which the programer does not want for some reason.

   Deduction from Rule. To elicit responses from the student which demonstrate that he understands what you mean and is speaking your language, you should use [formal/thematic] prompts.

   — — — — — — — — — — — — — —

   thematic.

3. For the average college student who has experienced visits to doctors, the mention of the common example (the knee jerk) is a sufficiently strong thematic prompt to elicit the word "reflex." Adding the formal prompt "re_____s" cannot increase the likelihood of an already strong associative response. On that basis, what do we mean when we say that a frame is overprompted?

— — — — — — — — — — — — — — —

(In your own words.) Some of the prompts can be subtracted without producing any change in the students' responses, or you can show that some of the prompts are unnecessary.

---

4. In Chapter 2, Section C, formal prompts were described as controlling "self-editing." In order to respond to a formal prompt such as the "serial-order prompt" in this frame:

> Like the American flag, the French flag is _____, _____, and _____.

or the rhyme in this frame:

> Nine times seven and just one more
> Is eight times eight or _____.
>
> (*Multiplication and Division Games*, TMI)

the student is in trouble unless he can produce a plausible answer or set of answers and see which one fits. The formal prompt helps him reject those that do not fit. The type of prompt that allows him to generate some answers so that he has something to edit is _____.

— — — — — — — — — — — — — — —

thematic. (This item is overprompted! However, I'm not apologizing for overemphasizing the distinction between the ways that the two kinds of prompts function.)

264 EDITING

5.
> A. A doctor tests your _____ .

As an introductory frame, that did not work. Students made a lot of errors. So the programer added prompts. Now it looks like this:

> B. A doctor tests your re_____es.

The error rate goes down to 5% and the programer is happy. He should not be. Why?

– – – – – – – – – – – – – – –

The frame is no more meaningful than before, although he has now helped the student guess what word the programer is thinking of.

6.
> A. A doctor tests your _____ .

A simple logical analysis of this frame should lead to its rejection before it ever gets to students. It is clearly underprompted. There are too many "correct, wrong answers," leaving the student to indulge in a guessing game.

> B. A doctor tests your re_____es.

In the sense that the train of thought suggested by the first thematic prompt leads to a fairly large number of potential responses, which can be thrown out because they do not fit, this is not quite so much of a guessing game.

> C. A doctor taps your knee (patellar tendon) with a rubber hammer to test your _____ .

THE ROLE OF THE FORMAL PROMPT 265

If both the second and the third frame have only one correct answer (assume they do), the student has enough information to get the answer. Which one is the more efficient frame? Which answer takes less time to get?_____.

— — — — — — — — — — — — — — —

The third frame. "Taps your knee" should produce "reflex," whereas the student may have to search through several words that he knows in order to find the answer to the second one.

---

7. When the first student works his way through the first draft of a program, many repairs are indicated. The programer's well-chosen statements of RU's turn out to be not so well-chosen. Examples turn out to be ambiguous. Points that were "so obvious" that they did not have to be stated turn out not to be so obvious. The program goes into rewrite. Data from the student govern what the programer does. Consider the following:

   (a) Errors are the data that help the programer revise. If he has not sufficiently prompted some response, will he find out about it when testing the program?
   (b) If he has more prompts than he needs, will he find out about it when testing the program?

   You create the rule for prompting in first drafts of programs.

   Write.

   _____
   _____

   Can you generalize from your rule about prompts to a similar rule about the amount of practice that should be put in a first draft?

— — — — — — — — — — — — — — —

If you said something like "A minimum of prompts should be used" (short of "what-am-I-thinking-of" frames), we agree. If you can generalize your rule to the amount of practice to be built into the first test version, you come out with "A minimum of practice should be written into the first draft."

SECTION F:
EGs, Non-EGs, AND THE MULTIDIMENSIONAL CONCEPT

This section describes what is perhaps the most difficult task in editing your first approximation. Once you can discriminate copy frames from non-copy frames, spot "Swiss cheese," and identify prompts when you see one, you can take the appropriate action whenever a misuse shows up in your draft. The problem discussed here is different: it is how to identify what IS NOT there but should be.

The material in this section hinges on all the previous material on concepts and principles. Although the term "concept" was used in its intuitive sense in Chapter 1, the first prime on this subject occurs in Chapter 2; further material is embedded all through Chapter 2 and 3, especially in the RULEG-EGRUL section, and summarized in essay form in Section D, Chapter 3. The problem we confront is insuring *both* adequate generalization and adequate discrimination of concepts and RUs.

1.
> A. When a word ends in a single consonant preceded by a single vowel, we double the final consonant when adding a suffix like *-ing* or *-er*.
> For instance, *sit* + *-ing* = *sitting*.
> Likewise, *bat* + *-er* = _____ .
>
> B. *Trap* + *-er* = *trapper*.
> *Clip* + *-ing* = _____ .
>
> C. From the way that we spell words like *bedding* and *furry* and *beggar*, we can state the rule:
> When a word ends in a _____ consonant preceded by a _____ vowel we _____ the final consonant when adding a suffix.
>
> D. Add the suffix *-ing* to *whip*: _____ .

A student is said to *discriminate* when he responds in one fashion in the presence of one stimulus and in a different fashion in the presence of another stimulus.

The above sequence rolls along in good RULEG fashion, terminating with an $\widetilde{EG}$. Can we now say that the student knows all about when to double final consonants in one-syllable words?_____. Why?

- - - - - - - - - - - - - - - -

No. We have evidence that he knows *how to*, but knowing *when to* also involves knowing *when not to*. Students with good memories and faulty logic (inserting a nonexistent "only") might be correct when spelling "fa*st*er," "*seat*ing," etc. But why not make the limits of the rule explicit?

2.
> Set A is a subset of B if every element of A is an element of B. Is the set $\{2,3,4\}$ a subset of the set $\{1,2,3,4,5\}$?

> $\{x, y, z\}$ [is/is not] a subset of the last seven letters of the alphabet.

> $\{$dog, cow, chicken$\}$ is a _____ of the set of domesticated animals.

In order to develop an adequate concept of subset, the student is here led to classify several subsets. Write an item leading him to discriminate between subsets and nonsubsets.

Write.

_____
_____
_____
_____

— — — — — — — — — — — — — —

Your item may display all sorts of originality as long as it satisfies one condition: the student has been given a smaller set in which *at least one* member of the set *is not* in the larger set.

3.
> An *element* of a set is a member of the set. a is an element of the set of the first three letters of the alphabet. x is n_____ an element of the set of the first three letters.

This frame contains two errors. Repairing the most obvious one is not all that it needs! What two errors are committed? (Do not repair them; simply name them.)

1) _____
2) _____

— — — — — — — — — — — — — —

The response is 1) overprompted, and what's more, 2) irrelevant.

268 EDITING

> An *element* of a set is a member of the set. *a* is an element of the set of the first three letters of the alphabet. *x* is n_____ an element of the set of the first three letters.

4. Assume that "member of the set" is meaningful, that this frame introduces the term "element," that the students know the alphabet, and that the purpose of the frame is to require a discrimination between elements and non-elements.

   Rewrite the frame to get a relevant response.

   Rewrite No. 1. Make it a RU + EG + $\overline{EG}$ (non-EG) frame in which the student discriminates rather than constructs the $\overline{EG}$.

   An element of a set is a member of the set.

   _____

   _____

   Rewrite No. 2. Assume your RU is well stated. Ask the student to make both discriminations.

   An element of a set is a member of the set.

   _____

   _____

   _ _ _ _ _ _ _ _ _ _ _ _ _ _ _ _ _

   No. 1. An element of a set is a member of the set.
           a is an element of the set of the first three letters of the alphabet.
           x [is/is not] . . .
           (or) Is *x* a member of the set . . .

   No. 2. The repair made on the third sentence should also be made on the second sentence. There is no reason why you cannot have one [is/is not] and the other a question if you prefer.

5.
   A. > Set A = $\{2, 7, 19, 6, 4, 25, 90, 106, 3, 18, 74\}$. Is the set $\{2, 3, 4, 5\}$ a subset of set A?

   B. > Set A = $\{$all the even digits$\}$.
   > Is $\{6, 8, 10\}$ a subset of set A?

   C. > Set A = $\{2, 4, 6, 8, 10\}$.
   > Is $\{2, 4, 9\}$ a subset of A?

   If the target population is, say, the fourth grade, one of these items is better than the other two as a test of the student's discrimination between instances and non-instances of subsets.

EGs, NON-EGs, AND THE MULTIDIMENSIONAL CONCEPT   269

These are *all* E̅G̅'s—non-EG's. Work through them yourself the way that a student would have to.

What is wrong with the other two? Why do they not represent good tests of the student's ability to discriminate?

_____ is not so good because _____

and

_____ is not so good because _____

- - - - - - - - - - - - - - - -

If you worked them out, you would recognize that A requires too much work to prove a small point in the student's learning.

B hinges on something that has nothing to do with sets—namely, the word "digit." (If training on that word was part of the objective of the program, this would be a good combination test item, but the student is likely to fail it here for the wrong reason—because he does not know "digit" rather than because he does not know "subset.")

---

6. A discrimination can be too hard. It can also be too easy.

> A pentagon is a closed figure with five sides. Label the pentagon below:
>
> ⬠   ∿   •
> ___   ___   ___

Suggest a better set of examples, which will require the student to make a finer discrimination.

- - - - - - - - - - - - - - - -

Two other closed figures, such as a quadrilateral and a six-sided figure (or a triangle) will do, but a really fine discrimination would include something else with five parts, such as a star or ∪ .

270 EDITING

7. > If a machine presents material to the student, requires a response from the student, and provides knowledge of results, then it is a teaching machine.

   When a student can discriminate that, according to the above definition, a film is not a teaching machine because it only presents material to students, can he then discriminate all negative examples (non-instances) of teaching machines implied by the definition? _____ .

   — — — — — — — — — — — — — —

   No.

8. How many characteristics define "teaching machine"? (How many things have to be true before a gadget is a teaching machine?) _____ .

   — — — — — — — — — — — — — —

   Three (stimulus, response, and knowledge of results).

Note: Please don't take that definition as an example of a good RU. It is not a very sophisticated definition.

9. The definition of a teaching machine is a good example of what is meant by a "multidimensional" concept. In order for something to be a teaching machine it must have
   property A and property B and property C.
   Any machine lacking any one of these properties is not a teaching machine.

   A student overgeneralizes when he generalizes erroneously to something that resembles but isn't an example of the concept he is trying to master. A programmer blocks such overgeneralization by including all appropriate non-examples.

   RU: *Good non-examples share some of the properties of examples BUT NOT ALL.*

   On the basis of this RU, you can work out a formula for frames that belong in the program. Your discrimination frames write themselves.
   The formula

   TEACHING MACHINE = A + B + C

   Non-examples: = A + B

                                    = _____

                                    = _____

   (Fill in the other required kinds of non-examples.)

   — — — — — — — — — — — — — —

   B + C and *A + C.*

10. The formulas you just constructed for non-examples of teaching machines are definitely abstractions. In the real world, some combinations of this sort might be missing. Or some might be absurd.

For instance, with A = Stimulus, B = Response, and C = Knowledge of Results, we have:

TEACHING MACHINE = S + R + KR

Non-examples   = S + R

                          = R + KR

                          = S + KR

You may be able to locate real machines (including paper as a "machine") which satisfy the first or second of these, but the third is absurd. How could you give Knowledge of Results if no Response had been made? So we scratch one kind of non-example.

Coming up with the other kinds of non-examples is what I had in mind on page 180 when I mentioned that "creativity" was involved in selecting examples and non-examples of concepts. Putting flesh on the bones of those formulas for "A + B + C" is work!

Now, among the principles you have come across in this book several times is:

> *The first draft should take the largest possible step*
> *that the programer thinks the students can handle–*
> *even a little more, if possible.*

Laymen as well as psychologists use the phrase "fine discrimination." Which of these, in terms of our formula above, is the finer discrimination in this pair:

_____The student will discriminate an EG (A + B + C) from a non-EG (A + B);

_____The student will discriminate an EG (A + B + C) from a non-EG (A).

– – – – – – – – – – – – – – –

The first one. A non-example that shares two properties is more like examples than a non-example that shares only one property. The discrimination is "finer" or harder.

11. The following concept was used in a demonstration program by Donald H. Bullock. (It is not really a nonsense concept—the real-life concept was a data word from a particular computer language.)

   A "glopple" is defined as a term which
   (a) must contain at least one letter;
   (b) may also contain other letters, numbers, and hyphens but NO OTHER characters on the typewriter keyboard;
   (c) MUST NOT contain more than 30 characters.

   Describe the kinds of non-examples that would be required to insure adequate discrimination of glopples from non-glopples.

   _ _ _ _ _ _ _ _ _ _ _ _ _ _ _ _

   You need three sets of non-examples: one set with no letters, one set with the prohibited characters, and one set that is too long.

Note. The problem of discrimination training is frequently solved by the nature of most subject matters. Discriminations between protons and neutrons, positive reinforcement and negative reinforcement, scalars and vectors, prefixes, suffixes, and roots, and so forth, literally write the discrimination sequences for the programer. When the subject matter is not so fortunately arranged, however, the programer has to be aware of *how many* dimensions define the concept that he is teaching and then include training on all these dimensions.

12.
   1. When the powers of two numbers are multiplied, the exponents are added.
      For instance, $(x^2)(x^3) = x^5$.
      Likewise, $(x^3)(x^4) = $ _____.
   2. $(x^3)(x^4) = x^7$.
      $(x^2)(x^3) = $ _____.
   3. $(x^2)(x^3) = x^5$.
      When the powers of two numbers are multiplied, we _____.
   4. $(x^3)(x^4) = $ _____.

EGs, NON-EGs, AND THE MULTIDIMENSIONAL CONCEPT   273

The absurdity of this sequence is a little too obvious, but it should suggest to you a common-sense rule about the choice of EG's. What?

Write.

_____

- - - - - - - - - - - - - - -

(In your own words.) Vary them. Not only should the student be led to see the limits of some rule or definition by seeing non-EG's, but he should also get an adequate sample of EG's.

13. To go back to our definition of "teaching machine," our abstract formula suggested that A + B + C (stimulus + response + knowledge of results) gave us a way to identify the best non-examples. To insure generalization, we also need to vary the examples in a somewhat orderly fashion. And we want challenging steps.

   If this were your first example:

   EG for first frame: a "talking typewriter," a large machine which provides picture and sound input, requires typing on a keyboard for the response, and confirms by moving on to the next step;

which of these is the bigger step in generalization?

(a) Second EG: a computer which types input onto a sheet of paper in front of the student, student responds by typing back, computer moves on to next problem;

or

(b) Second EG: a small battery-driven machine unrolls stored frames across a window, student pushes button for answer, is advanced to next frame if correct.

- - - - - - - - - - - - - - -

(b) As a second example, (b) varies both the size of the "machine," an irrelevant attribute, and the response mode (response itself is critical, but mode—constructed-response or button pushing—is not). An even bigger generalization would also have changed the way knowledge of results is provided. The computer example (a) changed only one aspect—the stimulus input. This would have been a smaller step in generalizing the concept.

14. *General Principles:* To select the biggest step you can in teaching a concept, you would: for discrimination, select a non-example (most like/least like) the example of the concept; for generalization, select a second example (most like/least like) the first example.

─ ─ ─ ─ ─ ─ ─ ─ ─ ─ ─ ─ ─ ─ ─

most like, for discrimination
least like, for generalization

---

15. At this point, consider what you have to do if, on testing your first draft, you have followed the rules and you find that you have pushed your student too far in each case. Is it apparent how to revise each frame? If so, how?

─ ─ ─ ─ ─ ─ ─ ─ ─ ─ ─ ─ ─ ─ ─

I hope you said yes. You would have to make the discrimination less fine—easier, in other words, by using a non-example that was farther away and less confusing. You would have to make the generalization easier by using a second example of the same concept that wasn't quite so different from the first one.

The above conclusion is an example of what was meant when, on page 186, you read "No one believes that much useful evidence can be gathered from 'undesigned' instruction. The programer must know what he is looking for." In these cases, you would know that you were stretching your student, and you would be watching for his reaction with a clear plan for making the discrimination or the generalization easier.

SECTION G: MAKING THE MOST OF AN ELASTIC PROMPT

1. Taking the sequence prompt into account, the programer has put these items at spaced intervals throughout a section of his program. Here they are removed from their context so that you may inspect the progression of teaching from the beginning to the end of the sequence on the definition.

1.	A vector is a quantity that has both direction and magnitude. Why is displacement a vector?
4.	Displacement is an example of quantities called vectors. Vectors have both _____ and _____ .
11.	Vectors have both _____ and _____ .
18.	Vectors have _____ .
29.	Vectors have m_____ and d_____ .
40.	What is a vector?

   Interspersed between these items in the program are items asking for other types of behavior indicating "understanding" of the concept: the student is being asked to give examples, label examples, give the term when given the definition, and discriminate this term from another contrasting term being taught concurrently.
   What is out of place in the above sequence? _____ .

   Item 29. It is much easier than some of the preceding items.

2. If data show the programer that it takes five steps to get the student from the initial step one (No. 1) to the final step six (No. 40), and if the programer chooses to leave item 29 as it is, where should he put it in the teaching sequence? _____ .

   Between No. 4 and No. 11 (the formal prompt is not likely to be as strong as the EG prompt), although you can make a case for putting it between No. 1 and No. 4, where a stronger sequence prompt would be operating.

276 EDITING

3. Programers, who like technical terminology as much as any other group, talk about "fading" the prompts in a sequence. Words such as "withdrawing" or "subtracting" will do as well. Whatever you choose to call it, the process is supposed to be done with some sort of logic. Logically, the more a student knows about a subject, the _____ prompts he needs to come up with the correct answer.

— — — — — — — — — — — — — —

fewer.

---

4. (a) $RU_1 + EG_1 + \widetilde{EG}_1$.
   (b) $EG_1 + \widetilde{EG}_1$.
   (c) $EG_1 + \widetilde{RU}_1$.
   (d) $\widetilde{EG}_1$.
   (e) $RU_2 + EG_2 + \widetilde{EG}_2$.
   (f) $EG_2 + \widetilde{EG}_2$.
   (g) $\widetilde{EG}_1$.
   (h) $\widetilde{RU}_1 + \widetilde{RU}_2$.

   No program really ticks off in such an organized fashion. If the process were that simple, however, you could write formulae such as the one above that would identify review items, give you a good look at your sequence prompts, and perhaps indicate where you had not given enough examples of one RU or had forgotten to ask for the $\widetilde{RU}$.

   If the above program involved five RU's and if all the review items, such as (g), were put off until the end, what do you think would happen?_____.

— — — — — — — — — — — — — —

Forgetting is a good hypothesis.

---

5. There are two ways out of this problem of forgetting. The best one, which we cannot illustrate in a single frame (take a look at the vectors program for one example) lies in clever arrangement of the material. If the subject has a structure (and many subjects do) the early steps are integral parts of later material and are being practiced without explicit review items. You cannot do long division without reviewing most of the basic arithmetic, for instance. The other method, of course, is to ask review questions.

   Would a $RU + EG + \widetilde{EG}$ frame be a good review question to use 40 frames after the original teaching? _____. Why?

— — — — — — — — — — — — — —

No. If you have to go back to the beginning, you probably have not taught much.

6. Here is another dogmatic statement. If a review item that appears out of context and much later cannot be answered by students unless prompts belonging early in the teaching sequence are added to it, *either*

(a) the teaching sequence was not good enough

or (b) the item is ambiguous.

If the item is ambiguous because the student does not know which of several plausible responses you now happen to have in mind, throw it out. Ask a better question. If the item is not ambiguous, you have to repair something. What? In line with the dogma stated above, you could:

(a) Add a large dose of prompts to the review item. Yes or no?_____.
(b) Lengthen the teaching sequence. Yes or no?_____.
(c) Insert a review item earlier in order to "keep the memories alive." Yes or no?_____.

— — — — — — — — — — — — — — — —

(a) No (it does not make the teaching any better and puts off the terminal item that much longer).
(b) Yes.
(c) Yes (you can always adjust the sequence prompt a little better).

SECTION H: BRANCHING FRAMES

The intrinsic school of programing, discussed in Chapter 4, sprang from a different philosophical background than the more dominant group to whom error on the student's part was a cause for revision on the programer's part. The old argument over frame-size has diminished, the classical intrinsic frame being quite outdone by the matheticists! The subject of error will remain a decision for each programer to make. Although we can hope that few programers will remain locked into one kind of frame and sequence design, always writing long paragraphs and multiple-choice questions, we can also recognize good reason for being able to use the techniques on occasion. Students do differ. Branching, even on a single question, is useful.

Many principles of good instruction are common to both kinds of programing, whether the frame will branch the student or not. An anonymous article circulated within U.S. Industries (parent company of many intrinsic programers) "How to Prepare a Branching Program for Automatic Teaching" will be liberally quoted. Along with advice relevant to all kinds of frames, it contains specific editorial guidelines for the intrinsic format.

> **On style, the anonymous author says:**
>
> The style of writing that has proved most successful is essentially informal. . . . If it is considered desirable for the student to take notes, say so. If something must be memorized, say so. Parenthetical remarks, warnings, encouraging comments, and even occasional flashes of humor are quite acceptable.

On clarity:

In preparing an elementary explanation of any subject, it is often necessary to indulge in "white lies." ... Whenever possible, of course, qualifying words should be used to mitigate the offense to pure science, but even qualifications can be misleading. There are pedagogues who would not commit themselves in writing to the proposition that "water flows downstream" because such a bald account of affairs fails to take into account eddies and whirlpools. However, the cause of education is not served by informing the student that "water sometimes flows downstream!" ... The foregoing is in no way to be interpreted as a justification for sloppy writing or ignorance.

On logical organization:

The fundamental problem in producing the main stream of "right-answer" pages for an intrinsic program is, of course, organization. In an ordinary teaching situation the occasional presentation of a fact before the student is equipped to understand it is seldom fatal. The student probably will cover the same material several times before being examined. ... In automatic tutoring, the student is tested on each concept immediately.

In writing the program itself, it is essential to know at every step just what the student knows, what he is being told to do with it, why he is being given this new material, what he is expected to do with it, and what mistakes he might possibly make. The programer, looking over a page of his work, can usually see several places where the student might be misled. The material should be rewritten to eliminate as many of these traps as possible. The possible misinterpretations that remain provide the basis for the multiple-choice question.

1. Linear programers would agree with almost all of these points. For the "frames-should-be-as-short-as-possible" school, there might be some disagreement with the comment about flashes of humor and parenthetical remarks. An informal style, of course, is a personal matter. There is only one point on which there would be fundamental disagreement. What is it?_____.

— — — — — — — — — — — — —

Leaving any room for misinterpretation (or leaving the possibility of an error in the frame).

2. *Rule.* "A good question requires the student to demonstrate his understanding of the idea presented."

---

24 (from 29)

Your Answer. The 2nd power of $5 = 5^2 = 5 \times 5 = 25$.

You are correct. The 2nd power of 5 means 5^2, which, of course, is 25.

Special terminology is used to describe a quantity written in the form of a power of a number. The number that is to be used as a factor is called the *base*. The number telling how many times the base is to be used as a factor is called the *exponent:*

$$\text{base} \longrightarrow 5^2 \longleftarrow \text{exponent}$$

Powers of numbers are very important in the study of number systems. We therefore need a convenient symbol to stand for the idea of powers. We shall use the letter b to stand for the *base*. We shall use the letter n to stand for the *number of times* the base is used as a factor. The letter n is the *exponent* of b. Thus, the symbol for any power of any number is

$$b^n$$

By using this symbol, we can make general statements about powers without needing specific examples, just as we can make general statements about addition or multiplication.

In the expression b^n

    b is the base and n is the exponent.   **page 11**
    b is the exponent and n is the base.   **page 17**

This question tests the student's understanding of the material. True or False? _____.

-- -- -- -- -- -- -- -- -- -- -- -- -- --

True.   Go to page 281, A.
False.   Go to page 280.

280 EDITING

Your Answer. The question does not test the student's understanding of the material.

You are correct. As it stands, the question is a copying frame, and we could translate it into nonsense words without affecting the error rate one bit (especially if we keep the italicized hints in).

The frame was taken from *The Arithmetic of Computers,* by N. A. Crowder, with editorial revision (in the wrong direction) of the question. The question as written by Crowder was

> If a quantity is written as a power, and the base of the quantity is 3 and the exponent is 2, what is the quantity?
>
> 8. page 11
> 9. page 17

According to the anonymous author,

> Another pitfall in the construction of a multiple-choice question is the temptation to ask a question which does not require thought but merely the ability to look back at the text and find the answer.

In other words, copying frames are out.

3.
> from p. 18A   23A
>
> You are correct. 4 is not the fourth component of the vector $(-1, 10, 4, 5, -7)$. The fourth component is 5.
>
> A vector with two components is often called a "two-dimensional" vector, one with three components is called a "three-dimensional" vector, etc.
>
> Which of the following statements is *incorrect?*
>
> (a) Vector *(a, b, c, d)* has four components. See page 17C.
> (b) *(X, Y, Z, U, V)* has six components. See page 17A.

The above frame contains a fundamental error in frame design. What is it? Does this error in an intrinsic frame remind you of a fundamental error in a linear frame? It should. What kind of error?

If you need some help with these questions, go to page 281, B.
If you have formulated an answer, go to page 282.

A (from page 279).

Your Answer. The question given in the intrinsic frame tested the student's understanding.

This is not correct. Although the frame is much too long for your author to translate it into nonsense terms, you will see, if you inspect it carefully, that it exactly parallels a type of frame that students can answer even if the material is written in nonsense words. Return to page 279, look at the frame again, classify that frame according to the type of frame it is (what type is it?), and choose the other answer.

B (from page 280).

> from p. 18A   23A
>
> You are correct. 4 is not the fourth component of the vector $(-1, 10, 4, 5, -7)$. The fourth component is 5.
>
> A vector with two components is often called a "two-dimensional" vector, one with three components is called a "three-dimensional" vector, etc.
>
> Which of the following statements is *incorrect?*
>
> (a) Vector *(a, b, c, d)* has four components. See page 17C.
> (b) *(X, Y, Z, U, V)* has six components. See page 17A.

Rule. "A good question requires the student to demonstrate his understanding of the idea presented."

If your problem was the question "What's wrong with the frame?", observe:

(a) The feedback gives you a pretty good idea of what the previous question was. What is the new material in this frame?
(b) Does the question test the student's understanding of the new material?

If your problem was the question "What linear error does this remind you of?", consider the following:

(c) The purpose of a linear frame is the elicitation of a response. If the text of the frame has nothing to do with the response, either the response asked for or the text is (?) to the purpose of the frame.

Now, here's the question again: The above frame contains a fundamental error in frame design. What is it? What kind of error in linear frame design does this error parallel?

Turn to page 282.

282 EDITING

Answer to Pages 280 and 281. The question does not test the student's understanding of the new information presented in the frame. This parallels the irrelevant response in a linear frame. It would also be correct to say that it parallels the introduction of irrelevant points into a linear frame. We could guess that perhaps the programer felt it necessary to give two questions on components (in which case he would need no new information in the frame), but slipped and included some irrelevant material.

Again, the frame was an editorial revision that damaged a good frame. The original came from *Vectors,* by R. Carman. Here is his question.

Which of the following is *incorrect?*

(a) Vector *(a, b, c, d)* has four components   (page 17C).
(b) *(X, Y, Z, W, U, V)* has six components   (page 17A).
(c) (4, 1, 7) is a two-dimensional vector   (page 19A).
(d) *(a, b,* 1, 2) is a four-dimensional vector   (page 20B).

The question requires the student to demonstrate his understanding of the idea presented.

---

4. At this point, you may be under the control of a prompt based on what has been going on so far: if a frame is not credited to some author, your author has revised it into some sort of monster. That is true. What is wrong with this one?

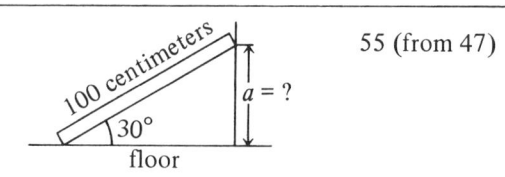

---

  55 (from 47)

  100 centimeters
  a = ?
  30°
  floor

Your Answer.   Yes, the length of side *a* may now be determined.

You are correct. Since we told you that in any 30° right triangle, the leg opposite the 30° angle is always .5 as long as the hypotenuse, you now have all the information that you need to find the length of leg *a* above. (You know the hypotenuse is 100 cm long.) How long is leg *a* in the diagram?

60°.   **page 53**
50 centimeters.   **page 56**
Can't tell.   **page 63**

The alternatives do not represent reasonable choices. They do not test "a possible misinterpretation."

5. Suppose the item were written this way:

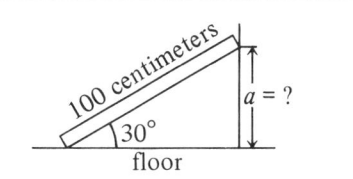

---

55 (from 47)

[Diagram: a right triangle with hypotenuse labeled "100 centimeters", a 30° angle at the base along the "floor", and the vertical leg labeled "a = ?"]

Your Answer. Yes, the length of side *a* may now be determined.

You are correct. Since we told you that in any 30° right triangle, the leg opposite the 30° angle is always .5 as long as the hypotenuse, you now have all the information you need to find the length of *a* above. (You know the hypotenuse is 100 cm long.) How long is leg *a* in the diagram?

  50 feet. **page 53**
  50 centimeters. **page 56**
  50 yards. **page 64**

What's wrong with this one? It tests a possible misconception, doesn't it?

— — — — — — — — — — — — — —

In the words of the anonymous advisor, "Programers should be warned to avoid questions centering around some trivial point." Even if feet vs. centimeters were a "possible misinterpretation" of the question, it is certainly a trivial one.

284 EDITING

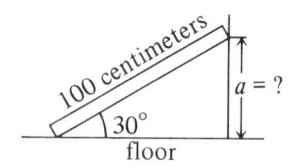

6.
> ```
>           100 centimeters
>                    ↑
>                    a = ?
>           30°      ↓
>           floor
> ```
> 55 (from 47)
>
> *Your Answer.* Yes, the length of side *a* may now be determined.
>
> You are correct. Since we told you that in any 30° right triangle, the leg opposite the 30° angle is always .5 as long as the hypotenuse, you now have all the information you need to find the length of leg *a* above. (You know the hypotenuse is 100 cm long.) How long is leg *a* in the diagram?

The student has a mathematical problem—one unknown to solve. This, of course, presents a situation fraught with peril. Think up at least one reasonable wrong alternative for this problem. (If you have experience teaching mathematics, you can undoubtedly think of several.)

The student has to do something with the numerals 100 and .5. The correct solution to the problem $a/c = .5$, when $c = 100$, has to be given as one alternative.

    50 centimeters (page x).
    _____ (page y).
    (optional)_____ (page z).

— — — — — — — — — — — — — —

There is room for variation in your answers. One very reasonable error would be 200 centimeters, which the student would get if he turned the equation upside down in order to solve it. Answers like 5 centimeters and 500 centimeters are highly likely errors when students are confronted with decimal problems, but their relevance could be questioned.

---

7. Consider this:

If you provide an alternative like 5 centimeters, permitting the student to demonstrate ignorance of the decimal system, you have to write at least one remedial loop on the subject. Do you believe that a remedial loop would be sufficient if the student did not know how to multiply by a decimal?_____.

— — — — — — — — — — — — — —

The question asked what you thought. I think not.

8. *If* an intrinsic programer provides an incorrect alternative, he *has to* teach. In a constructed-response program, errors in using decimals might very well arise in such a question. Most programers would feel it necessary either to require entering knowledge of decimals or to insert a remedial sequence in their programs. An intrinsic programer does not have to face this dilemma. What advantage does he have over other programers?

— — — — — — — — — — — — — — — —

In essence, he can pick and choose the errors that he will deal with. The multiple-choice question gives him this advantage.

---

9. *Review Question.* A multiple-choice alternative is a prompt. What kind of a prompt is it? Formal or thematic?_____.

— — — — — — — — — — — — — — — —

Formal. It specifies the form of the response, even to the decimal point!

---

10. In Chapter 2, a distinction was made between the logical strength of prompts and the psychological strength of prompts. Confronted with a blank that the programer knows may elicit twenty possible answers, students will pile up on one or two of the alternatives. On the other hand, confronted with a blank that has only one or two possible logical alternatives, students may break with logic and do some "original thinking."

Intrinsic programers talk a great deal about providing "reasonable alternatives" for their multiple-choice questions. These alternatives should give the programer a chance to eliminate misconceptions. In order to do this, he has to decide what misconceptions could arise. Suggest a way in which he could empirically determine what misconceptions could arise. What might he do with the first draft of the program?

— — — — — — — — — — — — — — — —

There are some delightful and agonizing reappraisals confronting any intrinsic programer who gives the questions to students without giving them the alternatives that he has in mind!

11. The following contains an error. Take the position of a student who has arrived at this item after a considerable struggle with a problem that he did not really understand.

> *Your Answer.*   20 is the 10th power of 2.
>
> It seems that you have been asleep or merely lucky to get this far in the program with such an idea as that. You must learn to pay attention.
>
> We will try once more. The power of a number is the number multiplied by itself as many times as the exponent shows. So the 10th power is $2 \times 2 \times 2 \times 2 \ldots$ and on to 10 2's. Now go back to page x and choose the correct answer.

What is wrong with this remedial loop?

— — — — — — — — — — — — — —

It is a pretty flagrant insult to the student.

In the words of the anonymous author:

> Writing "wrong answer pages" which the student sees after making an error demands extraordinary patience. The newcomer to programing, after spending a few days trying to produce even clearer explanations of matters he has already explained to his own satisfaction, may be excused if he feels a strong urge to print the same message on every wrong answer page: "No, dunderhead! Go back and think about what was said the first time."
>
>   A Crowderian program does the student the courtesy of assuming he made a sincere attempt to understand the material and failed for some good reason. The student is entitled to a further explanation, and just as some elusive point may suddenly be illumined by consulting a different author, so a slightly different approach on a wrong answer page may clear the matter up.

The words are equally true of any remedial branch, whether "intrinsic" in format or not.

This general rule might not apply, of course, to the aggressive students mentioned on page 236!

SUMMARY OF RULES FOR GOOD FRAMES AND SEQUENCES

Your task is to write a first draft for submission to trial by student in which difficulties with the subject matter are predictable and difficulties with the design are minimized.

A Checklist for first drafts

1. Frames should be written clearly in good English.
2. What is said should be correct.
3. Frames should be organized into some kind of logical order. Frames on the main track (if there is individualization) should present all the information that a student needs in order to master the new subject matter.
4. The response required of the student should be relevant to the purpose of the frame (based on the assumption that each frame *has* a purpose). If the student is to learn to *do* something, make him do it rather than talk about doing it.
5. If the question is multiple-choice, it should test the student's understanding of the material presented and should provide reasonable nontrivial alternatives.
6. The student's ability to handle demonstration materials, outside texts, etc., should be fully used to avoid telling him something that he can find out for himself. *Eliminate all* repeat-after-me copying frames.
7. Frames should be considered as units related to expected student behavior. If this means a large chunk of material, make it a large chunk. Make the response itself a meaningful step.
8. On the other hand, avoid introducing more points than can be responded to in any one frame. Digressions, if you choose to employ them for motivational purposes, should be somehow related to the issue at hand.
9. Use the wastebasket and scissors liberally to eliminate irrelevant material.
10. Provide a range of examples covering the variety of conditions that the student should be able to cope with. Where the subject matter itself does not provide appropriate contrasts, include *all* necessary non-examples.
11. Keep the strength of the sequence prompt in mind. Where the program is extensive enough, provide isolated review and test items as feedback to the programer as well as the student on how well the teaching sequence has gone. This requirement may be ducked if later materials require the student to actively practice earlier learnings.
12. Make use of thematic prompts (context) liberally and formal prompts (multiple-choice format excluded, of course) only when absolutely necessary. A first draft should have *none* of the latter.
13. When the student is branched to remedial instruction, the material should represent a restatement worded so as to indicate that the programer is neither condescending to nor exasperated by the student's error.
14. As large a step toward mastery as the student can reasonably be expected to take should be required in each frame. Let empirical testing tell you where the step is too large. On the other hand, hold irrelevant time-consuming activities, such as calculations and writing out long answers, to a minimum.
15. Let empirical testing determine the amount of practice necessary beyond the minimal range of examples. There should be *no repetition* of the same kind of problem within any short sequence on the first draft. (Review frames, mentioned in Item 11, are useful in long sequences.) The students will let you know how much practice should be provided.

Minor Editorial Caveats. English has a fair number of ambiguities which are to be avoided in writing frames. Here is one of them:

Question. "Is it raining or is the sun shining out there?"
Answer. "No."

The conjunction "or" is ambiguous. It clouds some issues. A frame with what looks like a multiple-choice design, because it includes an "or" (the programer intended the student to choose between the two categories), may not elicit multiple-choice behavior from students, even adult students. The repair of the frame is relatively simple. Be sure to ask "which," either in the statement of the question ("Which kind of animal is this—a cat or a dog?") or close to the blank to be filled in. Better yet, unless you are subtly trying to include spelling practice, label the categories and write the question thus: "Is this (a) a cat or (b) a dog? (a or b?)."

A question such as "Would you call this an *x*?" is ambiguous to most students because of parent-teacher behavior. They are forced to interpret the programer's behavior (does he want to know what I think or does he really mean "Is it an *x*?"). *If you are not interested in what the student thinks, ask the question straight out.* If you are interested in his opinion, be sure the answer space reflects this interest and allows him his choice. The question "Can you . . ." is always honestly answerable with "no." The student may also say "yes" and wait for instructions to do it at a later point!

Programers learned early in the game that the indefinite article operates as a formal prompt. In fact, if the item is essentially a choice between two terms, one of which begins with a vowel and the other with a consonant, a blank preceded by either "a" or "an" is all the prompting the student needs to help him make the choice. In an attempt to avoid this prompt, many programers adopted the convention "a(n)." Avoid it wherever you can. Use "the" if you can, or put the word into plural form if it can stand without an article in the plural. Better yet, ask a question. The fill-in blank is not sacred.

There is no absolute rule that a blank has to be at the end of a sentence. However, it is common courtesy to the reader-student to start his train of thought off with some well-chosen words. A sentence that begins with a blank is almost always an unnecessary imposition. Asking a question is always a way out.

Self-Test on Editing

Describe the error that has been made in each of these frames *and* repair the error. If you cannot think of relevant material in some area that you are not familiar with, indicate *what kind* of repair should be made. (*Do not* get involved with the subject matter. Stick to frame design.) The answers are on page 293.

> 1. An ABSTRACTION is an IDEA we have in our MINDS. Since "Essential Chairness" denotes an abstraction, it denotes an idea we have in our M____S.
>
>   (*On Abstractions,* D. Markle, 1962)

2. *Your Answer.* Love is not a numerical concept.

You are correct. There is no really meaningful way of assigning a numerical value to love. Temperature and intelligence, however, are numerical concepts.

We will define a VECTOR as a group of two or more numbers. Vectors are used to represent numerical concepts that require *more* than one number for their description.

Which of the following is not a numerical concept?

    The length of Route 66 (page 3).   Curiosity (page 9).
    The volume of a cube (page 7).

(revised from *Vectors,* Carman)

3. (*Context.* A poem is presented on a panel.)

In the second verse, the author describes a lovely scene. It is midnight and the full _____ is rising over the Yangtze.

4. The sine of an angle is defined as the ratio of the length of the leg opposite the angle to the length of the hypotenuse.

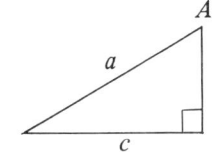

In this triangle, the sine of Angle A is a/c.

In the triangle below, what is the sine of angle P?

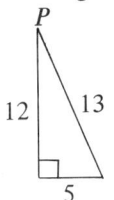

$\sin P = 5/13$. page 7
$\sin P = b/c$. page 11
$\sin P = 13$. page 14

5. The standard "dry Martini" consists of four parts of gin to one part of dry vermouth. An even drier Martini would contain 15 parts of gin to only one _____ of vermouth.

290   EDITING

> 6. The *mean* is the sum of the scores divided by the number of the scores.
>
> The *median* is the middlemost score in an odd-numbered set of scores or the midpoint between the two middle scores in an even-numbered set of scores.
>
> The *mode* is the most frequently attained score.
>
> Given the following set of scores:
> 199, 403, 211, 313, 158, 210, 217, 211, 314, 258, 284, 379, 211, 203, 311, 269, 315, 211, 248, 291, 207, 216, 212, 211, 201
>
> Calculate the mean.

> 7. *Your Answer.* I played the 10 of hearts.
>
> That was a very foolish move. You just trumped your partner's ace.
>
> Let us see if we can make this point clear to you *this* time. When your partner's card is the high card, you DO NOT, repeat DO NOT, play a trump card unless the person on your right trumps and you have to cover his trump. Now return to page 799 and play the hand more carefully.

> 8. An irrational number is a number which is _____ _____ of _____ _____ as an _____ or as a _____ of an _____ .

Outside Exercises

The following exercises represent some typical problems faced by programers in academic areas. The first is a "single-concept" program. The second pair are relatively complex principles which can be RULEGed or EGRULed. A more difficult task, in these cases, is to prepare a true discovery program. The third task is "observing behavior," teaching a student how to use cross-referenced tables or other complex information sources when the objectives do not call for memorizing anything. The fourth task is a chain.

Task One. *A multidimensional concept.*

Assume you are either a subject matter expert or that you have consulted one and have a complete description of the properties of the concept you are to teach. To put everyone on equal footing, the concept is a "nonsense" one modeled after Bullock's *glopple* (mentioned on page 272) but here redefined.

> Your objectives are: the student will identify examples of glopples and will be able to state why any particular non-example does not qualify. In other words, he need not spout the total definition in good "Swiss Cheese" fashion, but he must be able to say what is wrong with non-examples.

Glopples are "words" produced by combining (a) the ten digits, (b) upper-case letters, (c) dashes, e.g., –, and (d) spaces according to the following rules:

They *must* include at least one number.
They *may* include letters, dashes, and spaces *between* characters. (A space counts as one character. Spaces at the beginning and end of the "word" do not count.)
They *may not* include more than twelve characters including spaces.
They *may not* include any other characters on the typewriter keyboard.
The discrimination between the digit zero and the letter O is made by writing the letter O thus: ⌀

This is a fairly complex concept for which many and various examples may be generated.

1. Design your posttest for the two behaviors specified in the objectives. Check that the test covers every aspect of the concept—you are constructing a total criterion test, not a sample. The examples and non-examples you use in your criterion test *may not be used* in the teaching sequence. Check this again when you have completed the teaching sequence.
2. State your entry assumptions (can name asterisks, ampersands, etc., or can't, uses the terminology "upper-case" or doesn't, etc.) Recheck after completing the teaching sequence that you have not made any further assumptions about technical vocabulary or background knowledge.
3. Go ahead and produce the teaching sequence your own way—with or without an outline of what belongs in each frame.
4. Edit your draft. (I prefer to let it sit for 24 hours before doing so.) Compare your frames with relevant parts of the Checklist for First Drafts on page 287. Recheck test and entry behavior.
5. If you can find a critical reader to play editor, try it on this person before doing a student trial. (Ignore the editor's advice about how you "ought to teach"—but listen carefully to anything he says about the way you say things.)
6. Check your final product on a student.

Task Two. *Principles by RULEG or EGRUL.*

To make this a task worthy of a programer's effort, you need to select a relatively complex principle or rule. There are a couple of practice tasks that have been used for many years in programing:

1. A complicated double-contingency spelling rule, such as: In a two syllable word, the final consonant is doubled in front of a suffix beginning with a vowel if (a) the final consonant is preceded by a single vowel and (b) the accent is on the second syllable. (For non-enthusiasts of spelling rules, the following examples might come in handy: edited, emitted, bigoted, begotten, traveling, repelling, numbering, referring. I like to hold "programer" off for the posttest.)
2. A complicated mathematical trick, of which there are dozens: To square a number ending in five, multiply the part to the left of 5 by one more than itself and write 25 to the right of the product, e.g., 65^2 = 6 × 7 which equals 42, so write 4225.

In each case, determine the objectives you intend to reach (just application or rule statement too) and design your posttest to reflect your objectives. Design your program according to one of the systematic procedures. (You should be able to redesign it using the other.) Test it on a student.

As a more difficult exercise stemming from an EGRUL sequence on either of these types of principles, you might try having the *student* arrive at the rule in true discovery fashion. You will probably discover that it is extremely difficult to select examples which enable him to zero in on the appropriate properties! It is much easier to EGRUL than to discover. Any time you find yourself verbalizing what he should be looking for, you're EGRULing him rather than leading him to discover the generalization himself.

Task Three. *"Observing behavior."*

There are many times when the student is not expected to commit material to memory but is expected to be able to arrive at a correct answer using source materials. Airline reservation clerks, telephone company information operators, and long-distance moving company estimators obviously make their living by being good at such skills. Examples of such situations are:

(a) locating appropriate values in tables of mathematical functions;
(b) locating an appropriate word for a specific shade of meaning with both a thesaurus and dictionary;
(c) interpreting color-coded elevation and terrain symbols in an atlas;
(d) interpreting etymologies or pronunciation guides in a dictionary.

Select some information-location problem with which you are somewhat familiar (but not necessarily an expert) and design a teaching sequence to enable a student to obtain information with a specific low number of wrong moves and a reasonable time limit. These will depend on your estimate of the complexity of the task and the amount of cross-referencing necessary to solve your criterion problem.

Task Four. *Chains.*

Any procedure in which each step follows the one before can be considered a chain. Whether it should be taught in backward order is another matter. Your chained sequence does not have to proceed in a backward direction unless you see an advantage for doing so. Examples of chains in academic areas include:

(a) any procedure for preparing a machine for use, such as setting up a tape recorder or film projector;
(b) any relatively lengthy computation in which steps are taken in order, such as computing a square root or a rank order correlation;
(c) any sequence in laboratory procedures which must be done in order, such as certain sequences for determining the characteristics of an unknown substance.

Select a chain, divide the sequence of operations into reasonable chunks of behavior, given the appropriate kinds of students, and prepare a program teaching students to follow the procedure. (You may, as a teacher, question necessity for teaching such a skill up to a mastery level. This is only an exercise. In real life, perhaps the existence of "cookbooks" or directions for cooks, statisticians, and others should make us question objectives which require students to memorize procedures they can always look up.)

Answers to Self-Test on Editing.

1. This is a copying frame. (The subject matter is deliberately bad—see D. Markle, 1962.) The question should ask whether "essential chairness" is an abstraction, or, leaving that in as an EG, provide an $\widetilde{EG}$ or an $\widetilde{EG}$ and $\overline{EG}$.
2. The question does not test the new information. Either drop the new information, making this a practice frame, or write a question on the new information.
3. The item is so overprompted thematically that it can be answered without looking at the panel. Either ask for a "your-own-words" description of the scene in the second verse, or at least have the student identify the river or the time of day with no thematic prompts.
4. The alternatives represent an "idiot choice" situation (non-technical term for it!); no student who was paying any kind of attention could pick the third, and the second is a "trivial" misunderstanding—looking at the wrong diagram. Present two other ratios drawn from the correct diagram.
5. The response is irrelevant. Depending on your assumptions about what the students know at this point, you can either make a RU-EG-$\widetilde{EG}$ out of it or have the student fill in the "15." (Taking out the *one* and leaving the *only* is too strong a thematic prompt.)
6. The frame is overloaded—three definitions with only one response—and the numbers used represent too much work to get the point across. Either have the student calculate all three from an easier set of data or have him calculate only the mean and remove the other two definitions.
7. This is an insult to the student. The condescending tone ("*this* time," and the "repeat DO NOT") should be edited out, along with "foolish."
8. A Swiss cheese frame. Ask a question or leave a solid blank after ". . . a number which is . . ." (Prompting two definitions by leaving the "or" in is fine.)

Appendix

Your first draft, carefully edited, is an experiment. Each frame or short sequence is an hypothesis. The objectives of *Good Frames and Bad* have been to enable you to create a first draft in which you will be testing the best set of hypotheses that we know at the moment, the set from which student data will provide you with the most information. These hypotheses should be pretty familiar to you: that the student only needs to be told once, that he needs no hints, that his acquisition of the behavior you are trying to create in him can proceed in giant steps, stretching his ability to retain and to generalize what has been taught. Unlike other experimenters, the developmental tester hopes to be proved wrong. Each student who errs provides you with help in tailoring the instruction for a better fit.

When testing your frames, you are in a "clinical" relationship with a student and your preferred style of conducting the session is best. Some of us prefer to have the student do a great deal of talking about what he is thinking. Others prefer to watch the student (like the analyst behind the couch!), keeping out of his way unless a significant problem appears. If you let your first student work by himself while you stay out of his way, you may lose some data. In discussing his responses later, he may have forgotten some of the momentary problems that led to wrong answers or hesitations. If you talk with the student as he goes through, you need either a fantastic memory or a rapid shorthand for taking down everything that goes on. Gilbert (1960) recommended a tape recorder, and it is certainly worthwhile. When a problem arises, you will be trying out other ways of teaching the same point and you need to know exactly what you did that finally cleared up the problem. Remember, the spoken language is simpler than the language most of us write and you may have on your tape exactly the way a term ought to be defined—the way you said it off the cuff.

It is fashionable at present to videotape a new salesman's presentation or a student teacher's first attempt in order to "improve" their performance by showing them just how bad it is! A person testing a draft of a program is not front stage, of course—the program is. But a tape recorder might help with another problem that many of us have in learning how to get the most out of each student. You encountered, in Chapter 5, an extreme version of the "How-could-you-be-so-stupid?" remedial branching frame. When working with a student, your responses to his responses have to be masterfully tactful, never giving him the impression that you find his mistakes amazing or amusing or his comments, no matter how negative, out of order. This skill is *not* learned by reading admonishments such as this paragraph! As you listen to your tape recording, however, you might keep an ear out for the tone as well as the content of your own replies to the student. In fact, if the frequency of voluntary negative comments goes down as the session proceeds, perhaps there is a problem to be worked on.

The following are a few procedural hints (subject to your own way of handling things):

1. Be sure the student knows that the program, not he, is on trial.
2. Be sure that you have mechanical difficulties such as accidentally seeing the correct answer under control. (This is one reason for the advice to prepare your draft on cards or one frame per page with the answer on the back.)

3. Start your testing fairly early in the writing process if you are constructing a long program or if you are constructing a program for a group of students with whom you are not familiar. This prevents you from having the same mistake in your teaching appear in several places.

There is little doubt among practitioners (see Markle, 1967) that testing individual students significantly improves instruction. A great deal of important data will be lost if the programer looks only at answers written by students he has not watched and talked with. There is also considerable consensus that error rate within the program is not the important variable in judging whether the program "works." (Lumsdaine, 1963, 1965.) In developmental testing, the programer aims at reduction of errors, but he is always making a judgment about student idiosyncrasies when considering a particular student's error. Was it really careless? Was this student really representative? Was it a function of some disturbance introduced by the programer's attempt to repair off-the-cuff a previous bad frame?

The answers to such questions are arrived at in subsequent tests with further individual students and groups of students. And the kinds of answers one gets lead directly back into all the problems discussed in Chapter 4 on branching. Branching, of course (see Anderson's comment on page 223), cannot cure a problem caused by poor analysis of the subject or poor frame design.

When do you stop testing individual students and turn to group testing under more "normal" conditions? The answer, unfortunately, "depends." One factor is the programer's skill—in the design of the first draft and in the on-the-spot repairs he makes as each student goes through. Another factor is the complexity of the behavior he is trying to teach. A third factor is the standard of excellence which he intends the program to reach. (Roberson, 1963.) The more rigorous his standards, (for instance, in the case of the fire-fighters' program illustrated on page 169, where 100% accuracy is required), the longer the testing the program must undergo.

Students working with an interested observer hanging on their every word are a far different population than a group assigned a program as part of a regular course. There is still plenty to learn about the operation of the program when individual testing ceases and group testing gets underway.

A program, according to the definition presented in Chapter 1, is a validated instructional product. The purchaser can find out what the product will accomplish with students. The complexity of the validation process, as described in the AERA-APA-DAVI Joint Committee's *Final Report* (1965), is beyond the scope of this program. Suffice it to say that the programer's job is to describe *who* learned *what* in *how much time* under *what conditions,* "Who" is the students, what they were like, what they already knew when they started the program. "What" is defined by scores on the posttest or gain from pre- to posttest. "Under what conditions" includes such variables as what the instructor was doing, what motivation the students were working under, and such. For deeper analysis of these problems, see Lumsdaine (1965) and Markle (1967).

Bibliography

American Educational Research Association, American Psychological Association, Department of Audiovisual Instruction, National Education Association. "Criteria for Assessing Programed Instruction Materials. Final Report." *NSPI Journal,* Vol. IV, No. 8, 1965.

Anderson, Richard C. "Educational Psychology." In *Annual Review of Psychology,* Vol. 18, 1967.

Anderson, Richard C., and Gerald W. Faust. "The Effects of Strong Formal Prompts in Programed Instruction." *American Educational Research Journal,* Vol. 4, No. 4, 1967.

Atkinson, Richard C. "Computerized Instruction and the Learning Process." *American Psychologist,* Vol. 23, No. 3, 1968.

Atkinson, Richard C., and H. A. Wilson. "Computer-Assisted Instruction." *Science,* Vol. 162, 4 October, 1968.

Ausubel, David P. *The Psychology of Meaningful Verbal Learning.* Grune and Stratton, New York, 1963.

Basescu, Bernard. "More on Multiple-Choice Frames." *Programed Instruction,* Vol. 2, No. 1, 1962.

Bloom, Benjamin S. (ed.) *Taxonomy of Educational Objectives.* Longmans, Green, New York, 1956.

Bruner, Jerome S. *The Process of Education.* Harvard University Press, Cambridge, Mass., 1960.

Communicable Disease Center. *Life Cycle of Entamoeba Histolytica.* U. S. Dept. of HEW, Public Health Service, Atlanta, Georgia, 1964.

Crowder, Norman. *Intrinsic Programming.* Distributed by U.S. Industries (n.d.).

Deterline, William A. "Psychology and Instructional Technology." In Powers, P., and W. Baskin. *New Outlooks in Psychology.* Philosophical Library, New York, 1968.

Ely, Donald P. (ed.) "The Changing Role of the Audiovisual Process in Education: a Definition and a Glossary of Related Terms." *Audiovisual Communication Review,* Supplement No. 6, Vol. 11, No. 1, 1963.

Englemann, Siegfried. *Conceptual Learning.* Dimensions Press, San Rafael, Calif., 1969.

Eraut, Michael R. *The Development of Instructional Systems with Variable Input.* Office of Instructional Resources Technical Report 67-2. University of Illinois, Chicago, Ill., 1967.

Esbensen, Thorwald. *Working with Individualized Instruction: The Duluth Experience.* Fearon Publishers, Palo Alto, Calif., 1968.

Evans, James L., R. Glaser, and Lloyd E. Homme. *The RULEG System for the Construction of Programed Verbal Learning Sequences.* Department of Psychology, University of Pittsburgh, Pittsburgh, Pa., 1960.

Evans, James L. "Multiple-Choice Discrimination Programming." Paper read at American Psychological Association, New York, September 1961.

Evans, James L. "Programing in Mathematics and Logic." In Glaser, R., (ed.) *Teaching Machines and Programed Learning, II: Data and Directions.* National Education Association, Washington, D.C., 1965.

Ferster, Charles B., and Mary C. Perrott. *Behavior Principles.* Appleton-Century-Crofts, New York, 1968.

Forest Service. *10 Standard Fire Fighting Orders.* U.S. Department of Agriculture, Washington, D.C., 1965.

Frase, Lawrence T. *The Effect of Social Reinforcers in a Programed Learning Task.* ONR Contract Nonr1834(36), Technical Report No. 11, Training Research Laboratory, University of Illinois, Urbana, Ill., 1963.

Gagné, Robert M. *The Conditions of Learning.* Holt, Rinehart, and Winston, New York, 1965.

Gagné, Robert M. "Characteristics of Instructional Technologists." *NSPI Journal,* Vol. 8, No. 5, 1969.

Gilbert, Thomas F. "On the Relevance of Laboratory Investigation of Learning to Self-Instructional Programming." In Lumsdaine, A. A., and R. Glaser (eds.), *Teaching Machines and Programmed Learning.* Department of Audiovisual Instruction, National Educational Association, Washington, D.C., 1960.

Gilbert, Thomas F. "Mathetics: the Technology of Education." *Journal of Mathetics,* Vol. 1, No. 1, 1962a.

Gilbert, Thomas F. "Mathetics: II. The Design of Teaching Exercises." *Journal of Mathetics,* Vol. I, No. 2, 1962b.

Glaser, Robert. "Toward a Behavioral Science Base for Instructional Design." In Glaser, R. (ed.), *Teaching Machines and Programed Learning, II: Data and Directions.* National Education Association, Washington, D.C., 1965.

Goodlad, John I. "Thought, Invention, and Research in the Advancement of Education." *The Educational Forum,* Vol. 33, No. 1, 1968.

Gotkin, L. G., and Goldstein, L. S. "Programed Instruction in the Schools: Innovation and Innovator." In Miles, M. B. (ed.) *Innovation in Education.* Bureau of Publications, Teachers College, Columbia University, New York, 1964, pp. 231-248.

Gotkin, Lassar G., and Joseph McSweeney. "Learning from Teaching Machines." In Lange, P. (ed.) *Programed Instruction: 66th Yearbook of the National Society for the Study of Education, Part II.* University of Chicago Press, Chicago, Ill., 1967.

A Guide for Wiley Authors in the Preparation of Auto-Instructional Programs. John Wiley and Sons, New York, 1967.

Hartley, James, and Patricia M. Woods. "Learning Poetry Backwards." *NSPI Journal,* Vol. 7, No. 10, 1968.

Holland, James G. "Research on Programing Variables." In Glaser, R. (ed.) *Teaching Machines and Programed Learning, II: Data and Directions.* National Education Association, Washington, D.C., 1965.

Holland, James G. "A Quantitative Measure for Programmed Instruction." *American Educational Research Journal,* Vol. 4, No. 2, 1967.

Klaus, David J. "An Analysis of Programing Techniques." In Glaser, R. (ed.) *Teaching Machines and Programed Learning, II: Data and Directions.* National Education Association, Washington, D.C., 1965.

Knight, Stephen. "Programing for the Retarded Reader." *Programed Instruction,* Vol. 3, No. 3, 1964.

Lange, P. (ed.) *Programed Instruction: 66th Yearbook of the National Society for the Study of Education, Part II.* University of Chicago Press, Chicago, Ill., 1967.

Lewis, Brian N. and Gordon Pask. "The Theory and Practice of Adaptive Teaching Systems." In Glaser, R. (ed.) *Teaching Machines and Programed Learning, II: Data and Directions.* National Education Association, Washington, D.C., 1965.

Lindvall, C. M., and John O. Bolvin. "Programed Instruction in the Schools: An Application of Programing Principles in 'Individually Prescribed Instruction.' " In Lange, P. (ed.). *Programed Instruction: 66th Yearbook of the National Society for the Study of Education, Part II.* University of Chicago Press, Chicago, Ill., 1967.

Lumsdaine, Arthur A. "Some Problems in Assessing Instructional Programs." In Filep, Robert T. (ed.) *Prospectives in Programing.* Macmillan Co., New York, 1963.

Lumsdaine, Arthur A. "Assessing the Effectiveness of Instructional Programs." In Glaser, R. (ed.) *Teaching Machines and Programed Learning, II: Data and Directions.* National Education Association, Washington, D.C., 1965.

Mager, Robert F. "On the Sequencing of Instructional Content." *Psychological Reports,* IX, 1961.

Mager, Robert F. *Preparing Instructional Objectives.* Fearon Publishers, Palo Alto, Calif., 1962.

Mager, Robert F. *Developing Attitude Toward Learning.* Fearon Publishers, Palo Alto, Calif., 1968.

Mager, Robert F., and John McCann. *Learner-Controlled Instruction.* Varian Associates, Palo Alto, Calif., 1962.

Mager, R. F., and C. Clark. "Explorations in Student-Controlled Instruction." In Ofiesh, G. D., and W. C. Meierhenry (eds.). *Trends in Programed Instruction.* Department of Audiovisual Instruction, National Education Association and National Society for Programed Instruction, Washington, D.C., 1964, pp. 235-238.

Markle, David G. "Faulty Frames: in which it is demonstrated that a program that works may well be worthless." *Programed Instruction,* Vol. 1, No. 6, 1962.

Markle, David G. "On the Control of Runaway Programers." *NSPI Journal,* Vol. 6, No. 7, 1967.

Markle, Susan M. *A Programed Primer on Programing.* Vol. 2, *Practical Problems.* Center for Programed Instruction, New York, 1961.

Markle, Susan M. "Teaching Machines versus Programers." *Audiovisual Communication Review,* Vol. 10, No. 4, 1962.

Markle, Susan M. "The Lowest Common Denominator: A Persistent Problem in Programing." *Programed Instruction,* Vol. 2, No. 3, 1963.

Markle, Susan M. "The Harvard Teaching Machine Project: The First Hundred Days." *AV Communication Review,* Vol. 12, No. 2, 1964.

Markle, Susan M. *The Compleat Programer.* University of Illinois, Chicago, Ill., 1966.

Markle, Susan M. "Empirical Testing of Programs." In Lange, P. (ed.) *Programed Instruction: 66th Yearbook of the National Society for the Study of Education, Part II.* Univ. of Chicago Press, Chicago, Ill., 1967.

Markle, Susan M., and Philip W. Tiemann. *Programing Is a Process.* (Programed Film with Technical Manual.), University of Illinois, Chicago, Ill., 1967.

Markle, Susan M., and Philip W. Tiemann. *Really Understanding Concepts.* Tiemann Associates, Chicago, Ill., 1969.

Mechner, Francis. "Behavioral Analysis and Instructional Sequencing." In Lange, P. (ed.) *Programed Instruction: 66th Yearbook of the National Society for the Study of Education, Part II.* University of Chicago Press, Chicago, Ill., 1967.

Meyer, Susan R. "Report of the Initial Test of a Junior High-School Vocabulary Program." In Lumsdaine, A. A., and R. Glaser (eds.). *Teaching Machines and Programmed Learning.* Department of Audiovisual Instruction, National Education Association, Washington, D.C., 1960.

Oettinger, Anthony G., and Sema Marks. *Educational Technology: New Myths and Old Realities.* Harvard University Program on Technology and Society, Reprint Number 6, Cambridge, Mass., 1968.

Ofiesh, Gabriel D. *Programed Instruction: A Guide for Management.* American Management Association, New York, 1965.

Popham, W. James. *Educational Objectives.* VIMCET Associates, Los Angeles, Calif., 1965.

Popham, W. James. "Curriculum Materials." In *Review of Educational Research,* Vol. 39, No. 2, June, 1969.

Roberson, Paul L. "High Standards Needed." *NSPI Journal,* Vol. 2, No. 10, 1963.

Rummler, Geary A., Joseph P. Yaney, and Albert W. Schrader. *Managing the Instructional Programming Effort.* University of Michigan, Ann Arbor, Mich., 1967.

Schramm, Wilbur. "Programed Instruction Today and Tomorrow." In Schramm, Wilbur (ed.). *Four Case Studies of Programed Instruction.* Fund for the Advancement of Education, New York, 1964.

Skinner, B. F. "The Science of Learning and the Art of Teaching." *Harvard Education Review,* Vol. 24, Spring, 1954. Reprinted in Skinner, B. F. *The Technology of Teaching.* Appleton-Century-Crofts, Inc., New York, 1968.

Skinner, B. F. *Verbal Behavior.* Appleton-Century-Crofts, New York, 1957.

Skinner, B. F. "Teaching Machines." *Scientific American,* Vol. 205, No. 5, 1961.

Skinner, B. F. "Reflections on a Decade of Teaching Machines." In Glaser, R. (ed.) *Teaching Machines and Programed Learning, II: Data and Directions.* National Education Association, Washington, D.C., 1965.

Skinner, B. F. *The Technology of Teaching.* Appleton-Century-Crofts, New York, 1968.

Smith, Judith M., and Donald E. P. Smith. *Child Management: A Program for Parents.* Ann Arbor Publishers, Ann Arbor, Mich., 1966.

Thomas, C. A., I. K. Davies, D. Openshaw, and J. B. Bird. *Programmed Learning In Perspective.* Educational Methods, Inc., Chicago, Ill., 1964.

Tiemann, Philip W., Donald W. Paden, and Charles J. McIntyre. *An Application of the Principles of Programed Instruction to a Televised Course in College Economics.* NDEA Title VII, Project No. 5-0841. University of Illinois, Urbana, Ill., 1966.

Tosti, Donald T. "Behavioral Considerations of the Multiple-Choice Frame." Paper presented at the 2nd Convention of the National Society for Programmed Instruction, San Antonio, Tex., 1964.

Glossary

PROGRAMING TERMS

*Many of these definitions were drawn from the glossary prepared by the author for Ely, Donald (editor), *The Changing Role of the Audiovisual Process in Education: A Definition and a Glossary of Related Terms*, 1963.

Branch. A generic term for the point of choice at which students are sent to alternative frames depending on their responses to the particular branching point. This may include diagnostic test items, in-program frames with multiple-choice or constructed-response answer, student options, and so forth. The branch may take the student to a single frame (a remedial loop), a subsequence, or a linear sequence dealing with his particular needs. (*Note:* readers must determine from context whether a particular author is using the term "branch" to designate only the intrinsic model or whether he is using the broader sense of the term.)

Criterion items. See **Terminal behavior**.

Demonstrate. Gilbert's term for "prime," in which the process or the product is shown to the student for his imitation or study.

Error rate. The percentage of incorrect responses on a frame, a set of frames, or a whole program tested on a group of students. Most programers aim for a relatively low error rate, although there is little agreement on what is "low." Because spuriously low error rates are too easily attained by adding irrelevant responses, overprompted frames, and such and by eliminating criterion frames, error rate has fallen into disrepute as a measure of the program's effectiveness.

Error. A response not acceptable to the programer. Programers attempt to eliminate errors by revising the program. Erroneous responses may indicate: (a) a poorly designed item which fails to communicate and, therefore, needs to be rewritten; (b) a sequence in which prompts have been withdrawn too fast or inadequate practice given; (c) assumed previous knowledge which, in fact, the student does not have; (d) poor analysis of the subject matter, leading to a confusion not predicted by the programer. This definition assumes that responses which are errors in the subject matter are acceptable to the programer in some cases, for instance, as signals that the student should receive some differential treatment in a branching program.

Feedback. In intrinsic programing, the sentence or paragraph that discusses why the answer the student chose is correct or incorrect. In mainstream frames of intrinsic programs, this discussion follows the answer that the student chose and precedes the new instructional material. The device has been adopted by other programers as well when machine limitations permit.

Frame or item. The segment of material which the student handles at one time. It may vary in size from a few words to a full page or more. In almost all programing methods, it will require at least one response (overt or covert) and provide for knowledge of results before the student proceeds to the next frame.

Knowledge of results. A report to a student on the status of the response that he has made. It may be a verbal report, "Right" or "Wrong" (or lights, buzzers, etc., signaling one of these results), or a display (oral or written) of the correct verbal response. It may be a response of a manipulandum, particularly in those cases in which the operation of a device is the subject matter. Some teaching machines advance to the next item only when the correct response has been given. Since knowledge of results has been shown to facilitate learning in many situations, it is generally considered a subclass of reinforcement.

Mainstream frames. In intrinsic programs, the ordered sequence of frames that present the instructional material and branching questions seen by every student. If the student makes no errors, he will take a "linear" sequence of mainstream frames. The term can be generalized to include any set of frames in any kind of branching program which are taken by all students.

Mathetics. A systematic approach to analysis and frame construction devised by Gilbert.

Objective. A statement describing the behavior the student is expected to acquire. In Mager's (1962) and other formulations, a good objective specifies an observable response a student will make, the conditions under which the response will be given (such as kinds of problems to be solved, supporting materials and references) and the standards of accuracy or time that will be imposed.

Operant span. The number of operants (or responses) that a student can handle in one frame. Gilbert's term is closely allied to the more general term "step," with "exceeding the operant span" being synonymous with "a step too large for the student to take."

Panel. A lengthy segment of material presented in conjunction with a sequence of frames. While the term originally applied to texts too large to fit into the early teaching machines, it has been stretched to cover maps, globes, equipment, and any other adjunct material with which a student works as directed by the frames.

Prime. An introductory frame in which a student is told or shown precisely what to do in such a way that he can successfully imitate or perform on the first instance.

Programing, adaptive. A term the meaning of which varies depending on the user! Maximally adaptive programs would treat students differentially depending on student options, previous histories, preferred media, and so forth. Minimally adaptive programs are the fairly new group-paced programs. Most existing programs lie somewhere between the two extremes.

Programing, discrimination. A specific style of programing characterized by objectives related to discrimination rather than memorization of rules or generalizations, and by frequent use of multiple-choice responding to "critical incidents."

Programing, intrinsic. A programing technique developed by Norman Crowder, characterized by relatively lengthy items, multiple-choice responses, and consistent use of branching. If after reading the information section of each item, the student selects the correct response to the question based on the materials, he is sent to an item presenting new information. If he selects an incorrect alternative, he is sent to an item which provides information as to why his choice was incorrect. To the extent that the programer has correctly predicted the possible responses that the student population will make, the program taken by each student is under the control of his own responses, and will differ for students of differing abilities.

Programing, linear. Any program in which each student does every frame in the same order no matter how adequate or inadequate his response. Many present-day programs have branching points in them although the main sequences are essentially linear. In common usage, a linear program is taken to be a small-step constructed-response program with a low error rate, i.e., one of the classical Skinnerian variety. This would leave out linear mathetical programs with large steps, linear discrimination programs with multiple-choice responses, and others. (*Note:* again, the reader must beware when reading the literature in the field. Criticisms directed against "linear" programs may not always be aimed at the key characteristic. Often, the true target is small frames.)

Prompt. A stimulus added to the terminal stimulus to make the correct response more likely while the student is learning. It may be pictorial or verbal. Prompts vary in strength, i.e., in the probability with which they will evoke the correct response from a given population. The term is used synonymously with *cue* and is generally synonymous with the non-technical term *hint*. Prompts were classified by Skinner into two major types: *formal prompts* provide knowledge about the form of the expected response, such as the number of letters, the initial letter, or the sound pattern (prompted by a rhyme); *thematic prompts* depend on meaningful associations that make it likely for the student to give the expected response.

A distinction between *prompt* and *cue* is made by some writers. *Prompt* describes the function of a model of the response which the student copies, whereas a *cue* is a hint of a weaker sort. (Skinner specifically excluded stimuli to be imitated from the category "prompt.")

(*Note:* Since one use of the term specifically excludes that which the other use of the term includes, readers must determine which sense the author intends before interpreting one set of results as being in conflict with another.)

Release. Gilbert's term for terminal frame or criterion frame.

Remedial loop. In intrinsic programing, a frame consisting solely of an explanation of the error that the student made in selecting a particular answer. The frame refers him back to the item he just left for another chance at its question, but the frame itself contains no question. Also called *"first-order branch."*

Response, constructed. A student's effort to complete a sentence, solve a problem or to answer a question. A model of the response may be provided for the student to copy, but as long as he writes, says, or thinks it rather than selecting it from a set of alternatives, the response is constructed.

Response, multiple-choice. The student's selection of one of two or more alternatives. The provision of the correct answer among the alternatives prevents him from responding in his own words but does not necessarily produce a smaller step or an easier item than some constructed-response items.

Scrambled book. A book that presents an intrinsic program. The pages are not read consecutively. Following the information presentation, a multiple-choice question is given. The answer that the student selects refers him to a particular page for confirmation or correction. He may be sent either forward or backward in the text, the number of pages in either direction being randomized. Thus, no clue as to which alternative is correct can be found in the page reference accompanying each alternative.

Step. An indefinite, intuitive, but basic concept. A subject to be programed is broken down into items (steps). It is assumed that students cannot take later steps in a given sequence before taking the early steps, and that each item represents a step forward. If students cannot respond correctly to an item, that item is considered "too large a step." A step represents a combination of (a) a subjective judgment that an item represents progress in the student's mastery, and (b) an objective measure of the student's ability to respond correctly to an item. The size of the step is not necessarily related to the size of the response (a lengthy response may represent only a small step forward) nor is it necessarily related to the amount of material contained in an item. A programer generally increases the number of items in order to reduce the size of the steps.

Subsequence. In intrinsic programing, a sequence of standard intrinsic frames arrived at by making an error on a mainstream frame. The frames contain both new material and questions on that material which provide for further remedial instruction if necessary. At some point the student who takes the subsequence will be returned to the mainstream.

Terminal behavior. The behavior that the student is expected to have acquired at the end of a program or sequence. Evidence that such behavior has indeed been acquired is provided by successful responses to *terminal items* and/or performance on a *criterion test*. The *terminal items* contain no prompts and are placed far enough from the training sequences to measure more than immediate memory. Criteria vary in testing of programs as they do in any other learning situation. Criterion tests may involve multiple-choice items, fill-in items, essays, or performance of some task. If given immediately after the learning sequence, the test is a test of *acquisition;* if given considerably later, it is a *retention* test. Such tests may involve only the actually material explicity covered in the learning sequence, or they may involve extension, generalization, or application of the learned material, generally called *transfer*.

Terminal stimulus. The unprompted question, incomplete statement, or problem to which the student is taught to respond. This stimulus may occur as part of a prompted item which is not, therefore, a terminal item.

Validation. An experimental demonstration that the final version of a program does achieve its objectives, as measured by its criterion instruments, up to a certain standard of performance for a given population.

PSYCHOLOGICAL TERMS

Chain. An ordered sequence of responses in which each response creates the stimulus for the next response.

Concept. A class of objects, events, or relations which are grouped together in a subject matter and treated alike—usually by giving them the same name. (*Note:* this is a technical and limited use of a common word which is often used broadly, synonymous with "idea" and about as well defined!)

Discrimination. Differential responding to two or more stimuli in a set. In lay terms, the organism can "tell the difference" or "perceive the occurrence of the stimulus."

Generalization. Giving a response learned to one stimulus in a second situation slightly different from the first.

Operant. A class of behaviors which are defined by the reinforcer they obtain. Although they may differ in some properties, each one produces the same reinforcer (such as "door-opening behaviors").

Reinforcement. The process in which some stimulus, presented immediately following a response, increases the rate at which the response is emitted in a standard situation or increases the probability that the response will recur when the situation recurs. A stimulus having such an effect is reinforcing (is a reinforcer). Knowledge of results (feedback or confirmation) has been shown to reinforce correct responses of students in many learning tasks. When the student's correct response is followed by presentation of the correct answer, the probability that the correct response will recur is increased. When correct responses are not followed by knowledge of results, and when the student has no other way of determining what is correct, learning may not occur.

Considerable confusion has arisen because stimuli such as food, praise, or money are sometimes called reinforcers even in situations where they are not effective—i.e., no learning occurs when they are present or the same learning occurs even when they are not present. Experimental findings suggest that presentation of the correct answer may not be operating as a reinforcer in programed instruction. Learning has been shown to occur without confirmation of correct responses. The extent to which confirmation of the correct answer may truly be called a reinforcer remains to be demonstrated.

Educators should be aware that the psychological use of the term *reinforcement* does not parallel their own use of it. The two definitions are quite distinct. In both cases, a response is strengthened, but the procedures differ. In educational parlance, repetition or rehearsal is the procedure denoted by *reinforcement.*

Response. A general term for a wide variety of behaviors. It may involve the production of anything from a single phoneme or letter, word or phrase, to the solution of a problem requiring an hour or more. It may involve selection among alternatives (multiple choice) in which case the response often includes the nonverbal manipulation of buttons, keys, etc.

Response, covert. An internalized response which the student presumably makes but which is neither recorded nor otherwise available to an observer. A student who is producing an oral or written response must think of the response (i.e., respond covertly) before producing it.

Response, overt. A student's oral, written, or manipulative act which is, or can be, recorded by an observer. Whether such responses contribute significantly to learning or not, they provide the data on the basis of which programs are revised.

Stimulus. A class of events that impinge on an organism's sensory equipment and that experimenters can manipulate, describe, or hypothesize to exist. Stimuli are linked as observable (or hypothesized) antecedents to specific responses. In S-R (stimulus-response) psychology, the stimulus is a necessary antecedent to a response. Skinner's position places more emphasis on the consequent (reinforcing) stimuli than on the antecedents. In a program, the content of the item is the stimulus. This includes the terminal stimulus (the basic question or statement), any additional stimuli operating as prompts or models, and any external material such as panels.

Index

Aardvark "frame" 21, 23, 24, 88, 116, 235
Ameba Program 9, 104, 163-167, 168, 170, 173, 175, 254
Analysis of Behavior 128, 191, 262
Anderson, R. 8, 11, 88, 104, 118, 131, 223, 241, 296
Arithmetic of Computers (Crowder) 211, 214, 280

Basescu, B. 98
Behavior analysis 1, 14, 25, 56-58, 70, 74, 115, 130, 132, 137, 159, 160, 170, 172-175, 179-185, 210, 221, 296
    (See also Chain, Concept, Discrimination, Generalization)
Blackout technique 8
Branch 188, 193, 205, 210, 219, 221-236, 245, 250, 277, 286, 296
Bullock, D. 272, 290

Chain 56, 58, 60, 61, 74, 104, 130, 159, 160, 167, 171-178, 184, 185, 290, 292
Chaining, backward 172-178, 183, 185
Computer-assisted-instruction 223, 224, 229, 232-237
Concept 37, 38, 39, 44, 46, 48, 51, 54, 56, 57, 78, 92, 101, 103, 114, 115, 130, 132, 133, 135, 137, 143, 144, 150, 170, 179-181, 266-274, 290
Concepts, dimensions of 37, 51, 54, 180-181, 270-272
Conceptual structures 134, 181-183
    (See also Matrix)
Contingencies, double 106-107
Criterion frame, see Frame, terminal
Crowder, N. A. 187, 189, 191-194, 196, 204, 205, 206, 208, 212, 218, 219, 231, 280

Discovery learning 158, 171, 183, 292
Discrimination 11, 53, 56, 57, 59, 78, 86, 92, 97, 103, 106, 114, 115, 130, 144, 145, 149, 155, 156, 159, 160, 167, 170, 179, 184, 249, 251, 255, 266-272, 274

Efficiency 20, 58, 74, 148, 167, 170, 185, 227, 228, 230, 234, 239
EGRUL 151-159, 162, 182, 184, 234, 256, 290, 292
Elements of Bridge 198-209, 218
Empirical testing 3, 11, 15-16, 25, 40, 50, 53, 54, 101, 106, 108, 117, 124, 128-129, 137, 166-167, 175, 184, 185, 221, 228, 239, 265, 274, 285, 295-296

Englemann, S. vii, 56, 184
Entering behavior 16, 18-20, 25, 50, 54, 164, 166, 175, 193, 208, 216, 221-230, 238, 244, 285, 291
Eraut, M. 226-229
Errors 2, 11-20, 24, 53, 76, 100, 113, 117, 123, 128, 157, 167, 185, 187, 189, 194, 206, 222, 239, 265, 277, 278, 282-285
Error rate 16, 25, 117, 236, 296
Evans, James 11, 139, 157

Feedback 204-205, 209, 210, 211-213, 286
First draft 15, 25, 50, 160, 175, 185, 238-239, 265, 272, 274, 285, 287
"Formal" behavior 85, 86, 92, 130
Formats 24, 27, 42, 47, 95, 99, 113, 191, 196, 211, 212, 256
Frame, copying 45, 60, 62-64, 69-78, 85, 96, 97, 104, 108, 112, 113, 114, 127, 129, 130, 136, 139, 148, 185, 195, 213, 241, 243, 244, 248, 250-257, 258, 280, 287
    forced-choice 96-98, 101, 214
    "lecture" 258-259
    mainstream 193, 197, 205, 206, 216, 217, 220, 222
    NABB (BABOON) 101-102, 244
    review 6, 26, 39, 40, 47, 51, 52, 132, 208, 211, 216
    terminal 6, 44, 47, 56, 63, 65, 72, 78, 81, 82, 92, 93, 94, 98, 112, 130, 137, 138, 139, 149, 158, 164, 213, 238, 260
Frase, L. 236

Gagné, R. 48, 56, 183
Generalization 56, 57, 92, 114, 115, 130, 138, 159, 179-181, 183, 266, 270, 273, 274
Generalizations (See Principles)
Gilbert, T. 21, 104, 158, 159, 167, 172, 176, 178, 184, 247, 254
Glaser, Robert 139, 157, 232
Gotkin, L. 58, 111, 249

Harless, J. H. v
Hartley and Woods 177
Holland, J. G. 8, 128, 131, 210, 241
Homme, Lloyd E. 139, 157
Humor 110, 170, 249, 250, 277

Individual differences 2, 17, 19, 53, 106, 129, 186-187, 189, 206-210, 220, 229-234, 249-250, 258, 286

Klaus, David 21, 116
Klystrons (Kantor and Mager) 235
Knight, S. 109, 245
Knowledge of results 12, 20-25, 48, 146, 167, 177, 195, 204

Language of Computers 59, 60, 105, 111
Lumsdaine, A. 117, 296
Mager, R. 59, 60, 104, 111, 131, 235
Markle, S. M. 1, 23, 25, 48, 106, 118, 122, 128, 180, 186, 187, 245
Mathetics 159-178, 184, 186, 277
Matrix 131-139, 140, 181-182
Mechner, F. 56, 172, 178
Media 54, 57, 61, 110, 186, 220-221

Objectives 39, 44, 54, 65, 85, 86, 88, 89, 96, 102, 103, 110, 137, 156, 159, 168, 175, 184, 236, 238, 243, 247, 249, 250, 254, 261, 269, 290
 specific—of *this* program vi-vii, 54, 136, 179, 220, 229
Operant 160, 172, 173-175, 177
Operant span 160, 162, 164, 167, 168, 172, 173, 185

Pace (See Rate)
Pegasus "frame" 65-69, 80, 88, 119, 120, 124, 126
Popham, W. J., 111, 131, 186
Practice 17, 20, 26, 40, 52, 117, 137, 174, 185, 208, 211, 214, 216, 221, 224, 232, 233, 234, 265, 287
Priming 56, 58-62, 63, 65, 78, 104, 108, 130, 132, 138, 139, 142, 143, 144, 148, 159, 161, 162, 168, 171, 184, 232, 254
Principles 48, 132, 134, 138, 139, 143, 144, 147, 151, 155, 156, 158, 170, 179, 183-184, 249, 266, 291-292
"Problem of the first instance" 58, 60, 65, 98, 140, 146 (See also RULEG, p. 146)
Programmed English 73, 96, 112
Programing, adaptive 186, 220-237
 discrimination 57, 156, 158, 184-185, 186
 intrinsic 100, 187-220, 221, 227, 234, 277-286
 linear 1-24, 25-55, 186, 208, 221
Prompt 2, 14, 39, 42, 43-45, 46, 51, 54, 56, 60, 62-78, 99, 132, 138, 143, 148-149, 164, 167, 174, 195, 211, 213, 243, 256
 (See also Prompt, formal; Prompt, thematic; and Prompt, sequence)
 formal 79-94, 96, 114, 116, 121-124, 126, 167, 211, 214, 248, 260, 262-265, 275, 285, 287, 288

 sequence 111-117, 122, 127, 136, 192, 213, 257, 275-277, 287
 strength of 113, 114, 118-129.
 thematic 79-94, 109, 114, 116, 120, 125, 127, 128, 129, 214, 256, 262-263, 287
 visual 104-111, 130, 164, 176

Rate 3, 19, 186, 220, 236
Reinforcer 25, 110, 171
Response, active 3-11, 13, 24, 37, 48-49, 52, 53, 54, 146, 167, 177, 189, 209, 241
 constructed 2, 83, 191, 202, 223, 285
 covert 10-11, 87, 164, 167, 191
 echoic 60
 multiple-choice 2, 11, 13, 25, 83, 94-103, 130, 188, 191-192, 195, 196, 202-203, 223, 224, 256, 259, 277, 280-285, 287, 288
 observing 239-243, 245, 246, 253, 254, 290, 292
 overt 11, 168
 Procrustean 123
RULEG 138-159, 162, 170, 183, 184, 190, 213, 214, 234-242, 256, 266, 276, 290
 (See also EGRUL)
Rummler, G. 154, 159

Scrambled book 196-197
Sequencing 41, 46, 47, 117, 131, 134-136, 146-153, 158, 164, 167, 173-174, 235, 275-277, 278
 (See also Prompt, sequence; Matrix; RULEG)
Skinner B. F. 1, 2, 3, 13, 14, 19, 25, 39, 45, 47, 58, 60, 61, 62, 66, 76, 77, 79, 128, 157, 186, 195, 204, 263
Small steps 8, 18, 20, 26, 37, 44, 47, 75, 103, 106, 114, 147, 148, 160, 166, 185, 215, 231, 233, 254, 258
Smith, D. E. P., and J. M. 24
Standards, performance 25, 224, 230, 233, 296
Swiss cheese 48, 260-261, 290

Teaching machine 1, 2, 18, 24, 58, 110, 188, 196, 204, 221, 233-235, 273
 (See also Computer-assisted instruction)
Teaching Machines, Incorporated (TMI) 89, 108-109, 110, 157, 244, 254, 263
10 Standard Fire Fighting Orders 168-169, 224, 296
Tiemann, P. W. 25, 48, 180, 187
Thomas, Davies, Openshaw, and Bird 134
Tosti, D. 101
Trigonometry (Crowder and Martin) 191, 215, 218

Vectors (Basic Systems) 27-53, 70, 73, 95, 113, 116, 132, 134-137, 140, 151, 261, 276
Vectors (Carman) 282, 289

Words 53, 83, 84, 96, 98, 105, 122, 128, 143, 152

Yancy 154, 159